MANDELA'S CHILDREN

MANDELA'S CHILDREN

A NOVEL BY

Ora Mendels

Little, Brown and Company
Boston   Toronto

FIRST EDITION

Library of Congress Cataloging-in-Publication Data

Mendels, Ora, 1936–
Mandela's children.

I. Title.
PS3563.E475M3   1986   813'.54   86-10298
ISBN 0-316-54506-6

RRD VA

Published simultaneously in Canada
by Little, Brown & Company (Canada) Limited

PRINTED IN THE UNITED STATES OF AMERICA

For Joe, with love and thanks

All the characters in this novel are fictional except for those heroes and victims of South Africa who belong to history.

MANDELA'S CHILDREN

CHAPTER ONE

From the battered railing the sea was black, green-streaked. It smacked against the hull, churned powerfully away, rolled angrily upon itself. She clutched the rail tight with both hands as the deck shifted, shuddering beneath her feet. She looked behind to admire the smooth avenue carved by their passage between high walls of metallic water. Just beyond the swirling fall of water, she saw a long gray fish thrown up to the surface. A short stubby one floated nearby. Dragged along by the momentum of the vessel, dropping out of sight, surfacing again, they were joined a few minutes later by other, paler fish, all differently shaped. She wondered if they would swim all the way to the Cape and looked to see whether their heads were pointed in the right direction.

They had no heads. They were not fish. The stumpy withering lumps in the green-tinged water were severed limbs and trunks, remnants of drowned bodies. As she stared at the pieces of dismembered flesh, someone came behind her, grabbing her shoulders fiercely. "Come away, come away, there's nothing to see." She tried to resist, she had to see, she had to be sure; but, struggling on the deck against the liar, she felt that she would lose her footing, fall over into that fleshy water. In a clammy daze, she roused to the urgent voice of her neighbor on the plane. "You're having a nightmare," he said gruffly. "Better wake up."

It was three o'clock in the morning in a darkened British Airways jet hurtling high above Africa. He settled back into sleep after her muttered apology for the nightmare. It wasn't a nightmare, though, so much as a recollection; a memory of the event or, perhaps, of its recounting. She had never been sure.

Ruth Harris, folding her arms tightly around herself to contain the shivering, wondered why she'd dreamed her voyage on the *Umgeni* rather than the nightmare which belonged to South Africa, where she was going by choice, she reminded herself grimly, for the first time in over twenty years. The shadow of the South African nightmare, peopled by brigades of uniformed men with glossy high black boots, hovered over the pulpy flesh, vivid still upon the slimy surface of the water. Ruth shook her head sharply several times to wake herself fully, flicked the light for the air hostess, stretched out a trembling hand for hot coffee. If sleep returned her to the dreams, she'd stay awake. At least her conscious fears were real and immediate.

She ought not to be so afraid, she knew. She was an American now. She fumbled in the handbag at her feet, pulling out the dark blue passport from its zippered pouch to examine again its reassuring pages. Citizen of the United States, entitled to the protection of its representatives abroad. Ruth Fredman Harris, born 1939, naturalized citizen. Hair black, eyes dark brown, height five feet five inches, weight one hundred and twelve pounds. The passport had been routinely renewed the year before, so that her picture looked like she did now: wide-set melancholy eyes above prominent cheekbones, short hair brushed back at the sides, waving down onto the high forehead. You couldn't see the white streaks in the hair in the photograph but they were there. Ruth looked, she thought, austere. Not at all like the girl who had left South Africa twenty years before. Only the eyes were the same. When she'd first admitted to herself that she was thinking of making this painful, probably futile, certainly dangerous trip, she'd toyed with the idea of changing her name too, until she remembered that it was changed, partly at least. That had been enough trouble, she wouldn't look for more.

The stamps in the passport showed that she had traveled from Kennedy to Heathrow the day before. No customs official would bother to make the interpretation but Ruth knew it meant that she had not stayed long enough in London to visit her mother or her sister; among other, less compelling reasons, there simply wasn't time. The next stamp in the book would be Jan Smuts Airport, Johannesburg. She shuddered and turned back a page to the only other entry on the stiff, official, precious document. It revealed that she had spent a week in Vienna last summer. No security official in Johannesburg would know that the rubber-stamped dates showed that she had fled back to the States five days earlier than planned, landing at Kennedy with the unaccustomed relief of coming home. It was the encounter in Vienna with Max Hepburn that had begun the journey she now made herself endure.

She had first spotted him across the hall at the convention center, where she was lined up to register as a participant in the historians' conference that had brought her from Philadelphia. As soon as she identified him, she turned her back, digging in her bag for her documents. He was several lines away, registering also. She didn't think he'd seen her. She ran into old South African connections very seldom, going out of her way to avoid them. Not surprising, under the circumstances. She never knew how she'd be received; the few exchanges she'd suffered had hardly been reassuring. She registered and left without turning back again. The manicured, sweltering city was jammed with historians from the West; even with the Eastern bloc boycott, there were enough to fill the glittering anachronistic hotels, the chocolate-box cafes, the decadent palaces. She didn't even have to work at avoiding Max. She attended the meetings at the Hofburg, from whose porch Hitler had exuberantly hailed the *Anschluss*; and she presented her paper on failed revolutions of the twentieth century to the gratifying approval of her colleagues. Then, relieved that it was successfully behind her, she went on a tour to the Schönbrunn Palace. In the ornate gilded chamber where the Hapsburgs had gathered to celebrate their spreading hegemony, Max Hepburn had murmured, "It is Ruth Fredman, isn't it?" and, a nerve jumping in the back of her neck, she turned to find him close behind her.

He had aged, of course, in twenty years, but not much. The square face with pale distant eyes, coarse black hair cut to a short bristle, broad shoulders too hefty for the squat build, even the baggy corduroy jacket were all familiar.

"Hello, Max," said Ruth, too startled by his creeping up on her to pretend to be surprised that he was there at all.

"But how amazing to find you here," he said, nodding just the way he used to. "I was thinking about you. What are you doing in Vienna?" His South African accent had been neutralized by years in Britain. His voice was still thin, though his stance was less awkward, his manner more composed. Changed circumstances had forced some order upon him, Ruth thought irritably.

"The same as you, I imagine, Max," she said.

"You're in history?"

"I teach history, yes. At the University of Pennsylvania." Max was, she knew quite well, an Oxford don.

"Amazing, I had no idea." He put his hand on her arm to detach her from the group clustered around the guide, who was explaining the proliferation of the Hapsburg Empire by its marriages. They were annoying the others with their whispering. She let herself be drawn back behind the crowd. Max came to a halt under a massive tapestry depicting an idealized hunt. Ruth had already forgotten from whom it had been stolen.

"You aren't the Ruth Harris on the program, are you? Doing the paper on failed revolutions?"

"Yes, that's me. The paper was this morning."

"Damn, I wanted to go. Didn't know it was you, of course." His brows knitted, without leaving so much as a single indentation in his forehead. His skin was as obdurate as the rest of him. "I would have gone to it, but I had to be at a meeting. I'm on the review committee, you see."

This was, of course, predictable.

"Tell me, are you in touch at all with any of the old crowd?"

Ruth was startled. Max Hepburn was not a person who could ever have been regarded as sensitive, but, even for him, this was extraordinarily crude. Still, he'd come up to her, he was talking to her, he hadn't made a point of avoiding her.

"Hardly," she answered dryly and made herself meet his gaze.

"I'd like to talk to you," he said. "I told you I was thinking about you. Harris, is it? Are you here with your husband?"

"I'm alone, Max. I've been divorced for years."

"Oh, good, then you could come with me for a bite to eat and a talk."

Ruth laughed. He hadn't changed at all. Nothing existed for him beyond his immediate concerns. She didn't want to talk to him. There was nothing she wanted to hear from him. There was nothing he could tell her that she wanted to know. The only things he was likely to tell her were things that she certainly didn't want to know. She did not know how to avoid him.

"What about this tour?"

"Not very enlightened, is it? Still, if you're interested we could go on with it and then go somewhere."

But the idea of wandering through more halls and boudoirs and ballrooms dedicated to the acquisitive greed of the Austro-Hungarian Empire, and with Max Hepburn's bleak commentary in her ear, did not appeal to Ruth. Max was determined to talk to her, now that he had, as he would put it, discovered her; she would not be able to evade him and might as well get it over with.

They took a cab to the long winding public gardens on the Ring and settled down at an outdoor table under a huge tree at a cafe that boasted the biggest beer selection in the world and a lot of things *mit schlag*. Ruth detested beer and never touched *schlag.* The park was postcard perfect. Harmonious blends of color in the orderly ranks of flowers, not a weed, a root, a blown petal in sight. Not a crack in any of the winding paths, not a blemish on the green benches. The dark mulch was raked smooth. Even the discreet trash cans, carefully positioned, were immaculate. The trees and bushes were pruned to the exact dimensions of a landscape laboratory. The pond gleamed green.

Until their order was delivered by the German waiter, Max made perfunctory small talk about what Ruth knew he considered frivolous. He had, he said, married a London girl who was a successful potter. They had two small children, a decaying house in Oxford, and four cats, one of whom was currently pregnant. Ruth, who abhorred cats, told him that she had a son who was about to be a freshman at Penn. She was struck immediately by an image of Ken, his open dark brown gaze fixed on the ceiling on his bedroom in her apartment near the campus as he hefted weights, between unequivocal comments about the morality of sending advisors into Central America. He was so certain about everything. Missing him sharply, she didn't hear what Max was saying until a name jumped across the heaped table as boldly as if it had been raised in neon on a large screen. She jerked, blinked and clenched her hands together on her lap.

"I didn't hear, I'm sorry."

"I said, have you heard anything about Bernard Levine?"

"No." She knew it sounded cold. She knew she looked severe, eyes darkly impenetrable, narrow face expressionless. It couldn't be helped. It was the only way she could handle it.

"He's still in jail, you know." He nodded briskly. "More than twenty years now." He waited, his pale eyes fixed on her.

"It's hard to imagine." Her voice didn't waver.

"They moved him, you know. New long-term facility outside Jo'burg. He does some gardening, someone told me. Vegetables."

Ruth was preoccupied with getting away from this. She couldn't go on sitting there, drinking black coffee, while he spooned the pastry with extra *schlag* into his mouth between throwing missiles at her.

"You know Rita divorced him?"

"I didn't know." It was a whisper.

"You've really been out of it, haven't you?"

"Look, Max . . ."

"Anyway, what I was going to tell you, the son is in trouble now."

Ruth returned her cup to its saucer. No coffee spilled. She leaned back in the metal chair and waited, looking beyond Max toward a group of young men settling noisily into some serious beer drinking.

"I know about this through certain connections I have. I can't reveal anything about that," Max announced with his old pomposity. "It's very confidential, of course, but it won't be for long, the way he's carrying on."

"Carrying on?"

"He's deeply involved in the struggle." Max, leaning across the table toward Ruth, had lowered his voice. "He's mixed up in some very dangerous action. Nelson's playing with fire."

"Nelson?"

"Bernard's son, Nelson."

She felt her eyes widen further, her eyebrows raised beneath the sweep of flecked hair. He was watching her attentively; she wanted many things, but at that moment her chief desire was to avoid permitting him to read her thoughts.

"I . . . never knew his name," she said.

"Oh, yes. Rita said afterward that Bernard wanted to honor Nelson Mandela. The child was nominated, you might say, for the cause before he was born. Of course the stepfather didn't help. Nelson didn't want to be rescued by a white knight with his own factories, a mansion in Sandton and another on the ocean at Hermanus. As well as the right contacts in Pretoria."

"Max," Ruth said pleasantly, "why are you telling me all this?"

His stare didn't shift but he smiled slightly, for the first time. The smile did not make much impact on his stolid features.

"Well, Ruth," he said, "I think you should know. I told you before, I'd been thinking of you after I heard these things. I've been thinking for some time that you should know about this. But one didn't know where you were, don't you see? As soon as I saw you I realized I should take the opportunity to inform you."

"But why?" Her voice was stringent. She licked her lips.

"Surely that's obvious? After all, you have something to do with it. You haven't actually forgotten, have you? You have some responsibility, don't you? Don't you, Ruth?"

Now she understood his need to talk to her; she saw as clearly as she would recognize her own image in the mirror, the optimistic denial that had allowed her to let him do so. She opened her purse and withdrew some notes, which she put on the table next to the plundered mound of whipped cream; and turned and walked away, feeling his malicious stare slicing into her back between her shoulder blades.

She slept badly that night, raging at the flawed impulse that had exposed her to Max Hepburn's prosecution. She should never have let it happen. She should have known better. But her guard was down; her life, at last orderly and serene, suffused with the fresh glow Anthony's love had lately brought, had provided so much distance from her defensive fortress that she had allowed its walls to crumble so that even as weak and inept an avenger as Max Hepburn could penetrate. Ruth spent much of the night at her hotel window overlooking the ghostly park, whipping herself for her vulnerability and examining its causes. America. Her work. Ken. Anthony.

In the morning, she walked into the center of Vienna, ignoring the elaborate intricacy of St. Stephen's. She plunged through the clean, controlled boulevard studded with tables at which sleek tourists spooned whipped cream onto pastries and hot chocolate; and on just a little farther, until she arrived outside the rebuilt old synagogue in the heart of what had been the thriving Jewish quarter. The block was deserted now, except for two uniformed guards in high-topped glossy black boots. These days Vienna's police provided protection against terror. The new building and the empty communal headquarters opposite were tall enough to block all sunshine from the street; just beyond, there was a small open square bathed in summer light.

There was a plaque on the padlocked door of the synagogue. Ruth wanted to examine it, but was unable to because she would have to stand between the two cops. They glanced at her as she hovered uncertainly on the narrow pavement at the beginning of the block, where the angle of the building cut a sharp shadow against the bright morning light she'd come from. One of them might ask what she was doing there if she lingered; she would have to walk forward and pass them or go back.

Chewing the inside of her cheek, looking straight ahead, Ruth walked very quickly past them, on to the sunlit square beyond. One of its sides was bounded by an old two-story house whose entrance opened upon a small courtyard; Ruth stepped into it, out of sight of the watchful policemen. It had been an apartment building of some kind. The yard contained only a badly dented iron pail and a dusty pile of sacking. There was a stunted tree in its center. This must have been where the children played. Women hung their laundry out to dry on lines stretched from the tree to the railings of the narrow porches; dust rose when rugs were beaten over those rails; and over them, mothers called at their sons not to be rough, at their little girls to keep clean, to come in out of the cold; men came home after work through that courtyard in the evening air made fragrant by warm, fresh dumplings and the tang of sliced lemon for schnitzel and the crisp sweetness of flaky strudel.

Ruth closed her eyes and took a deep breath, but all she could smell was a sick sweet odor of blood, thickening on the cobblestones; she heard the thudding smacks of rifle butts, followed by weird piercing shrieks as bone crunched; she saw the round grave eyes of small children, holding each other's hands, silently waiting their turn to climb onto the back of the black smoking truck, looming huge in the shadows. In that place where victims breathed, burned from every abandoned room, every clogged gutter, every stained cobblestone, Ruth, her calves aching, breathing in short, jagged bursts, mourned all the victims she had betrayed, all of them, not only Bernard Levine. But most of all, Bernard Levine.

She opened her eyes to find one of the guards staring at her from the entry.

"Are you all right?" he asked in English. He could not have been much more than twenty years old. Smooth-cheeked boys in uniform, children in high shiny boots always shocked her.

"Yes. I'm all right," she managed.

He nodded, smiling. He turned away, back to stand guard outside the flat, windowless concrete wall of the empty reconstructed synagogue. His hand slapped briskly at the wide leather holster which held his weapon.

Ruth left at once. Walking very quickly, she returned to the hotel, where she cabled Ken, packed her bag, called the airport. She flew out of Vienna that afternoon. She'd had a great deal of experience in walking away, leaving fast. She had run away from South Africa; and, when it was time to make her move, she'd walked out fast on Brian, Ken's father in Boston; she'd taken off quickly enough from Max Hepburn's punishment the previous day. She'd escaped many times. Ken often said she left a room faster than anyone he knew. She ran from Max's malice and from the flimsy masks tacked onto Vienna's rotten, poisonous past, trying to leave behind the flaming guilt they had refueled.

On the flight back to the States she sank into a compulsive recital as practiced as a formal prayer learned in childhood. She would never know if Bernard Levine would have been in jail if not for her; it was likely but, she had to concede, not certain; she couldn't reverse what she had done, ever; there was nothing to be gained by reliving it; she had, in any case, no choice; well, not a real choice. Like an old puckered incision that had been irritated, her guilt prickled again.

Landing at Kennedy brought relief. In the citizens' line at customs, among familiar accents, recognizable clothes and signs and baggage and gum-chewing officials, security embraced her. Bag swinging against her hip, she strode jauntily out to discover Ken waiting for her. He'd received her cable in time to drive to New York to meet her and take her back. Just seeing him there added to her buoyant, relieved homecoming.

But being with Ken as she tried to settle back into her American life, as a mother and a history teacher, turned out to be unexpectedly difficult. Ken would be moving onto the campus in a couple of weeks, a college freshman. One night, sorting books and records before his move, they discussed the courses he would take. Her son looked so much like his father had when she first met him that Ruth was always surprised when he turned the full intensity of his smoldering brown eyes upon her. Those were her eyes, but there they were, along with Brian's big blond features and gentle manner, his slow, shy smile and broad untroubled brow.

"I hear there's a bunch of reactionaries teaching government," Ken observed, reminding her that he had more of her than big brown eyes.

"You'll handle them, Ken," she said.

He chuckled.

"I'll try. Got to start somewhere."

Ken could say what he thought. In public. To anyone. He could protest, march, sit in, resist. He would remain secure. Ken could count on all of this; it did not even occur to him that he depended upon it. Bernard's boy had none of it. He'd be older than Ken, of course, several years older. Nelson. The name was Bernard Levine's defiant gesture, surprising in so unsentimental a man. For the first time, she wondered if he had ever seen his son. She couldn't remember if prisoners in his category were allowed visitors.

"Why are you crying, Mom?" Ken asked.

"Dumb old weepy mothers," Ruth muttered. She had not been aware of the tears. She had not thought about Bernard's child for years; anyway, he'd never seemed real to her. Now Max Hepburn had given him a name and a legend. Nelson was in trouble, while Ken was preparing to reconstruct the world from the security of the Ivy League, where dissent offered respectable opportunity instead of solitary confinement.

Ken's quick perceptions and quirky humor made him a wonderful companion; suddenly he was also a nagging reminder of Nelson Levine, who had grown up fatherless, perhaps because of her. She wasn't innocent.

Flexing the muscles of his young manhood, trying on a new role as easily as a T-shirt, dropping it as easily for another, gaily poking fun at the establishment, boldly defending it against her attacks, free to come and go, Ken forced Ruth to remember that she wasn't innocent. Never more so than on a humid summer night of rumbling thunder when he brought a new friend home for dinner. It wasn't by any means the first time he'd brought a black friend home; but, Ruth thought, as she served the curried chicken he'd requested in advance, it was the first time it was a black girl. Her name was Sheila; she had merry eyes and a quick, responsive smile, her jeans and T-shirt were somewhat neater than Ken's; she'd been in his high school class, she was going to Penn also; they were going on after dinner to a party. All Ruth could think of was that if Nelson Levine took a black girl home for dinner or out to a party or anywhere else, he might, until recently, have gone to jail. She had known for twenty years that she had everything, Bernard nothing. Now she was forced to see that it didn't end with them.

She didn't think she had revealed her preoccupation to Ken, but the next morning he came looking for her where she sat at a round table in the little enclosed garden behind the apartment, making notes for a course.

"What was the matter with you last night?" he asked, towering over her.

"Nothing, Ken. How was the party?"

"The party was fine. A lot of kids leaving for Duke and Emory in a day or two. But look, I want to know. Did you have some problem? Did you object to Sheila?"

"Of course not, Ken. She seems very nice. Is she special?"

"Actually, no. Not at all. But you seemed so . . . I couldn't believe you'd object because she's black."

"Of course I don't."

"Well, then, what is it? Something's on your mind."

Raising Ken, becoming a historian, living in America, Ruth had developed the awkward habit of telling the truth. Though not all of it. Her son knew nothing of her life in South Africa; only that she had left and was glad to have done so. His maturing made his inquiries more direct than ever, his perceptions were more finely tuned, his sensitivity to her moods so accurate that telling the truth had become more difficult.

"Ken," she said, "I do have something on my mind, but it's nothing to do with Sheila, I promise you. Or with you."

"What is it, then?"

"Darling, I can't talk about it now. I have to sort it out."

He let it go, he was considerate as well as direct. But it was a relief she regretted when it was time for him to go up to Boston to visit his father before school started. It seemed unreasonable that the presence of her delightful son should force Bernard Levine upon her. She was pleased to be free of that for a few days; pleased also to accept an invitation to a party for a colleague going on sabbatical. She didn't know Bob Stern very well, but she liked what she knew of him. Sally Lemay, who was giving the party, was a close friend. The evening would renew Ruth's ties to her faculty friends after the long summer and help free her of the burdens she'd been unable to leave behind in Vienna.

At first the party was just right, the quick cure Ruth needed. Sally and Dick Lemay lived outside Philadelphia, in Merion, in a stone house with a pool and a barbecue and lawn chairs on the brick patio. Ruth arrived to find ten or twelve couples lounging at the pool. In the hazy summer evening, against the hush of dense, abundant trees beyond, they were colorful, ebullient, welcoming. They were all exchanging summer news; they wanted to hear about Vienna. Ruth told them about the conference, she asked Paul if his book was finished, she talked to Joann about her new baby, she heard about Peter's sail off Cape Cod, she lay back in a chaise sipping wine, too lazily comfortable to go in the water.

When Bob and Sara Stern arrived, the pace of the party picked up. They were brimming with stories about packing, passports, alternative routes, and a housing exchange. Bob had accepted a visiting professorship for his sabbatical. In South Africa. That, it now emerged, was where they intended to go.

"I had no idea," Ruth murmured.

"Nor did we, really," Bob told her. "They only made the offer about a month ago and of course we hesitated. Certainly don't want any part of the government over there. But the university's a private institution. Teaching history isn't playing Sun City. And we'll have Christmas in summer, that'll make a welcome change."

Pleasure raised scarlet streaks on Bob's normally salmon skin. There was even a glow on his forehead beneath the already receding yellow frizzy hair.

"What school, Bob?" Ruth asked, but she knew the answer before her lips could form the question.

"University of the Witwatersrand," said Bob. "Is that how to say it?"

"More or less. Call it Wits for short. My first college."

"Oh, really?" He sniffed the air like a tracking dog, head jerking attentively upward. "Tell us all about it."

"I've been away for twenty-three years, Bob. You'll have to

16

tell me all about it when you come home again." She shifted, folding her arms, her palms flat against the sides of her sleek black bathing suit.

"Can we take anything for you, Ruth?" Sara offered. "Gifts, letters for anyone?"

"I don't think so, thank you, Sara."

"Anyone we could get in touch with? Messages? Or, perhaps, any old friends we could meet?"

"No. No, thank you. I'm quite out of touch, you know. There's nothing . . . no one now. Look, excuse me, I'm getting chilly, I must go inside and dress."

She saw Bob and Sara exchange glances as she left. Everything was conspiring against her. Resentfully, she struggled to climb back into her armor while she put on her clothes. The last thing she needed was to be dragged into conversation about South Africa; it was all behind her, over; she wouldn't have come to Sally's party if she'd known the Sterns were going to South Africa. This wasn't an occasion she could walk away from either; she couldn't leave without giving offense to people who mattered to her.

She went outside to find them all gathered around a long buffet, piling their plates high, discussing apartheid and miscegenation, the Natal beaches and the game in the Kruger Park, the price of gold and the prawns in the Cape's restaurants, and, inevitably, the state of emergency. Ruth stood near the glass doors off the patio watching them from a little distance. Twilight had drained color from the sky and the water; the tops of the trees were huge smudges; everything was shadowed, gray, obscure, except the outlines of her friends in their bright summer clothes, clustered under a spotlight around heaped bowls of vegetables, steaming, skewered meats, breadbaskets and bottles of wine.

Threaded through the hum of conversation, she heard, wincing, code phrases she'd tried to seal away forever; and then, above it all, Sara's assured prehensile young voice.

"Of course there isn't anything we can really do, I know that.

17

But at least we can go and see for ourselves. It's all going to fall apart very soon. It'll be a bloodbath. This may be our last chance to see it."

Ruth swayed, leaned back against the glass door. She clenched her fists in the folds of her long cotton skirt. She pressed her teeth together tight.

"There may be things you can do," Sally said. "Learn all you can and then come home and talk about it, write about it, get people involved."

"We're excited," Bob said. "It's a hell of an opportunity for us."

Ruth walked over to the table in its circle of light. She spooned food on a plate, sipped a glass of wine, chatted with her friends. She spoke less than usual and the lines that curved from her nose around her mouth to her tilted chin were deeper than they had been, but no one noticed. None of them knew about her. They were colleagues and friends, some going back as much as twelve years, since she had first come to Philadelphia from Boston, yet none of them knew anything more than that she had been a South African and had left. She'd learned as she got older that people didn't have to know anything much about one to be friends. In America, at any rate, life's phases could be placed into compartments, labeled in code, sealed and stored away. No one here knew anything about her; she directed her remaining energy to keeping it that way. Her fortress had been painstakingly constructed; no chance combination of pressures was going to invade it.

But Ruth's dreams came back that night and the night after. Beardless young men in khaki, in the high-topped black boots which, marching in unison, made the pounding rhythm that first intruded them upon her, came from three sides onto the lawn around the palm tree; there was an opening on the fourth side, where the sweet flowery perfume of the yesterday, today, and tomorrow bushes spread over the high wood gate; she ran in their

18

direction, to be met by the sounds of more pounding boots, ranks of soldiers, coming for her. This time they chanted also, in the rounded, finished sounds of Sara Stern; "Last chance, last chance, last chance" gave the cadence for their march.

The day before Ken was due to return from Boston, Ruth called Bob Stern. She would like, she said, to take him up on his offer to do something for her in South Africa. She didn't want to be a nuisance; could she meet him somewhere convenient? Bob was delighted, no problem, he had books to return to the library, they could lunch somewhere on campus together, they should be wicked and gorge at La Terrasse.

Bob's robust frame gave evidence of frequent wickedness. Ruth was waiting at a table at a window on the verandah when he appeared, chunky, glowing, in the doorway. He bounced toward her, something reassuring and solid projected from his short sturdy figure.

"Sara and I were surprised you didn't have messages to send with us," he said. "Family, friends, whatever." But he attended to his priorities first, choosing the filling for his omelet after a lot of thought and nodding jauntily when the waitress asked about potatoes and bread. A carafe of wine would hit the spot, certainly. Ruth ordered a plain omelet and black coffee.

"You're sure? You're really careful, aren't you?"

"It's just habit," she said.

"You're so restrained, Ruth. I envy that." He leaned forward, propping his elbows on the table between them. His thick, freckled arms were sun-reddened. His ruddy face wore an amiable look of anticipation.

"Now tell me what we can do. We're delighted you changed your mind."

"I heard some news that has made me change my mind," Ruth said. "There is something I'd like you to do, but very discreetly, Bob."

His features adjusted to flushed gravity.

19

"Of course. Tell me."

"There's a man I used to know. He's in jail. He's been in jail for more than twenty years."

"Political?"

"Yes." She swallowed. "Treason."

Bob leaned farther forward, but made no comment. He had wondered for years about Ruth's South African life, ever since it became clear that she didn't care to discuss it. A lot of people wondered, he knew.

"His name is Bernard Levine," said Ruth. She had not spoken the name aloud for so long that it sounded to her like words in a foreign language.

"That's vaguely familiar," Bob murmured, gazing briefly at the hanging plant overhead as if an image in its swaying fronds would make the identification for him.

"The trial was rather sensational. It must have been covered in the media here. And he's become something of a symbol," Ruth said. "I'd like to hear any news of him you can get without embarrassment. But the main thing — what I'd really appreciate, Bob — is if you could try and find out about his son."

She stopped abruptly. She had planned what to say; she had decided what she would not say. But she wasn't sure how to continue now, with Bob's expression suddenly earnest and yet remote. She had to speak, though; the silence was becoming awkward.

"The boy's name is Nelson," she said. "He's about twenty-two, he was born during the trial. I heard from an ex–South African I bumped into at the meeting in Vienna that his mother had divorced Bernard and remarried."

Bob's eyes shifted, narrowed; his lips pressed together. She struggled for a tone of impersonal concern.

"Anyway," Ruth went on, "I heard the boy may be heading for trouble. It's bothering me, it seems very . . . sad. My source in Vienna is unreliable. I may be worrying for nothing. I thought you might be able to pick up some information and let me know if you learn anything."

She intended to sound casual. She didn't know if she was succeeding. Bob took his elbows off the table and attacked his omelet.

"I'll do whatever I can, of course. I have no idea how to go about it, though. Can you suggest any lines of inquiry?"

"Wits was a caldron of gossip in my day," Ruth said. "Johannesburg's a big city but the political community, the white one, I mean, is very incestuous. University people often know things they shouldn't. Some of the history faculty, other fields also, used to be . . . progressive. You'll be able to identify whom to talk to very quickly, I think."

When Bob frowned he did it with his whole face, scrunching it toward its center.

"I'll try, really I will. But wouldn't it be better if I got in touch with the mother, explained you were inquiring . . ."

"No, no," she cut in quickly. "Don't do that. That wouldn't do at all. One of the things I want to ask you is not to tell anyone I'm looking for information. I only want you to do it if you can keep me out of it."

Bob thought of himself as a measured and discreet man. He wanted to know more; he certainly wanted to help, but he didn't understand the mission, which would make it difficult.

"Isn't there anyone specific I could talk to?"

"There is one person." Ruth had hoped to avoid this. "He's in political science, very senior now, I think he's the chairman. His name is Gerald Gordon. He'd be likely to know about Bernard. And Nelson. But I'd rather he didn't know about me, Bob. I don't want you to do it if you can't manage to keep me out of it."

"I understand," said Bob.

"You'll meet him naturally, it's a very small community, comparatively. There'll be parties and things to welcome you, he's an obvious person for you to meet when you're settling down. You'll like him, by the way. He's very bright and he used to be very funny in a dry sort of way. He studied at Oxford, he's rather a star at Wits. It wouldn't be odd for you to ask him about Bernard. His name is very prominently linked to dissent, it's quite likely you would know it."

"I'll do my best," Bob promised. "I'll write as soon as there's anything to say; I hope I'll be able to be reassuring."

"I hope so, it's very kind of you."

It didn't occur to either of them that Ruth would be flying to meet him in Johannesburg four months later. After they parted, Ruth walked out into a hazy afternoon past buildings still closed in summer torpor, sidewalks deserted. It would all change in a week or two, when the students came back. She wanted to be ready for that; she drew a deep breath, jiggled her shoulders up and down, shedding the old, recalcitrant burden. She'd done what she could. She belonged here now, in Philadelphia, with Ken. Perhaps with Anthony also. She didn't want distractions, memories, guilt; she needed time and uncluttered emotions to discover whether she and Anthony could sustain the glowing connection they'd recently found, the enduring connection she had believed she could never make again.

With the discipline learned long ago as a tool for sanity, perhaps for survival, Ruth put Bernard Levine and his son, Nelson, into the cave in the dark ocean behind her mind reserved for ghosts and clung firmly to the framework of her painstakingly constructed American life. She had her priorities in order until Bob Stern's letters started arriving.

Bob and Sara had reached Johannesburg in late August. His first letter to Ruth was written in mid-September. Ruth, reminding herself that she had asked for this, skimmed the first page of tissue-thin airmail paper, covered with Bob's raptures about the beauty of the campus and the suburbs, the sophistication of the city, the glorious value of the dollar. He was struck by the eerie naturalness of pervasive apartheid, the comfort of everyday life. They'd met a lot of interesting people, including Gerald Gordon at a dinner party the previous night. Now Ruth read every word.

"He's a formidable guy. Everyone defers to him. You were right, he is head of the department, in fact he seems to be the most important English-speaking political scientist in the country. Even the Afrikaners respect him, I'm told. He's done everything: government advisory groups, international commissions, lectured and consulted all over the world, written a dozen books. He seems rather above it all at first but he's extremely witty and had everyone laughing uproariously over dinner. I talked to him for a while about the U.S. He's very knowledgeable. I didn't want to rush into a discussion about Bernard Levine, but don't worry. His very chic wife, Carolyn, who is British, has invited us to dinner soon and I'll have an opportunity. They're both intriguing and I am looking forward to it. I understand they live in a mansion."

Gerald Gordon had evidently made a huge impression on Bob Stern. Ruth thought that, apart from acquiring a chic wife and a mansion, he seemed much like the Gerald she had known rather well. Bob wrote a good letter and she anticipated the next one without anxiety. It came two weeks later.

"Sara and I went to the Gordons' for dinner last night. They live in a magnificent old house in a park-like setting in a neighborhood called Lower Houghton. Do you know it?" Ruth sniffed. "The arrangements are very lavish by American standards. There was a valet — black, of course — who took the car to park somewhere off the big circular driveway. We were received by a white butler in a tux at an entrance portico. The house is jammed with antiques and Persian rugs and a huge collection of art, including, would you believe, an original Renoir in the living room."

Ruth remembered it well. Gerald was obviously living in his parents' old house on the corner of Seventh Avenue. The chic wife must have added the valet. Gerald had once discussed the extraordinary intensity of the Renoir model's eyes, comparing their deep velvet texture with the luminous tones of the surrounding skin. When Ruth showed no interest, demonstrating by her wandering gaze some disdain for such superficial preoccupations, Gerald walked up behind her, put his hands on her shoulders, and steered her to an ornate mirror, bordered in gold leaf. "Look in there," he said. "Take a real look, for once. Stop playacting." Irritated by the accusation, she hadn't looked at all, leaping instead into denials that she was anything but utterly authentic. She hadn't understood what he was saying or couldn't hear it, then or later.

"I couldn't understand a university professor living like this," Bob's letter went on, "but one of the other guests, a guy I've gotten to know in history, whispered that Gordon inherited a fortune and Carolyn is a millionaire in her own right, daughter of an English lord or something. There were twenty of us at a long table for a formal dinner with three Cape wines and sherbet to clear the palate before the saddle of lamb. Conversation was pretty general, they all asked a lot of well-informed questions about the States. The talk turned to the media, responsible journalism, self-censorship and, by lucky coincidence, Levine's name came up naturally over the cherries flambé."

Ruth, who had been enjoying Bob's gossipy letter, raised her head and gritted her teeth together until her lower jaw hurt. It had always been impossible to visualize Bernard serving his sentence. It was impossible now. But she saw him eating, quite clearly. Not cherries flambé on gold-rimmed bone china set on a gleaming stretch of white damask, crystal glinting cool in candlelight; but strawberries, picked fresh from their tangled vines, spreading across the ground behind the stables in Sandown. They'd gathered the strawberries and carried them in a basket made by holding up Ruth's swingy blue skirt, all the way down to the willows next to the pond and ate them there, just like that, ate them from Ruth's lap and lay close together in the shelter made by the limp waving drifts of willow, all the long afternoon, breathing in unison, listening to each other's heart beat. Bernard ate the strawberries with devoted attention. "We didn't pick enough," he said mournfully. "They're never enough." Ruth didn't suppose there were strawberries or leafy willows in jail.

"They asked if we get news in the U.S. about their political trials. I said we get news about major events, not much about personalities. Then someone asked why there's so little pressure from the U.S. about long-term political prisoners like Mbane and Leshosi. And Levine. That gave me the perfect opportunity to ask about him. He and several others were moved from Robben Island to a new maximum security prison outside Jo'burg a while ago, no one quite knows why. He's now the only white facing life imprisonment. I was appalled to learn that he was often in solitary confinement . . ."

Ruth's hand was shaking so much that she could not read the handwriting. She put the letter down on the table near the kitchen window where she had been sitting, warmed by the brilliant sunshine of the early fall afternoon. She stood up, blinking, rubbing the back of her neck. The trees beyond were just starting to turn; the first haze of pale gold, the random spots of flaming red looked suddenly garish. She turned back to Bob's letter, standing over it.

". . . often in solitary confinement, sometimes for months on end, but much less in recent years. He is allowed books and is now permitted to write, though not, of course, for publication. He's a serious student of languages, which struck me as terribly sad."

Ruth didn't agree. She thought it was terribly optimistic. Idiotic, then, to be shaking and crying.

"I asked about his family and several people offered bits of information. His parents are both alive, he is divorced, he has a son, about twenty. I was pretty pleased with myself for getting to your mission so easily, so I asked about the son. There was an awkward hush, the first — the only — silence of the evening.

Everyone avoided looking at Gerald, who made a great fuss about uncorking more bottles of wine. Carolyn said something about talking of children and told a funny malicious story about selecting a good private school. I realized I'd put my foot in it and worried that I'd lost the chance to learn anything about young Nelson. But much later, after a dazzling array of liqueurs in the living room (or lounge, as they call it), Gerald came up to me. He suggested a breath of air, opened the French doors and led me outside onto a circular brick terrace, bordered by a rose garden, cunningly lit from beneath.

" 'Curious you asking about Bernard's son,' he said. 'May I ask why you're interested?'

" 'No special reason,' I said, feeling very uncomfortable. 'I've read a little about Levine, so . . .'

" 'I'm Nelson's guardian,' Gerald said. 'But I expect you know that.'

" 'No, I had no idea.' He was staring at me. 'Really, there's no way I knew.' It occurred to me that he suspected I was some sort of agent. I suddenly felt very foreign. I had to reassure him. 'Idle curiosity, that's all. I'm sorry. Everyone reacted at dinner as though I'd thrown a bomb. Forgive me for blundering.'

" 'Quite all right,' he said. 'People are very circumspect here. And some of them may know I have some difficulties at the moment. Nelson is . . . not easy.'

"I felt that I could not ask any more questions, but he seemed to want to talk about him.

" 'He's a medical student, you know. Very bright, too. Going through a bit of delayed adolescent rebellion, I'd say. Rather a worry to his parents.'

"He kept looking at me and I kept looking at the magnificent tea roses, grouped in blocks of color, glowing against the darkness because of the hidden lights.

"That was it, Ruth. I must say I feel that I was put on the spot. I don't like operating under false pretenses. I can't introduce the subject with Gerald Gordon again, but will certainly keep an eye and ear open for you."

Ruth went at once to the bathroom and washed her face several times. Rubbing it dry, she caught a glimpse of herself in the mirror, just a slice of her face, the bones of her temples and cheeks angled in a frame around her eyes, huge, so darkly brown they looked black, wide, vulnerable. She pressed her hands firmly together to reduce the tremor and then carefully applied fresh makeup, as meticulously as if she were going to a party. She returned to the kitchen and sat down at the table, her back to the high, clear light and the arching trees, to reply to Bob Stern.

She apologized for putting Bob in an awkward position; she'd had no idea that Gerald Gordon was Nelson's guardian. She certainly understood that he could not question Gerald further though anything he might learn accidentally would be very helpful. She did not tell Bob that his news had placed her firmly in the center of an evenly weighted scale: the desire to know more exactly balanced by the desire to keep out of it and prevent her American colleagues from learning anything about her own past.

Her letter crossed in the mail with Bob's next, hurried note.

"I want to let you know at once that your name has come up, unavoidably. A couple of days after the dinner party Gerald Gordon phoned to ask if I knew Ruth Fredman. I was reviewing a paper with a very sullen student at the time, didn't make any connection and told him I didn't know any Fredman. This morning I bumped into him in the parking lot, strange because he has a chairman's spot in another location. He asked if I knew Ruth Harris. It's just as well that I said yes, because he knows that you teach history at the same college I do. Didn't I know that your maiden name was Fredman? Of course I did not. He said he would appreciate a private conversation. It did not seem possible to question him or refuse. We have arranged to meet late this afternoon, at a place called the Wilds, to which he has given me directions. It may now be impossible for me to protect your anonymity in regard to Bernard and Nelson Levine. I am sorry, I am doing the best I can. I had no idea your request would turn out to be so complicated."

Ruth had not had any such idea either. She waited in brittle anxiety for the next letter. Her discomfort about embarrassing Bob, even her terror of what he might uncover about her, were now eclipsed by agitation. If Gerald wanted to talk to Bob at the Wilds he must be afraid that their conversation would be taped. What could he have to say that was dangerous? Was it possible, after all, that Gerald was in some trouble himself? The idea was bizarre; it had to be something about Bernard's son. But what did she have to do with it? How had Gerald traced her? She wished she could call Bob, but knew it was too risky. Twenty years ago the Special Branch monitored all overseas calls. She had to assume they did it still, just as she assumed they might still be keeping an eye on her.

Bob was conscientious. His next letter arrived two days later.

"I had a very disturbing meeting with Gerald Gordon," he wrote. "We met at a beautiful open park, almost deserted at five in the afternoon. Although there are lawns and ponds with interesting fish and lilies, he insisted on climbing up the winding paths of a very large steep hill. On all sides huge rocks are arranged to display an extraordinary array of gardens, all indigenous plants. All the way up, Gerald pointed out various local treasures, although I kept telling him I am not a naturalist. We passed very few people, a couple of groups of school kids coming down, giggling, and an elderly couple who greeted us as if we were all guests at the same country inn. Gerald made it clear he would talk of nothing but ferns and wildflowers until we reached the top. In spite of his slim build and pale, almost delicate appearance, he is extremely forceful. At the top, which is just a small, flat square, he stood and surveyed the slopes from every angle. There was no one in sight, no one at all in hearing distance. We sat on a large slab of rock and watched the sun blaze down, the colors more fiery as they concentrated above the horizon. I was glad to sit down. It was a brisk climb. Gerald seems to be in good shape. He waited until I had caught my breath. Then he said I must forgive him, life in South Africa must seem mysterious to an American, but he'd thought it best to make certain we could not be overheard. He wanted to know whether you had asked me to inquire about Bernard and Nelson Levine. I hesitated. You were so explicit about not bringing you into it. I'm not a good liar, Ruth. I have not had any practice. He saw me hesitate and said at once, 'Don't answer, it's all right. Let me just think a minute.' Then he asked if I know you well.

" 'I think so,' I said. 'She's senior, of course, but we've been colleagues for nine or ten years. We have many mutual friends.'

'Tell me about her,' he said. 'I haven't seen her for twenty years.'

" 'She's an intelligent, attractive woman. Solid teacher, exceptional scholar. She's done very well.'

" 'But what's she like? Personally, I mean?'

" 'She's well liked. She's rather a private person. Divorced before she came to Penn. She has a son, college freshman, very devoted.'

" 'She has a son, you say? She adjusted well?'

" 'To life in the U.S.?'

"He nodded. He was smiling, I don't know why.

" 'Oh, she's an American now. Except for her accent you'd never know she'd ever lived anywhere else.'

"There was a long silence. He whistled. I must say I've never met anyone quite like him.

" 'Bob,' he said quietly, 'do you think Ruth would like news of . . . former friends?'

"I wanted to tell him that you would like just that, but couldn't because of your prohibition. So I said I would ask you, and could I mention his name? He said of course, you and he are old pals. Then he really shook me up.

" 'There's a new disaster in the making here, Bob. Ruth might be able to help. The question is whether she will want to. Could you write and ask her? At once?'

"Of course I said yes. I asked a lot of questions, but couldn't get him to say another thing, except that the disaster involves both Bernard Levine and his son.

"I am mystified. I was glad to take on simple inquiries when you asked, but a great deal more seems to be involved. I hope you will not take offense when I say that I don't want to be used. You have set me up as a go-between when I have no idea of what is going on. I don't want to stand by and watch a disaster occur because I won't help, but I must know what I am doing. I don't understand, for example, why he doesn't write to you himself."

Ruth understood that very well. It was all the things she couldn't understand when she read the letter that brought the terror back into trembling hands and the nerve jumping arrhythmically in the back of her neck. She waited three hours, watching thin gold leaves drift down from the elm beyond her kitchen window. The elm was a survivor, one of the very few that had resisted withering disease; the leaves were as delicate as the tissues of hidden memory.

She was afraid to waste a minute longer. When she could hold her pen firmly enough to write she thanked Bob and apologized again. Your friend doesn't write directly because his letter or the response may be read by others. Your friend didn't create this situation, it is a fact of life. She wished she could clarify things, but was as mystified as Bob himself. She had no idea what disaster threatened. The request for her help was inexplicable. She and Bob's friend and the individual he was protecting had been close once, but had been without contact for twenty years. For old times' sake, of course she would help if she could, which she very much doubted. She hoped Bob would transmit his friend's request to her.

Arms folded, head bent, Ruth paced her apartment after writing her reply. She wanted desperately to send it by special delivery, express mail, radio, chartered flight, satellite, there must be some way to get it there fast, an interplanetary invisible courier, perhaps. After an hour's steady walking, up and down the center of each room, she acknowledged that even express mail was too dangerous. All she could manage was regular old airmail, several strong cups of coffee, and taut self-discipline.

During the sixteen days she had to wait for Bob's next letter, Ruth fought her nightmares by reciting poetry. She wasn't in jail now. She had books, she was allowed to read; she could switch on a lamp at will, she need not wait in darkness; she had a large bed, space around her, she need not lie rigid, feet cramping, in one position. But she retreated to the self-imposed compulsion she had learned, long ago, in the bleak days of her own solitary confinement.

In the dark, flat on her back, she recited quietly, "The highwayman came riding, riding, the highwayman came riding, up to the old something door." When she couldn't remember the words, she made them up. The thing had to scan. "I caught this morning morning's minion, kingdom of daylight's dauphin, dapple-dawn-drawn falcon, underneath him steady air." Or was it "riding high there"? She didn't look it up. She tried it different ways. She recited half a dozen more. Then, the familiar culminating lines. "Who can find a virtuous woman? for her price is far above rubies. The heart of her husband doth safely trust in her . . ." She couldn't remember how to go on; for this, she couldn't manufacture a substitute. But the lines reliably released tears from her tight locked terror until, at last, she could escape into sleep.

During the days she went about her routine with meticulous concentration. She made the most of every little task. She filled the hours with endless, consuming, mostly pointless activity. She made lists of things to do. Whenever the "disaster" clenched her stomach or blocked her swallowing, she did push-ups and knee bends.

She went home every day at lunch hour to check her mail, though there was no possibility of a reply for at least eleven days. On the sixteenth day, with no mail from South Africa, she returned resolutely to her office and concentrated on grading term papers. She was so absorbed that she didn't notice Sally Lemay come into the room until Sally was standing in front of her holding out a sealed envelope. The weirdest thing, she said excitedly, she'd had a letter from Bob Stern, enclosing a sealed one for Ruth. Strange that he hadn't mailed it direct. Ruth, blinking, stretched out a hand. She took the letter. Sally sat down to gossip. Ruth felt her eyes becoming larger. The bones of her face stretched her skin. It was difficult to speak. It hurt to swallow. Sally didn't notice. She was wondering if the dean realized how inflexible the chairman was . . . Ruth said she was sorry, she had to finish grading, she was already behind. Sally made a few more remarks about the chairman, Bob's sabbatical, the sleet icing up the roads, and left. Ruth got up and closed the door. She had been holding the letter since taking it from Sally. She looked at it and locked the door. She sat down and opened the letter.

Bob Stern was a fast learner. He used her title for Gerald Gordon. "My friend was pleased by your response," his letter began. "I am sending this by a means he has suggested. He did make several things clearer to me, enough so I feel I must continue in this role."

Ruth wasn't so selfless that she didn't take a few seconds to worry whether Gerald had made clearer to Bob the details of her own past. But she turned back to the letter very quickly.

"My friend was asked long ago, at the time of the divorce, to represent the father's interest with the son. The boy has been rebellious for years. Managing him has been much more challenging lately. His behavior will be familiar to you. My friend says he pushes the limits further."

Ruth, who had been slumped over the letter, jerked upright.

These were Gerald's phrases, but what did they mean? Nelson was behaving the way Bernard had, only more so? What more was there to do? Had anything more been invented?

"My friend wants to make alternative arrangements for the boy, for his own health and his father's. That is how you can help. He will consult the father for permission. I will then get in touch with you. I hope I am making all this clear. I also hope I will not regret what I am doing."

Ruth could only speculate about the meaning of Gerald's cryptic message. She had theories to match every mood. She thought up new ones every day. No theory explained why Gerald thought she could help. Or why Bernard, of all people, might want her to do so. The news that Gerald would talk to Bernard was utterly bewildering; trying to guess what would pass between them was impossible. That didn't prevent her from trying, though. She dreamed at night of high black boots, marching in time to the jarring shout "Last chance, last chance" around the outside of a barbed wire cage, from whose upper edges raw and jagged wires dripped dark blood. She could not see inside the cage. She tried, but she always woke up, rigid, drenched, too soon.

She waited three weeks for the next letter. When it came, it answered no questions, it only asked new ones. It was addressed to her apartment.

"I am writing to invite you to visit us over the Christmas vacation. Sara and I would enjoy showing you around and spending time with you. Our house has plenty of room and this sabbatical gives us a great opportunity to reciprocate all your hospitality. Sara joins me in sending regards . . . P.S. You wanted to make it up to Ben."

A rush of hot tears splashed down onto the postscript as she read it. It was, of course, Gerald's message. "I'll spend the rest of my life wanting to make up for it" had been her last words to him before she left him at Jan Smuts Airport to fly to the United States twenty years before. Ben had been her private name for Bernard.

Now watching from the window as the British Airways plane flew into the first streaky gray light of dawn, she had to brace herself for meeting Bob Stern again, this time at Jan Smuts Airport, where he insisted he would welcome her. She'd known perfectly well, when she'd asked him to find out about Nelson Levine, that he might also learn a great deal about her. She hadn't thought it likely; but in any case, though she hated the idea, it was a risk she had been prepared to take. She had not expected Bob's letters to become signals on the road that would return her to South Africa.

She hadn't ever gone back. Not once. Not even when her father was dying. Not that she knew; they kept it from her so there was no chance she would appear. Not even for his funeral; it had not been very difficult to accept her mother's insistent plea on the phone that the risk of arrest wasn't worth it, now that he was gone. The judgment that she'd injured him so much in life that her attendance at his funeral was redundant was not explicit, but Ruth heard it clearly. She accepted it. She did not return for her little sister's wedding either; or to help her mother sell and pack up to move to London to be near Rachel's growing family.

Now she was going back. Beyond the window, the plane was banked by coral-swept cumulus. The screen of early morning cloud obscured the land beneath. She didn't know what she would find when she got back; she only knew, sadly, that she had no choice. It might be her last chance. It wasn't only Max Hepburn's attack in Vienna or the alarming success of Bob Stern's inquiries that returned her to the place from which she had only barely, and at terrible cost, escaped, just before Bernard's trial and the birth of his son, Nelson.

She was returning also because of Anthony Brill, who made her laugh, fed her chocolate, rubbed her calves; Anthony, who said he loved her, lent her his toothbrush, got out of bed at four o'clock in the morning to follow her to the kitchen and ask why she couldn't sleep and, when she couldn't tell him, stayed with her anyway; Anthony, who waited up with her all night when Ken, driving back to Philadelphia in a winter storm after a visit to his father in Boston, came home five hours later than the absolute latest she'd expected; Anthony, who told her his life. It was Anthony who said he intended to marry her, who said that she could trust him; and did not understand her pain when he said that he trusted her. She had told Anthony that she had unfinished business in South Africa she could not explain. When he accepted this without hesitation, he confirmed her own horrified recognition that she had to go back.

The pilot announced their descent. The fall toward land began. As the plane lurched, steadied, and angled down, Ruth understood the reason for her dream of severed limbs and trunks floating on turbulent water. She'd been four years old on her only other trip into South Africa, traveling from England on the *Umgeni* with her mother, who was desperate to abandon the bombed rubble and shelters of London and return home to her family in sunny South Africa, now that her husband was somewhere in Europe with the Royal Army Medical Corps. For Ruth, her father was a gentle memory of restrained amusement and a formal photograph in full dress uniform. She was not aware of missing him. She was also not aware at the time that the *Umgeni* had to sail the long way around, taking in New York and Montevideo on its way to the Cape of Good Hope, which some people on the boat also called the Cape of Storms. Taking the long way around did not avoid the German subs or bombers, which left other boats ripped to pieces, along with their crew and passengers; wartime regulations forbade the ships to stop for rescue missions, so that the bodies floated until they sank. Sometimes she thought they'd been calling out, crying for help, she thought she heard their voices pitifully through the crashing waves, she thought she should have helped them.

When Ruth first arrived in South Africa, she settled down with her mother in her grandparents' suburban home in Johannesburg. She was an alien. Her straight black hair was cut too short, her fingernails were too long, her accent was wrong, she did not belong, she was foreign. She had been a foreigner of one kind or another ever since; and would be now, she knew. As the plane touched down and rode the runway, slowing for her return, she combed her hair back with her fingers, straightened her narrow black sweater over her jeans, swung her pouchy leather bag over her shoulder. She was an American now. Alien. This time it was better that way.

CHAPTER TWO

Ruth walked down the steps onto the runway into the crisp air of Johannesburg summer. She was at once enclosed by sunshine and suspicious unease. Her point of escape had been a dusty, flat, sprawling building, cut out of the veld. Now Jan Smuts was a huge international airport. The massive customs hall with its counters and loudspeakers and curved bright plastic chairs and slippery floors and ramps and signs were the same as all big airports everywhere. The same, but not quite the same. Here the officials spoke English with the raw whine of their native Afrikaans; there were more men with mustaches and shiny suits and guns in their armpits; the black porters sounded awkward and unfamiliar, until Ruth remembered that in Philadelphia blacks spoke like whites; in South Africa their first language was Zulu or Xhosa.

She was clammy when it was her turn to go through the foreign entry line. She stood at the glass window and pushed her American passport through the slot at the uniformed official. He had a gun in his belt, a large, drooping mustache and small dark eyes glittering among pads of thickened, sallow skin. He spent a long time looking from Ruth to her passport picture.

"What is the purpose of your visit to South Africa?" he inquired lugubriously.

"I'm just visiting," she said.

"Visiting who?" he said, staring at the picture.

"An American colleague. He's teaching at Wits. I'm going to stay with them. I'm just touring." Her voice fell away as she heard she was talking too much. He was staring at her now.

"You're a South African," he said flatly.

In twenty years she hadn't lost her accent. It marked her foreign in Philadelphia, it identified her unmistakably here. She hadn't even thought of it when she'd fondled the American passport like a security blanket.

"I'm an American," she said, gesturing at the blue passport.

He sniffed, turned the pages over, sniffed again.

"When were you last here?" he savored each word.

"I left in nineteen sixty-four," Ruth said.

"You haven't been home since then?"

"No."

She wanted to look behind to see if Special Branch detectives were approaching. She was afraid to turn away.

"Well," he said, "everything's much bigger now. But still pretty, the best. You will be here two weeks?"

She nodded.

"Have a nice holiday," he handed back the passport.

She walked rigidly to collect her bag. The old terror, shooting through every nerve end, was back in place as if it had never left. Terror of talking too much, saying the wrong word, fumbling into a trap. By the time she'd moved mechanically through customs and zippered her bag, free to leave the airport and return to Johannesburg, she had forced enough composure upon herself to go out and look for Bob Stern. If an ordinary airport clerk reduced her to a paranoid quivering sponge, she might as well turn around and get on the next flight home.

Bob's crinkly yellow hair and bright plaid short-sleeve shirt looked wonderfully foreign in the crowd waiting for passengers outside customs. His shouted "Hi, Ruth, right over here" was resoundingly American. No South African handshake either, there was a hug and a warm kiss on her cheek, he grabbed her bag and started chattering immediately, as they went to find his car. Had to buy one, of course, sell it when they leave; Sara wasn't with him, the mornings were a bit difficult, she'd explain herself; how was the flight, the weather on Christmas Day when she'd left, wasn't the sun wonderful? There was so much to talk about, she must be bushed, breakfast would be waiting at home, the house in Westcliff was very convenient, did she remember the neighborhood? When they were settled and on their way in the bright orange Volkswagen, she remembered to ask politely about his work.

"It's different here," he said at once, shifting in the driver's seat, one elbow thrust comfortably out of the open window into the December summer. "Besides all the obvious things, very few black students or faculty, university much more isolated from the real life of the city, I don't mean all of that. Everything's much more formal. The kids are kind of respectful. And teaching them, well, you can't read them as easily, d'you know what I mean?"

"The surface of everything is much denser here," Ruth said quietly.

Bob turned eagerly toward her, nodding, then looked back at the broad highway, land falling away flat and green on either side, the gray outlines of the city ahead.

"You're right, that's it exactly. People don't react as fast or as openly. Faculty too, we've met a lot of people, they're very hospitable and friendly, but it's harder to figure them."

"You can't identify people the same way, can you?" said Ruth. "I wonder how much that's being a foreigner and how much it's the white South African obduracy you're up against?"

"Can't tell. But you'll be able to. You're not a foreigner, Ruth."

She closed her eyes, feeling the skin around them tight and drawn.

"I suppose not," she said. "But I feel like one. You know,

Bob, I never really belonged here, I never felt like a South African."

She felt his glance on her and opened her eyes again. Ahead, the mine dumps rose, bulky outlines littered with rubble, pebbly sand, discarded paper, cans, bottle tops at their base. They didn't look as big as she remembered. Pale yellow dusty hills, that's all they were, debris from the pulsing heart of the gold mines. Above, the sky was a steady, pervasive blue, a solid blue like nowhere else on earth that she had seen, though she'd searched for it.

"Ruth," Bob said. She heard a warning signal and sat up straighter, staring ahead. "I gather you decided to come to . . . look into this problem with the Levine boy. Of course, we'll help if we can."

"Thank you," she made herself whisper. "Thanks for all you've done."

"I assume you want to see Gerald Gordon as soon as possible."

She had no idea what Bob Stern knew about Bernard and his son. Or about her. He gave no clue.

"We thought of inviting him over tonight, if you'd like."

Ruth didn't know what to say. She didn't know how to handle Bob. And Sara, mustn't forget Sara and her appetite for other people's secrets.

"I know you must be very tired, but you don't have much time."

"You know I have to be back for the beginning of the semester, Bob. I've got a normal two-week vacation, that's all. I'd rather go back sooner if I could."

"Yes, well, that's why we thought . . . would you like to see the Gordons tonight?" He was choosing his words carefully.

Traffic was heavier now and the green open land had given way to the miserable little cottages and shacks and warehouses and dry dusty strips of yard that litter the outskirts of every city. Nothing was familiar, except the high blue above.

"Does Gerald know I'm here?" Ruth licked her lips.

"Of course, Ruth." Bob cleared his throat, shifted uncomfortably, and brought his arm inside the car, stretching it straight out toward the steering wheel.

She needed to know what Bob had learned about her, she wanted to know how much he'd found out, how distorted it was, how he judged her, how to measure the damage; but she couldn't think of a way to ask. Anything she said might reveal more than he knew already. She had territory to defend, she mustn't get careless. Bob Stern would return to Philadelphia and tell everyone about her; the less he knew, the less he could repeat, analyze, embellish. How could she talk to Gerald Gordon in his presence, then? And how could she not, after all he'd already done, running messages between her and Gerald? She was trapped, as always in this ambiguous, distorted place, trapped by her own muddled intentions.

"Perhaps," she said softly, "I could phone Gerald and chat a little. Then we'll see if tonight's a good idea."

"Whatever you say," said Bob evenly and then they were out, away from the approaches to the city built on gold, driving past neat suburban houses, set back behind evenly cut lawns, surrounded by bright flowers, shrubs dense with blossoms, canopies of trees. Here and there the sheen of a swimming pool glistened. There were fences around every house, bars on every shining window, double and triple locks on every well-hung door. As they drove deeper into the northern suburbs, Ruth saw dogs romping with children in the shade of huge jacarandas, purple drifts touching the sky. Nannies in starched white uniforms and perky white caps supervised the play.

"We were lucky to get a house in such a good neighborhood," Bob said. "The owner's a computer engineer, doing research in the States this year. He took his family, left us the house, the dog, and the maid. Worked out just right for us."

He turned into a driveway edged by a deep bed of dark blue agapanthus, interspersed with pale lilies. Ruth had forgotten how things grew here. Dripping lushly off the broad front verandah, massed golden trumpet-shaped flowers exploded from dark green vines. Bob brought the car to a halt right in front of the verandah just as Sara stepped out, waving above the folds of a billowing maternity smock.

"Ruth, how lovely to see you." They touched cheeks. Then, answering Ruth's look of smiling inquiry, Sara said, in a hushed voice, "Yes, four and a half months already. That's why I couldn't come with Bob to get you. I'm still having the morning wobblies, can't stand the car early in the day."

She led them through the hall, past a sunny, comfortable living room, to a dining room whose French doors opened to a stretch of lawn with a fishpond ornamented by a stone cherub and huge lilies floating on its surface. The polished table was set for breakfast. As soon as they walked in, the maid appeared through the swinging door from the kitchen. She carried a large tray with coffee, tea, orange juice, and a steaming silver casserole, whose cover she removed so that they could inspect the bacon, eggs, and toast beneath. Ruth smiled at the maid, who did not acknowledge her presence. Sara said, "Ruth, this is Ellen. This is our visitor, Mrs. Harris." Ellen set the dishes carefully on the table.

"The servant comes with the house," Sara explained as soon as she retreated behind the door. "We'd never have hired one ourselves, of course, but the owners wanted to keep her."

"And she lives here, of course," Bob added quickly. "You know, Ruth, she has her own room in the backyard. Certainly didn't want to dislocate her."

Ruth admired the house, congratulated them on the expected baby, drank three cups of coffee, made an effort to eat. They wanted news from home, they talked about people they'd met, places they'd visited, sights they'd seen. No one mentioned Bernard Levine. Or his son. It was only after she'd given up all pretense of eating and pushed her coffee cup firmly away, slumping wearily against the back of her chair, that Bob returned to the purpose of her visit.

"Well, I know you must be exhausted," he said. "How about calling Gerald Gordon, so we can make plans, and then you should take a nap, that's what you need."

Sara rang a small silver bell for the maid to come and take away the dishes. Bob moved flatware around, lining it up in different patterns. There was a long silence.

"All right," Ruth said.

"Perhaps you'd like privacy for the call?" Bob suggested.

"Thank you."

He led her to a small paneled room near the front door. There were a lot of books, a chess table, a desk, comfortable chairs, and a telephone. A notepad lay next to it. On it was written "Gerald Gordon 42–2796." Bob was certainly well prepared. He left her there, closing the door firmly behind him. Even if Bob was manipulating her and had made some arrangement with Gerald or had some concerns of his own he wasn't sharing, she had expected all along to begin with Gerald. As if sitting down would pamper her reluctance to call, she stood wearily at the desk and dialed.

The number turned out to be Gerald's campus office. Professor Gordon was at a faculty meeting, would she care to leave a message? No, she'd call back later. When she went out to the front verandah to tell Bob and Sara that she couldn't reach Gerald for another hour or two, she watched them exchange glances.

"Is there something I should know?"

"No, no problem," Bob said quickly. Sara pulled a wilting flower off the vine. "Wouldn't you like to take a nap?"

"I'd love to."

"No one else you want to call?" He wasn't looking at her.

"Not now, thank you," she said steadily.

Sara showed her the bedroom they'd arranged for her, off a hall in a different wing of the sprawling one-story house. There was a bathroom next door, just for her. She should make herself comfortable, they'd see her later and "really talk," Sara said meaningfully.

Ruth walked over to the window to stare out at the laden fig tree beyond a stretch of thick lawn. She had sat with Bernard Levine once on damp spring earth under a fig tree, sacs of fruit hanging from its low branches just above their heads. A pale shaft of light from the streetlamp near the gate half a block away had picked out drops of water still shimmering in darkness after a late afternoon rainstorm. "You're so lovely," Bernard whispered, two fingers trailing down her neck into the open V of her white cotton blouse. His fingers went lower, under the blouse, tracing the line of her breast. "You feel so ripe." He bent closer to kiss her neck just above the collarbone and she felt his warm, urgent breath. She was amazed. She'd never thought of herself this way. She'd never thought of him this way, either. It hadn't occurred to her that Bernard, whom she'd known for only a few weeks, was interested in her for anything more than taking minutes as the freshman rep on his Liberal Association committee. Now here was this dark lean celebrity, pointed out from a hushed distance to new students, eyed respectfully as he moved nonchalantly through the halls, always surrounded by the best-looking girls, the brightest guys, the people who stood for something, always coming from somewhere, going somewhere important, here he was, now, in the darkest, furthermost corner of her parents' deep garden, reduced by her, Ruth Fredman, to physical disarray. The world, which had been looking new and different since she had started college a few months before, shifted further still from the assumptions of her seventeen years. That night her perception of herself changed forever, she saw herself through senses surging sweetly in answer to Bernard's flattering urgency. More than that; she tasted the discovery that he was human too, she could make the leading politician on campus tremble, she could bring a glow to the skin of the dynamic rebel; she could deliver a glazed and hooded look to the intense leader; she could, with suddenly acquired countless deft little touches or with lowered head and an upward glance of dark brown eyes, tease more passion from the courageous student than even the most oppressive acts of the Nationalist Government could arouse. Ruth saw herself new and fresh that night. It was the first of many gifts that Bernard gave her. She treasured it so much that she offered him ardently everything she was and hoped to be. First love. It was going to last forever. Tears blurred the outlines of the ripe fruit on the tree beyond and she blinked and turned away.

Stripped in the bathroom, she stood before a full-length mirror and examined herself. What would he think if he saw her now? She was thinner, the roundness had been chiseled by the years, there were bones where he'd felt softness. Her collarbones stuck out, angular lines marked her hipbones, she could trace her ribs. Pale shining streaks lightly scarred the skin of her abdomen; Ken had been a big infant. But her long thighs were firm. She cupped her breasts in her hands. Not much different really, perhaps not quite as full, still high, though. Suddenly embarrassed, she stepped quickly into the shower, enclosed herself in hot water and steam. Why was she examining herself this way? She ought to be thinking about Bernard's son, not about her body. It wasn't, she recognized with pain, as if there were any chance she would see Bernard or should if she could. But she would, of course, be seeing Gerald Gordon soon. With a harsh tightening inside, she admitted to herself that it mattered to her how she looked to Gerald. It mattered what he thought of her. It always had. She had never, not in the beginning, not later, risen to pure dedication to social justice, never been free from her insatiable search for approval, never soared above her need to be desired, never, like Bernard, submerged herself for a greater good. She had not even detached herself enough to measure the alternatives, calculate the rewards and make a clear choice. Like Gerald Gordon. Whose judgment still mattered. Gerry, whom she was going to have to confront. Whose help she still needed.

She wrapped a towel around herself and, still dripping, pulled from her big pouchy bag the leather folder holding Ken's photograph. Under it, folded evenly, hidden beneath a layer of leather, were the letters Bob had written to her about Bernard and Nelson. And Gerald. Like a student frantically reviewing notes before a big final, Ruth looked at the letters again.

Bob's descriptions of Gerald tugged her back in time, tapped nerve ends long dormant, quivered at the wispy edges of memory. Ruth resisted. She struggled against the invasion of the past. Coping with the present was more than she could manage, she didn't need to wrestle with the past as well. The facts, she urged herself, skimming the letters again, only pick out the facts. Keep the priorities clear. For now, get ready for Gerald. Nothing but the facts.

There were only three: Gerald Gordon was, astonishingly, Nelson Levine's guardian. Nelson was in danger. Bernard needed her help. Or Gerald thought he did.

She owed Bernard anything that she could do for him, anything at all. She had no doubt of that. But the notion that she could do anything more for Nelson than his guardian Gerald Gordon could do was inconceivable. She had no influence, no resources, no connections. She couldn't imagine what it was that they thought she could accomplish.

Sprawled across the bed in the Sterns' guest room, Ruth wasn't sure that she should have come back to South Africa. The decision to accept Bob Stern's invitation and with it the challenge in the postscript from Gerald had been weighed down by pain and fear and had turned, finally, on Anthony's serene confidence that her mysterious unfinished business was worthwhile. "Won't you hate yourself if you don't go?" he'd asked her, without even knowing that she had betrayals to pay for. "Yes, I'll hate myself more," she'd said. "Well, then," said Anthony gently. So she had come. But she couldn't believe that there was anything she could do; she was afraid that this was one of those expensive, complicated flurries of activity that turned sour and left trailing trouble behind, like so many early schemes. Anyway, even if she did nothing, just being there was dangerous. In Philadelphia, not coming had seemed uglier than coming; in Johannesburg, that wasn't clear. But she was there, in the Sterns' house. She had to face Bob and Sara and whatever they had learned about her, however they judged her. She had to face Gerald Gordon and whatever he wanted from her. And she was going to have to face, at last, herself.

High bright sunshine slanted through the window, warming the skin of her back. She rolled over, the towel fell away, and soothing steady heat settled on her face and breasts. Outside, near the fig tree, huge purple plums glowed in golden light. It must be midafternoon already. Ruth hoped Bob and Sara thought she'd been asleep. She got up and dressed quickly. She couldn't postpone it any longer. She had to contact Gerald Gordon.

This time, he answered the phone himself. His voice dissolved the years. Hearing him, Ruth was a girl again, time was limitless, right and wrong were white and black, everything between despicable. He sounded tranquil and controlled, as he always had. He knew she had arrived that morning and had been waiting for her call. He was delighted to talk to her at last, she sounded exactly the same. Yes, they should certainly meet as soon as possible, he said, with the old tone of oddly nonchalant precision. Without mentioning her name or anyone else's he made plans. Thank you, but he could not accept her host's invitation for the evening, he had a dinner meeting he was obliged to attend. However, perhaps later, around nine . . . good, his wife and children were out of town for a few days, perhaps she would join him for a nightcap? Could he send a driver to collect her? She heard the deepening in his voice as he said how much he was looking forward to seeing her.

Bob and Sara didn't seem to mind. They'd extended their invitation; they relaxed when they heard it had been declined. Ruth thought at first that they were relieved to be spared the challenge of entertaining so grand a guest as Gerald, but as Bob avoided her gaze and as Sara, with ingenuous, dogged questions, prodded for information, it occurred to Ruth that they were afraid of getting further involved in foreign subterfuge. From Sara's little interrogation and Bob's flushed refusal to tell her what he'd learned from Gerald about the Levines ("I think you should hear it from Gordon," he said roundly), Ruth drew some comfort from tentatively estimating that they had not discovered much about her own role in the activities that had kept Bernard Levine in jail for twenty years. Sara would surely not have contained herself if she knew. But even this brought no relief from Ruth's constant awareness of being watched, measured, and judged, so that she settled into the leather upholstery of the backseat of Gerald Gordon's Jaguar as if it were a chariot of deliverance. Getting away from Bob and Sara Stern untied knotted muscles, halted jumping nerves, and lifted the tension of choosing her words. In Gerald's car, Ruth was so much soothed by the comfort of escape that she forgot to panic at the prospect of Gerald's inspection.

The low black car swept into the circular brick driveway, curving around the side of the gabled main building. It halted at the foot of flagstone steps to a side verandah, screened in lilac wisteria made silvery by a pool of light in which Gerald stood waiting for her, an arm stretched out. His curving smile and steady blue eyes were sharp against the pallor of his skin. Ruth ran up the steps and into a surprising hug. "Wonderful," he murmured against her hair. "You look wonderful." He waved to the driver, led her inside, hugged her again and then steered her into the lamp-lit library.

Heavy chintz drapes covered the tall windows. Hidden speakers yielded the stately chords of Beethoven's Fifth. Alone in the book-lined refuge, standing near a carved rosewood desk, Ruth and Gerald stared openly at each other. Ruth's self-consciousness made her the first to turn away.

"You've worn well, Gerry," she said. "A true aristocrat."

She heard herself fall immediately into her old tone of mild mockery and disliked the younger self he had revived. He *had* aged well. He was as lean as he had been twenty years before, he carried himself with the same upright yet relaxed bearing, his worn tweed coat was as perfectly cut, his manner as contained and poised, with the addition of an extra air of authority. His pale, nearly translucent skin, dotted now with high color above the cheekbones, was marked by a few lines, but Gerald didn't look as if he had done a great deal of grimacing. The feathery sweep of reddish-brown hair did not entirely hide the deeper lines carved on his forehead; his hair, while no less abundant, was tipped by telltale sandiness. His eyes were as disconcertingly penetrating as they had ever been, his gestures far more assured.

"You look wonderful," he said, with an enthusiasm she did not remember. "Better than before."

"Gerald," she laughed, "how can you say that?"

"But it's true," he said gravely. His gaze frankly swept her up and down several times, lingering, at last, on her narrow face, tilted toward him, caught between flattery and amusement. "You've fined down. All those good bones. Elegant," he said crisply. "And more of the eyes, too." He looked at her carefully, a blue beam of inspection. "I know what it is, you fit yourself better, you've come into yourself."

He had changed, more than she'd guessed. He'd never have managed that twenty years before. "Thank you," she said, which was decidedly not what she would have said long ago.

"I'm glad you're here." He led her to a big chintzy club chair. She waited until he leaned back into the one opposite and asked, "Why exactly am I here, Gerald?"

"Because you're still Ruth, just as we hoped you would be." He smiled faintly, but his gaze was steady, serious, a piercing blue.

49

"We?"

He pursed his lips, raised an index finger and put it in front of them, shook his head gravely. Then he pointed to his ear.

"Later," he said. "Let me pour us a drink. And let's catch up, I want to hear about your life in America."

He poured the drinks from decanters sparkling on a sideboard, raised his glass to her, murmured "To old friends" and drank.

"Tell me," he said, "what you've been doing all this time."

If his house was bugged, as he seemed to suggest, how was she going to find out about Bernard and his son? They were evidently going to do it his way. She shrugged slightly.

"I went to cousins in Boston, people none of us had ever met," she said. "I wasn't . . . well. They were very kind, they tried to understand." He looked uneasy, but he needn't have worried, she wasn't going to explain the difficulties of her recovery from one hundred and thirteen days of solitary confinement. She understood that she must speak for the hidden discs of the Special Branch. "I got a job, teaching history to pubescent Catholic girls." Gerald laughed and shook his head. "I met Brian Harris through one of the other teachers. We got married. I was married within the year, Gerald." Brian was her well-lit, solidly constructed, secure sanctuary, she thought.

"Catholic?" His eyes were wide.

"Lapsed. Very lapsed."

"And then?"

"We had a son. His name's Ken. He's . . . he's a great kid." They both laughed. "I went to school, history, doctorate, research, all that, then got divorced."

"What went wrong?"

"We had nothing in common except my need for security and his need to provide it." She hesitated, then added, "We never knew each other."

He jerked forward.

"You mean you never . . .?"

She knew what he couldn't risk asking.

"Never." She had never told Brian what had happened to her. "Nor anyone else. At all."

He took a long drink, put the glass down, leaned toward her. "You poor dear," he said.

"I'm not sure about that. It was a conscious choice." She bent her head, blinking, thinking that if she came out of this safely she might be able to tell Ken about it all. Ken; perhaps Anthony also.

"Your turn," she said.

He filled their glasses. With his back to her he said diffidently, "I've been very fortunate, able to do what I like most of the time."

"You've done well at Wits," she ventured.

He turned to face her, smiling.

"I moved up quickly through the department, I've headed it for years. Last year they created a special endowed chair for me for life. Not unacceptable." He was pacing the room now, measuring his story to fit his stride. "There've been interesting opportunities, also. I've done a lot of government consulting, advice on border issues, trade, foreign relations."

"Here or abroad?"

"Both. Here, of course, and Britain. A great deal in Africa."

"Gerald, what fun!"

"Breaks the routine of teaching and university infighting very pleasantly," he said, satisfaction seeping from every tissue.

"And your family?" she asked, as she was obviously supposed to do. She wanted to move him along, help him set the record straight, get the amenities behind them, so that she could discover the disaster he'd summoned her to solve. She wanted to dispose of it somehow; she needed a magic wand to return her to the predictable order of her life in Philadelphia.

"My parents live in Europe now," Gerald said, sitting down opposite her again. "I have the house, as you see. My sister lives in London, painting unusual portraits. She's done very well for herself."

"I've heard that Julia's a sensation," Ruth murmured.

51

"My Uncle Harry is still the most respected progressive in Parliament, still the nearly lone voice of dissent."

"More like a benign patriarch, isn't he?"

How like Gerald to report on his parents and sister and uncle before mentioning his wife; that was the secret of the diamond-hard durability of the Gordon clan, the core of its anachronistic survival.

"You married an English girl?"

"Yes, Carolyn." He seemed suddenly uncomfortable. "About ten years ago. We have two children." Gerald glanced about, jumped up and brought a silver-framed studio portrait from the rosewood desk over to Ruth. "Here they are."

Carolyn, in riding habit, was a creamy English rose, with more than a dab of imperial gem-like hardness. Two small, pale, and pretty children were arranged on ponies behind her. Gold gleamed in the air above.

"Lovely," Ruth smiled. "They're all away?"

A flush mounted furiously upon Gerald's cheeks. Inexplicably off balance, he nodded, jumped to his feet again to return the picture to its place of honor. He was not, she saw, collected enough to speak.

"So, Gerald," she said, as gently as her urgency allowed, "you're really the academic you wanted to be?"

"Absolutely," he said rather loudly, with an emphatic nod.

It didn't fit with his messages to her through Bob Stern. She still had no idea why he had maneuvered to get her to return. She tilted her head to one side, smiling, eyebrows high.

"I am an observer. An analyst. Not a participant," he declared.

"Gerald in an ivy-covered tower." Ruth had made this observation many times before.

"Detached," he said firmly, pouring blue rays at her.

Forty-three blacks had died in unrest in Soweto alone in the past week. Seven had been burned and hacked to pulp for collaboration. Five presumably contaminated infants had been tossed into a burning shed. The others had perished as police maintained law and order during a funeral for those killed the week before. Twenty-four had been shot in the back. Although Ruth and Gerald were sitting not much more than thirteen miles from Soweto, it might as well have been another planet. Not that it wasn't happening, not that it wasn't real. It was all, simply, very far away, enclosed in distant sadness. The distance was as great as the one that stretched between American spectators at fund-raising rock concerts and the victims of Ethiopian famine.

"Sitting watching from Mount Olympus," Ruth said derisively. "Not pulling any strings, then?"

Gerald turned away, but she saw the blood gather again beneath his transparent skin. She couldn't understand it; she had intended nothing more than the mild taunts that had spiced their early friendship.

"Ruth," he said after a long pause, "let me show you Carolyn's greenhouse. She's a keen horticulturist, grows orchids, cultivates her own hybrid. The greenhouse is in a separate building."

They walked back through the house, down the long hall through the butler's pantry, the square kitchen, the plant-filled sun porch.

"I see you remember the way," Gerald said, following her.

"Of course. I was here a lot."

"And George? Remember when George taught you to drive?"

They were outside by then. Ruth hoped the darkness hid her shame. She mumbled and moved ahead. She had fallen immediately into the white South African tunnel vision. George was a black man, that was his identity, he was otherwise faceless. The man who had just driven her from the Sterns' in Gerald's car had taught her to drive, he'd been there all the years she'd known Julia and Gerald, but when she swept into the Jaguar, he was just the driver. She had managed a polite "Good evening," nothing more.

53

The greenhouse was some distance from the main building and was tucked away out of sight of the low line of flat-roofed servants' quarters, screened off by a high stone wall. Gerald opened the greenhouse door by juggling two combination locks. He nudged her inside and pressed a switch. Dull blue light hovered at bench height. Eerie shadows crept from bulky cacti lining one glass wall. The central trestles were covered with potted orchids, mottled burgundy, wine, mauve, splattered silver. On the other side, banks of proteas and bromeliads loomed in shadow, leaves blue-tipped, flowers like spiky weapons.

"Gerald, it looks like *Star Wars* in here. I want to see it all, can't we have decent light?"

"I brought you here so we can talk safely. Forget Carolyn's plants. If you really want to see them, she'll be delighted to show you another time. No one can see in with this light, that's the thing."

"Gerald, do you think anyone's trying to?"

"No, I don't really. But it's a sensible precaution."

"Is your house bugged?"

"Ruth, I just don't know. The phone has been tapped since . . . well, lately. I can't tell about the house. I don't want to have it swept in case it attracts attention."

Ruth was astounded. When she had known him, Gerald had done nothing that could qualify as dissent, even in excessive South African terms. He had made a point of keeping his hands clean, as he called it. They'd argued about it many times. He and Bernard had quarreled furiously because of it. Gerald had always maintained that he wasn't going to get involved.

"Have you changed so much, Gerald?" Ruth said quietly. "Or is this just a dose of standard paranoia because you're talking to an ex-detainee?"

He backed away a step, pulled a leaf savagely from a fat, complacent succulent and squished it with a sharp stamp.

"Neither of those," he said. "I am still an observer, nothing more, I told you that. And I suppose they'll let you out again, won't they? You're an American now?"

"Yes. Or I couldn't have risked coming. So what is it, Gerry?"

"It's Ben, dammit. And the boy."

Ruth propped herself on a small stool and waited for the new disaster to be exposed. Damp warmth settled upon her. The blue light made Gerald's skin look bruised. He shoved his hands into his pockets, leaned a shoulder against a metal frame in the curve of glass, and poked at the brick floor with the toe of his soft suede shoe. When he spoke at last, the baffled unease was gone from his face and voice, his equilibrium restored.

"Nelson was born during the trial, you know, just after you got away. Then Bernard was sentenced to Robben Island for life. Rita had to make a life for herself and the baby, she had a very hard time. She hadn't really signed on for it, she never had any idea of what she was getting into." He wasn't looking at her.

"Gerald, surely I'm not the best person to be sympathetic about Rita's problems?" The nerve in the back of her neck jumped feebly once, then gathered momentum.

"I'm not sure about that. Anyway, it's beside the point."

Gerald raised his eyes, purplish in the blue haze and stifled her objection as if she were a nit-picking student. "Bernard's parents tried but they couldn't stand her, they never got over his marrying a Gentile, they never let her forget it. They blamed her for Bernard's trouble, there was no way to persuade them that she was utterly innocent."

Ruth laughed raspingly.

"It is ironic, isn't it? They've always said, if only he'd stayed with you. Anyway, they had no sympathy for Rita and no money, of course. Her parents were divorced, broke, disapproving, hated Bernard for destroying Rita's life. I tried to help a bit."

"*You* tried to help?"

He nodded. "Bernard asked me to, before they took him away. That's friendship, Ruth, not revolution."

Ruth had forgotten, or had not thought of it for many years. Gerald and Bernard had been friends, an unlikely combination, first drawn together by their frivolous attitude to team sports; they were spared ridicule and bonded together because they were both good tennis players. It was odd how much they'd had in common, just as it was odd for them to find themselves in the same school, considering where they came from. Gerald only went to the government school because his father considered it better preparation for what he briskly called the real world than the private school Gerald's mother preferred. "Gerald's got it all," his father told his mother over cocktails beneath the Renoir, Gerald eavesdropping behind the open French doors. "Looks, brains, money, breeding. He's part of the elite whatever school he goes to. He needs a chance to know what people are like, he'll need that in the real world." She'd said dubiously, "Parktown's very *mixed*," but in the end she capitulated, it wasn't worth making a stand. They didn't anticipate Bernard Levine, but even if they had, they would not have predicted Bernard's development. "He's from the wrong side of the tracks, of course," Gerald's mother noted, with her dainty little shoulder shrug, after he first brought Bernard home. But Bernard didn't eat with his hands or use vulgar language, so he was all right. Young Levine had quick reflexes and put a lot of topspin on his balls, so Gerald's father didn't complain. The friendship had endured beyond adolescence; beyond the increasingly strained quarrels about ivory towers and the real world; beyond, apparently, the different choices they had made.

"You stood by him, then?"

"There was nothing I could do for him then. But I promised I'd keep an eye on Rita and the kid. I helped her find a job as a receptionist at the Prince Edward Hotel and got the grandmothers to take turns with Nelson until he was old enough for nursery school. Rita developed a talent for flower arranging and then for decorating, she did very well, the hotel management kept promoting her and sending her to other hotels all over the country to spruce them up. She met Derek Brand at the Regis in Cape Town. He owns fourteen of them, no, sixteen now, I think."

"Surely, that's not who . . ."

"Yes, it is. She wrote to Ben and told him she was getting a divorce, he'd made his choices and they weren't hers, she couldn't spend her life alone while he was incarcerated on Robben Island and so on and so forth. She didn't tell him about Brand until the divorce was through; then she wrote and told him Nelson would be well cared for. Brand was willing to adopt him."

Ruth closed her eyes and tried to imagine Bernard reading the letters; she thought she glimpsed him, stretched out on a cot, face turning darker as he read the lines, fists pounding the rough gray blanket, but the image was gone before it was fully formed, she couldn't hold it, she had never been able to visualize Bernard in prison, never, not even at first, and she couldn't do it now. When she opened her eyes, her cheeks were wet. Gerald watched her curiously.

"It was long ago," he said. "Nelson was five when they married. He's over twenty now."

"How did Ben take it, Gerald?"

"It's hard to know. He got permission for me to visit, but it took months to move the papers of authority through the system. He'd used his visitor's privileges for the family until then. I'd never been, so when I did get out to the Island it was almost six years since I'd seen him. He'd had time to adjust to the divorce. He said he didn't care about Rita."

Ruth knew that, of course; she had a hefty share of responsibility for Ben's unlikely marriage. Greenhouse heat lay like an added skin upon her. She swayed and Gerald put a hand briefly on her damp shoulder before he went on.

"He knew Nelson would have an easier life, brought up in comfort with two parents. What scared him was Derek Brand. The idea of a man like that raising his child horrified him. He'd told Rita he wouldn't agree to the adoption. He asked me to act as Nelson's guardian. He seemed to think I might be able to moderate Brand's influence." He paused. Then, his voice rising slightly, he said, "Ben seemed to think Brand and I would be able to get along." Resentment briefly curled his lip.

"And did you?"

It seemed most unlikely. Like anyone who read the newspapers, Ruth knew something about Derek Brand. She'd been about ten years old when he burst upon public consciousness, where he had remained ever since. He'd been a flamboyant millionaire before he was twenty-five, having parlayed his design for a hand-held rocket previously unimagined into the foundation of a personal munitions empire. The son of a nearly always destitute, always drunk farmer, whose first language approximated English more closely than anything else, and a genteel former hairdresser of sturdy Boer stock, Derek Brand had injured his father permanently with his rocket experiments on the veld behind the farmhouse, taken his mother's name, and catapulted himself out of the scrub of their northern Transvaal farm and into the broad welcoming laps of the country's defense and security chieftains, the toughest, most durable clique in the Afrikaner establishment. Brand would do anything, it had always been said, if it would make money. He must have done a great many things since the first factory for manufacturing rockets was hailed with Cape champagne and guarded, electrically charged fences, because his wealth kept multiplying. There were always headlines: Brand opens new factory, Brand in billion-rand deal with this country or that organization, Brand honored at a banquet after the opening of Parliament, where his patriotism had been applauded. There were always magazine articles: Brand's new mansion here, his new seventeen-room cottage overlooking the Indian Ocean near Hermanus, his new stable, his new wife — for there had been at least two before Rita. Once there was a photograph of Brand with his mother, at a state ceremony. She was quoted as saying that "family duty and the security of the *volk* are what Derek has really worked for all his life." Brand traveled the world, advising new governments on how to handle insurgents; sometimes he advised insurgents on how to handle governments. His connections with the government were so formidable that he was often able to obtain a favor for a friend or client, frequently a foreign corporation. His empire had expanded long ago to include construction; it was hinted that he had large and secret mining interests; hotels, too, it seemed. The notion of Rita as the consort of this baron was absurd; friendship between him and Gerald Gordon was surely impossible.

"I've tried, Ruth, for Nelson's sake." Gerald dabbed his moist forehead with a white handkerchief. "Brand and I get along all right. It's Nelson that's the trouble."

Ruth felt sweat edge down her sides from under her arms. Her blue cotton dress was wet. Her underwear stuck to her skin. She was afraid that if she suggested leaving the hothouse he wouldn't go on talking; she had to find out why he'd wanted her to come. She waved her hands in front of her face, gulped warm air, leaned toward him.

"Tell me about Nelson now, Gerald. Please."

"Nelson's always been provocative." He was looking down at the brick floor again, banging the toe of his shoe against a rough edge. His face was a bleary blue but his voice cut crisply through the cloying air. "Bright, very sharp, but rebellious. When he was younger, he used to argue with everything on principle. I asked him once why he did it, why did he insist it was nighttime in the middle of the day? 'Practice,' he used to say, 'I'm practicing to win all the arguments I get into.' For a long time he didn't like to visit Bernard. He never said so, but it was obvious, he used to make up excuses too intricate to be believed. Bernard wrote to him as often as he was allowed, which wasn't much. Nelson was always in trouble at school."

"What kind of trouble?"

"Everything. Looking back, I think that he just tried one thing after another to see how far he could push. He usually charmed his way out of it. He played hooky, didn't turn up at school.

Once he took a friend and hitchhiked almost all the way to Durban before I found them. He was ten or eleven then. He stole cars for a while. Not stole, borrowed, he used to call it. He'd borrow a car for an evening out, before he was old enough to drive. He always returned the car in good order a few hours later. I only know this because he told me. He was never in trouble with the police. Not then, anyway."

Gerald sighed deeply and wiped his face again.

"Drugs?" Ruth asked.

"I don't think so. He started drinking a lot one time, he must have been about fourteen, partying and getting smashed on all kinds of muck, but he gave that up, he had better things to do."

"What were they?"

"Plotting revolution, I imagine," Gerald said wearily. "He began to take an interest in Ben, he became as devious organizing visits to him as he had been at avoiding them. He read everything he could find about the trials, he even asked me to get him transcripts from the lawyers. He stopped all the petty bad behavior entirely. He read all the time, history, politics, biographies of Che, Trotsky, Mao. He learned to speak Xhosa. He astonished Rita and Derek with the news that he wanted to be a doctor. He's done well at medical school." Ruth thought Gerald looked more miserable than the blue light and moist heat warranted.

"So what *is* the problem, Gerald? It sounds as if he pulled himself together."

What did Gerald expect? Nelson's father had gone to jail before he was born, his mother was a nitwit, a high-pitched groupie, his stepfather a thug with a thick coating of platinum veneer. Kids became wild adolescents with less cause. Bernard's son seemed to have come out of it, settled down in spite of his awful start in life. But Ruth couldn't separate thoughts of Bernard's boy growing up without him from the old tortured questions about her own responsibility for his imprisonment. She wriggled on the high stool, curling her ankles around its legs. She seemed to have made a career out of depriving boys of their fathers, though Ken's loss wasn't comparable to Nelson's. Surely divorcing Brian hadn't forced Ken to grow up without a father, she'd been very careful about that, always. Visits and vacations weren't the same as living with both parents, but Brian wasn't locked up for life, Ken and Brian had a relationship, a continuing connection. Irritably scratching her damp head, she wished she could prevent her own guilt from injecting itself everywhere. She was so absorbed that she missed Gerald's next words.

"Excuse me? I didn't hear."

"I said Nelson outgrew petty crime. Turned big-time. He's in a packet of trouble now."

Nelson, it seemed, had discovered his father and racial oppression at about the same time. Derek Brand had always been an outsize domestic tyrant; when Nelson identified him as a fascist, a fat capitalist, stool pigeon for the bloody Nats, Bernard's resistance became at first intriguing, then fascinating, ultimately compelling. When Nelson learned that Brand's fortune rested on munitions and that he would supply anyone who could pay, he also learned about the Africans who couldn't scratch out a living from the phony homelands in which Brand's buddies in Pretoria had resettled them. Nelson absorbed whatever he could about Bernard from newspapers and trial transcripts and snatches of banned books; he couldn't hear about it all from his father because it was forbidden to discuss these matters in jail and letters were censored. When Nelson was able to visit his father, usually fresh from a scene with Rita, pleading with him not to aggravate Derek, he saw Bernard through the screen of courageous commitment reflected in his statements at the trial; they never spoke of these things, but Nelson saw the purposeful man who had rebelled absolutely, defiantly, proudly.

Nelson gravitated naturally into the fringes of the political underground. By the time he entered medical school he was painting slogans on walls, pushing pamphlets under doors, keep-

61

ing watch for cops while banners were hoisted; within the year, there was the first black girlfriend, still illegal then under the miscegenation laws. They escaped capture only because the girl's mother, a bank clerk with a strong sense of priorities, sent the girl packing to an uncle in the Free State. Nelson wrote articles for banned underground papers, went to parties that illegally served alcohol to racially mixed groups, attended meetings of banned organizations, visited black townships without a permit time and again, transported fugitives about the country in the Audi Derek had used as a bribe for good behavior on his eighteenth birthday, been photographed in a sea of black faces at an illegal political gathering, broken the petty apartheid laws a thousand times, mocked them publicly.

"Gerry," Ruth said softly, "isn't it all just normal student stuff? Don't you remember all this kind of thing?"

"Normal?" Gerald's lips curved, blue, thin. "You know very well only a minuscule fraction of white students ever gets involved at all. Most of them couldn't care less, Ruth, and you know it. It's always been that way."

"Yes, but those that do . . ."

"Some of them wind up in jail, Ruth. Or run away."

"I know," she whispered. The greenhouse air was so close now it was hard to breathe easily. Her mouth was dry. The odor of decaying roots hovered in the moisture now, hanging above the blue light, seeping slowly down through the plants and mulch and fertilizer through her hair and clothes to settle on her skin.

"Anyway, that's not the point. It's out of control now, much worse." As if the subject of Nelson or the damp close air of the hothouse had become unbearable, Gerald moved on briskly, clipping his words, hurtling to the end.

"Nelson has made several trips to the camps in Angola, and at least one to Lusaka. He's bought and transported medications for the guerrillas. Medications and who knows what else. He's done quite a bit of recruiting. He's been seen by the wrong people with the wrong people. His current girlfriend is Victoria Naidoo.

They've changed the sex laws, but there's no getting around who she is, a fiery, prominent radical who refused publicly to stand for election for the new Indian chamber of Parliament because she says it's tokenism, window dressing for the Nats. She's fifteen years older than Nelson. Nelson's done enough already to put him away for life. It's a miracle he's still going about. It can't last."

"Do Derek and Rita know about all this, Gerald?"

"Rita knows a little. I'm not sure about Derek, but I'll tell you this. If he knew it all, he'd turn Nelson in himself, Ruth." He paused, folded his arms, stared at her deliberately. "I've got to get him out of the country, Ruth. And fast."

Images of Bernard tumbling hot through her mind, too fast to be grasped, she asked quietly, panting from lack of air, "Will he go?"

"No. He refuses, of course."

"But then what . . ."

"That's the point, Ruth." There was a mild suggestion of professorial method. He had led her carefully to this moment, where the conclusion was evident. "We need you to persuade him. And to take him to America and help him continue with his studies and . . . take care of him."

"Why me? Why America? How can I take care of him, he's grown up?" She flapped her hands about, trying to make air. "Gerald, can't we walk about outside, I can't breathe in here anymore."

"Just a few minutes more," he said. "Look, I've tried to persuade Nelson, Ruth. He laughs at me. It's dangerous for Bernard to discuss all this with him. But he's heard about you, from Bernard. And from questioning me."

She was startled.

"Nelson knows about me?"

"Not a great deal. But enough. Enough to trust you."

"To *trust* me? Come on, Gerald."

"He knows Bernard loved you. He knows you were involved.

63

And Ben has asked him to give you a hearing. We think you can convince him, Ruth, if anyone can. When you see him, you'll understand."

She stood up, legs cramping after their long twisting on the stool. She stood on one foot and shook the other. She blinked several times. She reversed feet. Then, pacing the narrow aisle between spiky blue plants, she said, her back to him, "And why the U.S., Gerald? Why not Britain, where so many refugees are still fighting the good fight in exile?"

"That's just why. Before we knew it, he'd be back in Lusaka, making bombs or something. In America he can get involved with the anti-apartheid movement at a safe distance, he may even achieve something there. At least he won't be destroyed. Bernard wants the kid to live, Ruth. He's lost most of his own life, you know."

She turned to look at him again. His chin was thrust out, his head high, his eyes purple, penetrating.

"You're a respected professor at Penn, Ruth. We hope you'll use your influence to get him into medical school there to finish his training. And keep an eye on him."

"Gerald, he's grown up, with a mind of his own."

"Not quite grown up. He needs a safe place. Someone who cares. Who understands. You must represent Bernard, Ruth. That's what he wants."

As the tears, which had been gathering behind her eyes for some minutes now, rolled over onto her cheeks, as her shoulders shook to contain the sobs, as her hands clenched and unclenched, Gerald moved next to her, an arm around her, a reminder of long, loyal warmth.

"Let's go outside now," he said quietly.

"Just tell me one thing first," she said, rubbing her eyes with the tips of her fingers. "If the house may be bugged, what about this greenhouse? How do you know they haven't been listening all the time?"

He laughed as he steered her firmly toward the door.

"George swept it for bugs, Ruth. He suggested this spot. You remember how he loved Bernard? Well, he's even crazier about Nelson and he tries to take care of him. He knows why you're here."

She heard this as a blow in the stomach, shaking the last air from her. Then the blue light dimmed at last and she stumbled into the cool clean dark beyond.

$\mathbf{N}$elson Levine stood alone at the iron railing around the seals' pond. He could have been Bernard, waiting there for her, forearms resting lightly on the waist-high rail, dark curly hair close to his head, long lean body effortlessly graceful. Rounding the corner some distance away in bright sunlight, Ruth saw him watching three seals cavorting on the surface of the water. His profile was turned toward her, the same dark eyes under heavy brows, the same narrow head and high temples, the surprisingly full-lipped mouth, the same triangular chin, bisected by a tiny cleft.

Ruth stepped backward and stopped abruptly, staring, blinking against the summer sun. Gerald had chosen the meeting place; Gerald had insisted upon lending her one of his cars the night before, following her back to the Sterns' to make sure she was safe, leaving the car for her so she could get about easily; Gerald had planned to bring Nelson to meet her. She certainly didn't need help identifying Bernard's son, but Gerald was supposed to be there for the awkward confrontation. He was nowhere in sight. All she could see was a young Bernard, idly watching the seals.

Perhaps they were being watched, perhaps it was dangerous for Gerald to be there, there were risks everywhere, threats in the clumps of flowering bushes, the little lanes, the curving gardens of the zoo. There were corners tucked everywhere, hiding places for the Special Branch, listening posts for informers, sheltered spots for ambitious security officers on the watch for a flashy catch. She was crazy to get herself dragged into it all again. The old ache crept back behind her calves, the nerve in the back of her neck twitched its warning, she glanced about, looking for the cops, on the edge of turning back toward the big iron gates and the parking lot across Jan Smuts Avenue when, from under the shade of a huge jacaranda, Gerald emerged, carrying cans of soda, ambling in the sun toward Nelson, a man out with a young friend, nothing to it.

Ruth watched Nelson turn to take the soda. He leaned back against the railing now, talking to Gerald, both of them glancing about. As they noticed her, she walked toward them, waving briefly in response to Gerald's delighted smile.

"I was beginning to worry that you'd forgotten how to find the zoo," Gerald said.

"That's not something I'll ever forget." She turned at once to Nelson Levine. "I'm so happy to meet you," she said.

"Hello." He shook hands easily, looking directly at her.

"I hope you won't mind me saying you look very much like Ben, like your father. When I knew him. Long ago."

"I don't mind at all. He looks much the same now." He glanced at Gerald. "Except for his hair, of course."

"His hair?"

"It's white now."

Ruth bit her lower lip.

"How is he?" she asked.

"He was fine when I saw him two weeks ago." Nelson frowned briefly, a dark gathering of bushy eyebrows. "He told me you were coming."

"Did he tell you why?"

"Gerald did. More or less." He laid his open palm briefly upon Gerald's shoulder, a tolerant touch to match his slight smile.

They did get along, these two, they did connect in spite of everything. "My dad asked me to listen to you and think about it." He hesitated, then went on quickly. "He told me you always had good judgment and had persuaded him many times."

"But not always," Ruth said ruefully, blinking.

Gerald was staring off into the distance. His hair, glazed redder by the sun, stirred in the light wind. He looked as if he were leaning out of himself, stretching away beyond them, removed from their conversation, separated from their preoccupation. But Nelson fixed his dark gaze upon Ruth, forcing her to meet his eyes.

"Dad gave me a message for you," he said deliberately.

"Yes?"

"He said I must tell you the slate is clean and thank you."

She closed her eyes quickly to hide them from him as much as to check their sudden filling. The first time she and Bernard had quarreled, hurt each other and made up, she had said she didn't want their fight to poison things between them, she wanted to wipe the slate clean, start again. After that, a whispered "Clean slate" had always marked the end of estrangement. It was their phrase for forgiveness, a declaration of parity. But this was the message of a man desperate to save his son, willing to use her guilt, as she was, to get Nelson out of South Africa. Bernard could never absolve her for what she had done. When she opened her eyes she found them both watching her, waiting.

"Well," she said, taking a deep breath, "tell him I'm happy there's something I might be able to do."

"If I ever see him again," Nelson said brusquely. "If you have your way I'll probably never see him again, have you thought about that?"

Now she saw the rage that simmered behind his eyes, the fury that gathered beneath the taut young skin, the tumult seething in the shoulders and the long restless legs. He had learned somehow to keep that anger chained or he couldn't have hidden it so well until now.

Her glance at Gerald was an appeal.

"Let's walk," he said at once, "there are interesting spots to visit." He stepped between them and, with a hand on one of each of their elbows, guided them along the path that led past the seals' pool toward a bird sanctuary.

"You always liked the zoo," Ruth remembered. "We used to come here a lot."

"My dad too?"

"He and I used to come often when we were still in school," Gerald said, steering them beyond the birds, past dazzling peacocks, along a large open stretch of lawn bordered by bright flower beds. "Later, Ruth came along as well."

"Why do you like it?"

"It's open and anonymous. And untainted. And . . . " He was smiling, but he wouldn't go on.

They wandered down a familiar broad avenue, leading on one side to a little lake. It was hidden from view among stands of willows, thicker and more profuse than Ruth remembered, utterly secluded. The water was clotted with rare lilies and inhabited by small, innocent, jewel-colored fish. On its banks, large birds strutted, their arrogant long necks arched majestically. There was no one else in sight. Gerald loosened his tie, took off his jacket and slung it over his shoulder, halting at the edge of the lake.

"Lovely, isn't it?" he murmured. "It's always shadowed because of the trees. But the colors of the lilies and fish flash brighter in shadow; look down there for a minute."

Ruth looked obediently, but Nelson gazed grimly forward, his tilted head a clear message that he was prepared to wait out the social amenities only so long, no longer.

"There's a bench around the curve," said Gerald. "Let's go and sit down."

Ruth, feeling hopelessly ill equipped to debate with Nelson, sat tentatively on the edge of the bench. Gerald sank down beside her. Nelson threw himself on the grass in front of them, stretched out, head propped on an elbow, waiting, as his father had done, many times. He was not exactly like Bernard, of course; he was lighter, more mercurial, his face was a shade softer, he was perhaps less controlled than Bernard had been. But she was thinking of Bernard when she last saw him; he had been older then than Nelson was now. The comparisons, the memories, the new responsibilities were so consuming that she could not concentrate on what she was there to accomplish.

"Nelson," said Gerald, in his most detached professorial tone, "I've explained to Ruth that I think you should go to the U.S. and that you don't want to. Your dad and I are hoping she'll be able to convince you."

"I told you she's wasted the trip," Nelson said grimly, pulling up blades of grass one by one, blowing them off his fingers. "No one can convince me to cut and run. If you and Dad can't, how can she?"

Just what Ruth was thinking herself. But Gerald had anticipated Nelson's challenge.

"Your dad can't speak freely, Nelson, he can't risk saying all he wants to. And my arguments are compromised, aren't they? A silent witness is as bad as a collaborator, an academic in an ivory tower is a conspirator too, isn't that it, Nelson?"

So young Nelson had hurled Ruth's own taunts at Gerald. He'd had his hands full with this boy, but he kept on battling, he had chosen his personal battlefield and still tried to hold the ground. Nelson didn't even blink. He just nodded, once. He was used to this.

"That's it," he said.

"Well, that's why we want you to listen to Ruth. She can speak freely, it's something she's very good at; and her positions aren't compromised by detachment, like mine. No one who spent one hundred and thirteen days in solitary confinement before the

Sandown trial because of her political beliefs can be described as a collaborator, Nelson."

A smile briefly curved his lip. Then he said, "Actually that's something I'd like to know. Why did they . . . ?"

But Ruth knew what he was going to ask; she wasn't ready to answer, she didn't know if she ever would be, so she cut quickly into his question with one of her own.

"Nelson, won't you tell me why you don't want to leave?"

"I'd have thought that was obvious," he said roughly.

He was evidently easy to divert, young enough to distract. This provided her first relief. She was freed to concentrate on the problem of getting him away. She was, after all, not incompetent, she could handle him, she'd handled a lot of people successfully, including bright, intense young men. Which led her at once to her own Ken, whose image she caressed in her mind before turning back to Nelson.

"South Africa's my country, I owe it something," he declared flatly.

"That's such an abstraction, isn't it?" Ruth murmured.

"These are my people," said Bernard's son, waving a narrow hand about at the trees and lilies shimmering on the shadowy lake. "I was born here, raised on the fat of the land and the profits of slave labor, by the way, while all around me people are deprived, starving, desperate, oppressed. Do you know how bad things are here now?"

"I know some of it."

"If everyone who can make a difference just takes off, what will happen?"

"The same thing that will happen anyway, I think."

"What do you mean?"

"I mean I have been quite certain for a very long time that nothing will prevent a violent revolution in South Africa."

"Damn right," he said excitedly.

"Then, if it will come anyway . . ."

"I'm going to be part of it, can you understand that?"

71

"Oh, yes, I understand that very well. That's what Ben said. He agreed that it had to come, of course, but he thought he could make it come sooner. He even thought he could make it less convulsive."

At that, Nelson sat up straight and smiled fully, for the first time. He raised a clenched fist in the air and shook it energetically once or twice.

"Exactly," he said. "Couldn't have said it better myself."

Ruth looked away and swallowed hard. He was very young. He'd had a terribly complicated, splintered youth. He was greatly burdened. If she ever used a tone, even a nuance of authority, she would be consigned to that contemptuous limbo he reserved for all the authority figures in his young life. She didn't allow herself to confirm that Nelson could not have said it better himself. Instead, she said gently, "But you can't be any use at all in jail, Nelson."

"Oh, they won't get me," he said, hunching his knees up and wrapping his long arms around them. "Don't worry, I'm careful."

She'd heard it all before, of course; she'd even said it once or twice herself. But looking at the mobile young mouth, the lively eyes of Bernard's son, she could not believe he had never thought of it, feared it, grappled with it. His own father had been in prison all the years he had been alive; didn't that give him pause, didn't it, in the hidden crevices of his most private fears, threaten him, terrify him at all?

"Your father thought that too, and look what happened."

"Oh, we've learned a lot since those days," said Nelson, with a jerk of the head that was like a little swagger. "We've learned to specialize, no one tries to do it all anymore."

Ruth wanted to ask what he meant; Gerald leaned forward to comment. But Nelson jumped up suddenly, walked a few steps away and stood quite still, head bent low, hands deep in his pockets. Gerald's open palm moved up and down, silencing Ruth. Beyond, a tall bird with delicate silver tracings on its deep blue feathers eyed them contemptuously, stretched its neck, turned away in disgust; and in the same instant Nelson turned back toward them.

"I wish you could understand," he said, his voice low and firm. "I know it's difficult, things have really changed a lot since your day."

Ruth bit her lip and avoided looking at Gerald, whom she felt shift beside her.

"I don't mean that the way it sounds," Nelson cried. "Please listen to me, let me try to explain." He drew a deep breath, sat down again, holding his knees against his chest, leaning toward them. "In the fifties the ANC was legal, trying for peaceful change, not very big, not really a mass resistance movement. Then, you know better than I, you were there, after Sharpeville the Congress was banned, went underground, gained wider support, started attacking hard targets here and there, screwed it up most of the time. There were the trials, the government intimidated every-one, got rid of a whole generation of responsible leaders. They ran away or died or . . . went to jail." He jerked his head back, looked at the sky, paler now that the sun drifted away. "It was all much quieter for a long time. Twenty-four million people went on submitting to the rotten deal five million laid on them. They accepted it. They went on struggling for survival, hungry, sick, powerless, pushed around, exploited, a huge labor force to maintain white supremacy. But a new generation was growing up and all the countries around us were liberated. We even got television at last, we could see blacks who're people, family com-edies where black men live with their wives and children in decent homes. The rest of the world seeped into South Africa somehow. New leaders appeared. People got caught and tortured and killed and their martyrdom gave the resistance more impetus. Teenagers got involved, even kids. They're angry, they won't submit. They're Sharpeville's children. There's a mass resistance movement now, people won't just take it anymore, it's all changed." His dark eyes burned passionately, his face flushed as if with fever. "Harvest time's coming, it can't go on much longer."

Ruth, who agreed with everything he said, who had predicted it all long ago, was too moved to speak. But Gerald murmured, "Why you, Nels?"

"Wait, I'm explaining," he said. "There's another battle going on besides the obvious one, government and people. There's a massive fight amongst the people. It's always been there, of course you know that, but now that things are coming down to the wire, it's fierce. Some kids are running wild in the townships; they're enraged and destructive and don't think about the future. Then the Azanian crowd wants black rule, no cooperation with whites, all that stuff. The United Democratic Front and the ANC and most of the unions want a democratic multiracial society. There aren't many white progressives around for them to cooperate with; if we all run away we'll be caving in to a new version of racism, another fascism, don't you see?"

"I see," said Gerald calmly, "that now they're killing each other."

"Not quite," Nelson shouted. "Not exactly. They're killing collaborators, black cops, turncoats, informers. They aren't killing each other because they disagree about the future."

"I don't agree," said Gerald.

It was a mistake. These two had fought this battle many times and had failed to shift each other by a fraction. Nelson wasn't going to submit to Gerald in front of Ruth, he wasn't going to permit Gerald to set the agenda, he wasn't going to be manipulated. He stood up again, waving his arms about.

"I don't think anything useful can be achieved by having this conversation right now," he said, looking at Ruth as if Gerald weren't there. "I told Dad I'd listen and I will, but it'll have to be some other time. I'm late for a clinic anyway."

"Could we have dinner together, Nelson?" Ruth said quietly. "I'd like that."

"After clinic. I have to go to . . . I can't till later. How about nine o'clock?"

"But where?" said Gerald suddenly.

Nelson turned to him then, eyes glittering, slits of spiky light under bushy brows.

"I'd like to meet Ruth alone, Gerald."

"Oh, quite. Absolutely. I was just thinking you might avoid attracting a lot of attention if you choose your spot carefully."

Nelson looked at him as if he'd crawled out of the lake, covered in fungi, dripping dead leaves. After a long minute, he turned back to Ruth.

"There's a pizza joint near the old Med School in Hillbrow. Doney's on Kotze Street. Could you meet me there at nine? If you don't like it, we can go on somewhere else."

He waited long enough only to see her nod, then turned and strode quickly away, disappearing into the trees with a shouted "See you," leaving Ruth and Gerald limp on the bench in the fast-fading light.

"Well, Ruth," said Gerald, turning his blue scrutiny upon her, "you see what Nelson's like." He barely managed his customary nonchalance; irritation or some deeper glumness threaded the air.

"Ben; but not really Ben," Ruth said painfully. Then she thought of Gerald's long unwavering commitment. She put her hand on his arm. "He's passionately sincere, decent, open. You've done a remarkable job, Gerry."

"Listen to me." He seemed to rouse himself, gather his bones together. The flush above his cheekbones surged. "We've got to find a way to get him out. That's all that matters. He's got to go, I tell you, it's absolutely vital." His eyes were rounded, intensely, coldly blue. "You've got to understand. This is it, Ruth, absolutely imperative, mortal."

She stared at him. She had never heard this urgency from him, never, not when he tried to persuade Bernard to value life and Bernard had insisted that was his purpose; not when he struggled to prevent her from going back to Bernard, warning her how high the price would be; not even when he put her on the plane to the U.S. at last. Taut desperation carved hollows under the newly steel eyes, tightened the curving mouth, squared the narrow shoulders as he clenched his hands so hard upon his knees that the knuckles gleamed white.

"Why?" she cried, "Why do you feel this so much? You've tried and he won't go. Why's it so crucial?"

He turned and gripped her shoulders as hard as he had held his own knees.

"I'm responsible, that's why," he said, face flaming now. "I took him on, for Ben. I'll see it through, whatever happens. I won't be stopped now."

He heard the words and their intensity at the same second she did; her shocked expression told him he'd revealed more than he'd intended. He loosened his grip so abruptly that Ruth rocked back hard against the slats of the green bench as he jumped to his feet and walked quickly to the edge of the lake in front of her.

In the enclosure made by the hugely drooping willows, the light had drained away as the sun dipped. The long sweeping branches, motionless in the still air, the drowsy birds and spreading, drifting lilies dense on the water, were all hushed, gray, suspended between day and night. Gerald, hovering at the water's edge, half turned away from her, seemed caught too, a tentative, bleached figure wavering between impossible options. His pale skin looked ghostly now and in the soft wave of hair above his forehead, the sandy tips overtook the ruddy haze.

While he stood there, trying to decide how much more to tell Ruth, a majestic bird, its proud serrated neck stretched tautly forward, stepped delicately between the trees beyond, halting as soon as she saw him. He saw moisture on her beak, spite in the glittering eyes. She appeared to be inspecting him. Something about the bold, inquisitive stare, the arrogant long curve of neck and the brilliant blue of the feathers, threaded by silver tracings shining like wire, barely muted by the faded light, reminded Gerald of Carolyn, who had announced two days before that she had decided to take the children out of school and drive down to the Valley of a Thousand Hills. She loved the misty light there and wanted to transplant some proteas on the terrace behind the cottage. Besides, she had said, her Oxford accent more crisply defined with each word, if he was going to be messing about with an old girlfriend she'd just as soon get away. Nonsense, this was a question of doing something about Nelson, he said, as she very well knew. Well, she wasn't too keen on that either, she'd leave him to enjoy his mission of mercy. He detested her caption for his stewardship, he was not really sorry to have the space. Early the morning before, Carolyn had supervised the disposition of their four-year-old daughter, seven-year-old son, two maids, and a gardener into the large station wagon, waved and driven off, her long golden hair crowned by sunshine. Carolyn's disapproval of Gerald's connection with Bernard Levine and his son had become more than a nuisance. It was a threat. Watching the arrogant bird examine him, it occurred to Gerald that he might explain his outburst to Ruth by means of his marriage. He experienced a tremor of distaste at having to compromise his natural reserve, but he recognized that it was the safest option. Besides, it was the truth, or part of it; the whole truth must be snapped as firmly tight as the bird's rigid, pointed beak. He had to try to manage without it.

Gerald turned and walked slowly back across the grass to Ruth, who smiled and held out a hand toward him.

"Tell me," she said. "I want to help."

"I do feel enormous responsibility to Ben for Nelson," Gerald said quietly, "but there is something else. My marriage . . . " his voice fell away in a hush as he watched her expression shift, her slight nod, which told him both that she respected his diffidence in speaking of personal problems and that she had been aware there were some. If he handled it right, this would convince her, this would be enough to get her roused, energetic, determined to take Nelson away before it was too late. He looked at Ruth, whose fine dark eyes were wide with the sympathetic attention that had always been a large part of her appeal.

"I'm afraid Nelson's putting great strain on my marriage," Gerald said, sitting down again next to Ruth. "Carolyn's fairly hostile."

When he married Carolyn, and brought her to live in South Africa nine years before, she had dismissed his guardianship of Nelson as a "mission of mercy." She expressed admiration that Gerald "kept out of politics" and declared that she would "never mess about with things that weren't her concern." Watching Ruth's face closely Gerald confirmed that, as he had expected, Ruth recognized the code and identified his wife accurately. He was surprised to find that this made it easier to continue talking about his private life. Carolyn, he told Ruth, often professed amazement at people who "got involved," "took risks," "stuck their necks out" and was sometimes actually annoyed when these misguided people made it more difficult for the rest of them, trying to get along and mind their own business. "It's not my problem," she often said, with a dismissive flick of her pretty wrist, not unlike that of the tall bird, turning her head away from her contemplation of Gerald.

"This was all quite acceptable to me," Gerald said. "I know it wouldn't have been to you."

Ruth smiled, shrugged.

"It's the attitude of most white English-speaking South Africans, after all," she said.

For nine years Carolyn had fitted Gerald's life as smoothly as her French silks and supple Italian leathers fitted her. An avid tennis player, a dedicated horticulturist, a gracious, even a scintillating hostess. "She collects people," Gerald told Ruth. "She does it with such flattering interest that they don't object, in spite of . . ." He did stumble here. He'd had no practice. He wasn't used to discussing his wife, he had barely articulated his thoughts, even to himself, it simply wasn't his style to analyze his own life, those energies were devoted to the dissection of power structures in political struggle.

"I suppose a different person might cause resentment about the British upper-crust glamour," Ruth murmured helpfully.

"Yes, quite so. But she gets around it, she has people falling over themselves for her friendship."

She had been just right. Her antagonism to Bernard Levine hadn't mattered. She had shrugged irritably in the days when Gerald had flown to Cape Town occasionally to take a shuttle boat out from the harbor to Robben Island to visit Bernard. She'd never asked about his life in his ocean-bound jail. That was fine with Gerald. But her disapproval had increased as the difficulties with Nelson mounted. Carolyn couldn't understand why he was so particularly troubled about Nelson lately. "He's been making a damned nuisance of himself for years," she observed cheerfully. That was certainly true, but his current activities were dangerous, Gerald pointed out. "If he's determined to get into trouble you can't really stop him, can you?" she said crisply. "Anyway, perhaps he needs a good paddywhacking to teach him to behave."

Repeating this to Ruth, watching her little grimace, quickly suppressed, Gerald swallowed an extra dose of annoyance. It was hardly conceivable that even Carolyn, with her blinkered vision, wasn't aware that the Special Branch's methods were more than the equivalent of six of the best on a quivering adolescent rump in a headmaster's sanctum. Besides, Nelson's activities were dangerous to others as well. He wasn't about to discuss that with Ruth, he must avoid that as if it were radiation. He certainly hadn't discussed it with Carolyn, but the danger weighed so heavily upon him that he couldn't help liking her less. Her trip to the mountains was probably better for him, after all. He found it very difficult to imagine introducing Ruth Fredman to Carolyn.

"The thing is," he said slowly, making her departure more threatening than he believed it was, "she's so fed up, she's taken off. Packed up the children and left."

"Because of you trying to help Nelson?"

"Mm. More or less. She knows I got you out here to help get him away, she didn't want to be around when all this was happening." He hesitated. Then, without choosing to, he added, "She refers to you as an old girlfriend."

Ruth's eyes widened. She wasn't quite sure what he was intending to say. His expression, in the shadowy light, was as troubled as she'd ever seen it. She took the kind of flying intuitive leap that had both graced and damaged her in the past and, honoring the moment, said, "Gerald, I've often thought that if things had been different, if we'd been somewhere else, that might have been true for us. And, if it hadn't been for Bernard."

As soon as she said it, she was afraid. But Gerald smiled at last; his face rearranged itself and found an approach back to its more natural detachment. He leaned forward and kissed her cheek.

"I've always thought so too. I'm glad you agree. It was long ago and another life, Ruth."

"But now . . ."

"Now my phones are tapped at home and at the office. It's quite possible there are bugs in my house. I've thought, sometimes, that I'm being followed. I had chosen not to get involved and now my responsibility for Nelson is messing up my life. Nobody's really free from surveillance anymore, Ruth, there's a more or less continuous state of emergency, the police have extraordinary powers, no one's immune, not even if they have a prominent MP for an uncle, an impeccable reputation and loads of money. My wife . . ."

"She must be afraid?"

"No, not really. She believes in her own immunity like the divine right of kings. It's not that. She's concerned that I'm making a fool of myself and, by what she regards as unfair implication, of her too."

Ruth could think of no response that wouldn't wound him further. She clasped her hands tightly together and waited. After a long pause, he went on.

"This trip to the mountains is a temporary separation, to give me time to sort it out," he said glumly. "If I can't find some way to get Nelson out of here, I think it'll be permanent. She won't stand for it. You may find this strange, but I'd prefer to keep her and the children."

"Not strange at all, Gerry." Ruth cleared her throat, blinking. "Besides, it seems you're in some danger yourself."

"I must get him away, I must." His voice dropped, he poured all the intensity of what he'd told her, as well as what he hadn't, into his appeal. "This is the best chance, you must help, Ruth."

"I will. Of course I will. I'm going to try, very hard. By the time I meet him later, I shall have prepared more carefully. Now that I've talked to him, I have a better idea of the problems. I'm going to do everything I can."

Glancing at him, Ruth watched his oddly meticulous nonchalance return, his pale, milky skin evenly restored, his eyes change to sharp, brilliant blue as if he had wiped a renewing chemical over the surface of his face. It only took a few seconds; then, with his curving, ironic smile, he turned to her and said that it was almost time for the zoo gates to be locked for the night.

"I think we should leave separately; why don't you go ahead?"

He didn't want her to call him after she'd seen Nelson; he would, he insisted, get in touch with her, it was better that way. She left him sitting there on the bench, leaning forward to watch the movement in the water. As she moved away into the densely sheltering willows, she turned back to wave, but Gerald wasn't looking at her. With his head bent, he was rubbing the tips of his fingers up and down over his temples.

Walking back toward the main gate, Ruth looked quickly about, up and down in every direction across the broad lawns and several paths converging at the main road leading to the entrance, looking, checking for watchers. She wondered whether Gerald had any real basis for his fear, any grounds other than the pervasive threats, the gray persistent cloud of intimidation that loomed over South Africa. She couldn't be sure. She went on looking, checking, inspecting, trying to appear untroubled, just in case. It was almost closing time, people appeared from different routes, making for the main gates. Several young women pushing strollers, a group of schoolgirls, their blue summer uniforms and panama hats limp in the heat, shepherded by a squirrel-faced teacher with a high, alarming voice; two black men in dungarees, eating peanuts from the shell; an elderly couple strolling briskly, efficiently tapping identical walking sticks in unison; and a tall thin man in a tan suit, a camera hanging from his neck, approaching from her left with a steady stride, a gleam of teeth below a clipped toothbrush mustache. Ruth, enclosed immediately in a burst of heat which left her damp and dizzy, walked straight forward, toward the gate, forcing herself not to run. She had to pause to let the group of schoolgirls file out together. As she waited, the man in the tan suit drew up and in the little crush, jostled against her, close enough for her to smell tobacco and feel the edge of the leather camera case against her back.

"*Jammer,*" he said loudly.

She didn't turn or answer.

"Sorry," he said, changing to English when the Afrikaans apology didn't draw a response.

She nodded once, moved out beyond the gate. She couldn't look at him.

"Did you have a nice time?" he said in a tone of teasing suggestion that brought the hot rush back.

She walked away at once and sat down on the bench at the bus stop in front of the gate, staring in the direction from which the bus going into the city would approach. She was surrounded by schoolgirls. The man in the tan suit stood on the sidewalk nearby, staring ostentatiously at her. She thought she heard a camera click. Then, just as the bus came into sight, far down the big avenue, he moved away, crossed the road to the parking lot, climbed into a bruised gray car and drove off, in time for her to be able to avoid getting on the bus.

By the time she flung herself into the car Gerald had provided, locking herself in, switching on the ignition, the heat panic had subsided, yielding to cold fingers on the back of her neck, cold knots in her muscles, cold shivers that set her teeth chattering. She couldn't tell if he was security or a man on the make. What would have been obvious anywhere, almost anywhere, she corrected herself, mechanically trying to be fair, was inexorably masked here.

Too shaken to face the Sterns just yet, she decided to drive around until she was calmer.

She was struck by how well she remembered the streets off Jan Smuts Avenue, hardly changed in all these years, how easy it was to return to driving on what had become the wrong side of the road. She turned into Parkview, drove past the corner cafe where she used to come with friends after school to drink cream sodas and repudiate school regulations by removing her panama hat in public. Hers was always creased and curling at the edges, its original white always dingy from abuse, its elastic always hanging in shreds. She had been proud of it, she remembered ruefully; it was an early signal of nonconformity.

A few blocks farther into the settled suburban quiet, she identified the broad driveway leading to her old high school. Its stolid red brick facade was as uninviting as it had ever been, its hugely sprawling sports fields spread out for miles in front, a reminder of five years of compulsory after-school sports for all girls unable to produce a verifiable medical certificate. After all those years of propriety and regulations, surrounded by females, reciting by rote in formal musty classrooms the archaic English translations of the Latin classics or the raw patriotic gushing of early Afrikaans poetry or the dry stately rules of the Queen's English or the official sanitized version of South African history, after all that, it was little wonder that leaving it behind for Wits had been so liberating. Whatever her parents and their secure upper-middle-class professional world had left undone, Parktown Girls High School had completed, readying her more truly than anyone intended for the convulsive gulping freedom she plunged joyfully into from the first time she climbed the long shallow steps of the University's Great Hall. Perhaps Nelson Levine had also deluded himself, entering an enclave where tolerance and the open exchange of ideas were trumpeted, that he was free to believe what he chose and act accordingly.

Glancing compulsively at the rearview mirror, checking that neither the tan suit or anyone else was behind her, she lingered outside the school only long enough to recognize the old claustrophobia. Then she turned back, driving up Jan Smuts Avenue toward the turnoff for the Sterns.

Approaching Westcliff, she passed the black bus stop and the long, ragged lines that waited there. It was in the same place it had always been, the lines were at least as long, the end-of-day expressions as blank. There were patches of noise here and there, men drank soda from cans, heavy women clutched shopping bags, muttering, shifting dusty feet, their heads covered by scarves, caps, or printed turbans. Some of them had been waiting an hour or more, the lines were so long it would be several more hours before all were accommodated, the journey would take an hour or two. Then they would clamber off the bus at some point along the bumpy ride through the littered streets of one of Soweto's divisions and walk the rest of the way, avoiding the gangs of knife-toting, delinquent *tsotsis*, calling to friends; they would arrive at eight or nine o'clock at shacks without electricity, often without water, in time to prepare to leave for work again at five or six the following morning. It was the same, all the same, as if the lines were carved in stone, but for two perceptible differences. People were a shade better dressed than Ruth remembered, a touch less downcast; and, riding high and solemn on either side of the lines, were two mounted policemen, weapons hanging off wide leather belts, boots high-topped and gleaming in the last light. These days, in white residential neighborhoods, where all workers but those domestics who huddled in bleak cells in the backyards of their employers' homes had to be gone by nightfall, perhaps they judged it safer to supervise the exodus to the townships.

Riots had become, at last, as fixed a feature of South African life as sunshine. Everyone's expectations had adjusted almost imperceptibly as the lines hardened; the police had shifted their concentration from harassment to the more urgent job of confining riots to the black ghettos that ringed the cities and to the mine dormitories and resettlement camps.

A few yards beyond the top of the bus line Ruth heard a radio crackling from a police car parked illegally, a cop on the road muttering into a transmitter, another swatting a fly, listening. A car idled nearby, a battered car that might have been driven by a thin man in a tan suit with a camera around his neck. It was fully dark as Ruth passed it, rigid behind the wheel, the old creeping fear settling like dust upon her skin. She turned off with relief on the street that led to the Sterns' borrowed house. She craved a hot shower, quiet and space to repair herself, a chance to plan how to influence Nelson.

She checked the rearview mirror: there was no one behind her as she pulled up in the Sterns' driveway. But there was someone waiting for her. Lights blazed from the house, the front door swung wide open and Bob Stern stepped onto the verandah as she walked up. Under the light his skin was polished salmon, his frizzy yellow hair settled in wiry clumps. His greeting was delivered with a certain urgency.

"Good, we were worried, glad you're back." He was blocking the doorway, she had to stop.

"I'm sorry to be so late," she murmured.

"Are you all right?" he asked, staring steadily at her.

"Yes, of course."

"Did you meet young Nelson?"

She hadn't told them where she was going, she hadn't really talked to them since her meeting with Gerald the evening before. She understood that Bob was reminding her that he had helped for months and felt entitled to information.

"I did, yes. I'm going to have dinner with him later."

She had forgotten again to ask Gerald what he had told Bob Stern about her; she had no idea, either, what Bob knew about Nelson Levine. She hated to risk antagonizing him, but she was determined not to reveal more than she must. Hesitating, muddled, and frightened, she saw him watch her, wait her out. She had to say something to get him out of the doorway.

"I'm trying to do what I can to help Gerald Gordon," she offered, hoping that mentioning Gerald's name would invoke enough of his prestigious mystique to satisfy her inquisitor. It did not appear to satisfy him.

"Step inside, would you?" he said, shifting at last. "There's something I am forced to say."

He led her into the small study and closed the door.

"I'm hoping to avoid getting Sara into this," he said roughly. "She's easily upset, what with her pregnancy and all."

Bob Stern propped a well-padded haunch on the edge of the desk, folded his arms tightly over his stocky chest and looked at Ruth with a grimness undiluted by his high color. He seemed oblivious to the tight set of her shoulders, the drained, determined severity with which she faced him.

"Just for the record I'll say that I never knew what I was getting into when you asked me to inquire about Bernard and Nelson Levine."

"Nor did I, Bob," she reminded him quietly.

New color rose in his neck and face, staining it pumpkin.

"Let's face it, you knew a darn sight more than you told me back in Philadelphia."

She was at a multiple disadvantage, especially since she had no idea what he knew. She started to remind him that she'd known nothing about Gerald Gordon's relation to Nelson when he interrupted her brusquely.

"Whatever, it's water under the bridge now." He jerked his square chin upward as if pushing away a bothersome bug. "Now I'm stuck with a feeling of responsibility for helping bring you back here. And you're a colleague and . . . " — his hesitation was just noticeable — "a friend. I'm afraid you're going to get into a lot of trouble again."

Again. He knew a certain amount, then. More than anyone else in Philadelphia. But she couldn't judge how much.

"I'm obviously more detached than you, perhaps I see it more clearly." His tone softened a little. "Whatever it was like here twenty years ago, Ruth, it's obvious to the most ordinary observer that it's all much worse now." To her raised eyebrows, he added, at once, "I mean that these days dissent involves being willing to put one's life on the line. That's how it seems to me as an outsider."

Just for a few seconds, a memory of Bernard obscured Bob Stern's chunky figure, the book-lined room, the wispy edges of new threats; Bernard, pacing his small bedroom in his parents' flat in Yeoville, dark eyes snapping in the passion of his argument with her. "I'm not talking about being ready to die for change, Ruth, don't you see, I want to live for change." He'd come, of course, to a limbo in between. There were, she thought of telling Bob, alternatives to dying. She blinked and sat down opposite, waiting for him to issue his declaration.

"I don't know where you've been or what you've been doing," he said, resentment curling the edges of his words. "But you must realize that for a woman in any circumstances to be wandering about alone after dark in this city is very dangerous, we were terribly worried about you."

Ruth couldn't believe this was all. She apologized at once, she had been with Gerald and Nelson, she should have called to let them know when she'd return, she appreciated their concern. Bob jerked his chin up and down once or twice.

"Now you say you're going to have dinner with Nelson later. Is that wise? Isn't it dangerous? This boy is a rebel, Ruth. I wonder if he's even stable."

"Oh, I'm quite sure he's stable," Ruth said briskly.

"Well, that depends on one's point of view, doesn't it? Anyway, the kid's a radical all right, no doubt about that. Meeting him for dinner might attract the notice of the security police, don't you see? Maybe you've been away too long to understand the danger. In the few months we've been here, I've talked to a whole lot of people. Let me tell you, you're walking into trouble. I've got to tell you that."

There was a contagion in the air of South Africa, Ruth thought limply. There was an epidemic disease that infiltrated the minds even of visitors like Bob. It wasn't paranoia, that was healthy realism, of course; the disease was the incorporation, as subtle yet measurable as osmosis, of the value system, along with the codes to define it. Nelson was opposed to apartheid and the suspension of the rule of law; therefore he was a rebel, a radical, and, yes, unstable. Bob Stern's affiliations with university history teaching and liberal democratic politics had not taken long to erode in the high dry air of Johannesburg.

"I really appreciate your concern, Bob," she said, as evenly as she could. "You know, I came to help Gerald with Nelson because his politics are likely to lead him into trouble. I understand what you're saying, that's why I'm here."

"I understood you were coming to take him home with you," Bob said sharply. "I understood Gerald Gordon was sending him to the U.S. to finish his education. Very sound judgment, if you ask me."

"Well, that's what I'm trying to accomplish." She was bewildered.

"I didn't know that you would use our house as a headquarters going about secretly until all hours, having late-night assignations."

"Oh, Bob, surely 'assignation' is a bit exaggerated, all I . . ."

"Not in the context of the situation here, it's not exaggerated at all. Sara and I are guests in this country, Ruth, we didn't undertake any political commitments, we're not looking for any embarrassment."

He had visions of harboring a terrorist, Ruth thought wildly.

"And how would I explain to the guys at home if you wind up in jail again, Ruth? While you're my guest?"

"Come now, Bob, having a meal with a medical student committed to civil rights isn't going to land me in jail, don't worry about it."

"Is it quite so innocent, that's what I want to know. I have a right to know."

"You're not suggesting . . . " but her voice tailed off as, with flaring anger, she understood that he was implying she was engaged in terrorist activity herself.

"Let's face it," he went on, bluntly, immune, "you may be an American now, but they're still not going to let you aid the underground, they won't keep still for it, Ruth."

"The underground?" she said shrilly.

"Aren't you an ANC supporter? It's a banned organization." She was overcome by déjà vu, she was briefly returned to her parents' house in Saxonwold, grinding fingernails into palms as she tried to fend off similar commentaries. She was not a dependent young woman anymore; Bob Stern was not her parent. She didn't have to submit to this. She stood up, thinking that she owed him a response.

"Bob, whatever you may have heard about me, I am here for one purpose only and that is to help Gerald Gordon persuade Nelson to return to the U.S. with me. I think it would be best . . ."

"There was a phone call for you," he interrupted. "In fact, two. The first time, he just asked for you. By your maiden name.

'Can I speak to Ruth Fredman?' Then, a few minutes before you arrived, he called again. 'Not back yet?' he said and laughed. No, he wouldn't leave a number for you to return the call, but he'd be glad to leave a message. 'Tell Ruth to hurry up and get out. She should have learned her lesson, didn't she have enough before? You just tell her that. And we don't want Americans messing in our business.' Then he hung up. He said this to Sara, who is now resting."

Ice cold, braced to disguise the tremor, she said, "I'm terribly sorry, Bob, I can't imagine . . ."

"This is the point."

"What . . . kind of voice? No one knows I'm here. Who . . . what about the accent?"

"Sara isn't sure. It was a mature male voice. White, almost certainly. Not a strong accent, could have been Afrikaans or English."

"I have no idea what it's all about, Bob. Honestly."

"I believe you. But it doesn't alter the fact that you're endangering yourself. You may be endangering Sara and me."

"Bob, I was going to say before and I feel even more strongly now that I ought to move out of your house. I shouldn't be imposing on you. You've both been very kind, but I must move out at once."

His glance wavered. For the first time, he unfolded his arms, pressing fleshy palms as flat as they would spread on the polished surface of the stinkwood desk.

"We'd rather you didn't do that, Ruth," he said, without enthusiasm. "We don't approve of apartheid and Gerald Gordon's story of your ordeal made us admire your courage. I feel very sorry for Bernard Levine. With reservations, naturally."

He didn't want to say more, but couldn't avoid the question in her eyes.

"He tried to overthrow the government, Ruth. He'd have been imprisoned in any other country, you know."

It was, Ruth thought drearily, a little more complicated than that, but a quick seminar wasn't likely to be helpful and she didn't think she was up to it herself.

"I should leave, Bob."

"I was just saying, we think it's right to get the boy out of here before he gets into more trouble. I respect you for coming and trying to help Gerald with that. I wouldn't have helped if I didn't see it as the decent thing to do. But I understood this was a personal thing, helping an individual with a family problem. I didn't see it as political."

"It's not political, Bob." Her voice was faint. She shifted, sat straighter.

"I'm not going to be manipulated, Ruth."

"Oh, Bob, I'm not trying to manipulate you. But I do have to go out and meet Nelson. He has refused to leave. I'm here to try and persuade him. If I don't keep tonight's arrangement, it'll kill any chance."

"Well, I hope you'll be careful. Alert to the risks. Those phone calls show that people know you're here and know who you are. I feel entitled to ask whether you're involved in any . . . illegal activity?"

Despising herself for responding, she said, "Of course I'm not. I'm only trying to get the boy away. Bob, I think I should move somewhere else."

"No, my judgment is that your position would be more precarious if you do that. I think ours would be too. I've thought about it. I don't want to be responsible for that. I undertook to help with getting the kid out of here, if that's all you're doing there's no sense changing the arrangements now."

"I'm sorry to be causing all this trouble," she said.

"Good luck," Bob said roundly. And then, astonishingly, his voice rising a notch or two, added, "I hope you pull it out."

"Thank you," she said helplessly. "Please apologize to Sara for me."

If she hurried, she would just have time for a shower before driving to meet Nelson in Hillbrow. She dismissed the anonymous caller with no difficulty; she struggled to dismiss worrying what Gerald had told Bob Stern about her; she concentrated on finding a way to persuade Nelson to go back to the States with her.

CHAPTER FOUR

There was no sign of Nelson.

Outside Doney's in Hillbrow there were narrow-hipped, tightly trousered men, talking Italian and Spanish; American tourists weighted down with cameras and packages; girls with multicolored hair in exclamations, earrings dangling huge against curving necks; couples window-shopping, Polish, Australian, Latin, sometimes snacking from a bag of dry, salty deer *biltong* or a slab of chocolate; cops on every corner, police cars cruising, cars from Germany and Japan, Italy, England, and America bumper to bumper on the neon-scarred street; money changing hands, little packages passed along in brown wrappers, people all shapes and sizes and colors with at least the common urge to eye each other.

Ruth stood on haunted ground. In the dense center of Johannesburg's nearest thing to Greenwich Village, the clotted traffic and cosmopolitan, drifting strollers merged with her memories. A block away, the secondhand bookstore beckoned still, though its name was different now and its intriguing, shabby window had been spruced up; once, you could buy Doris Lessing's early novels there for a shilling, even the banned ones, crammed innocently among physics texts or musty essays on mysticism.

A couple of blocks to her right were the old Medical School and the General Hospitals, European and non-European, once acceptable titles for whites and for the conglomeration of everyone else; across the street, the red brick jail, the Fort in its sandy courtyard, behind spike-tipped walls; and farther down, all the way down at the bottom of the hill, Wits University spread out for mile after mile between shaded avenues and grassy banks, serene stone buildings gleaming like ivory towers.

Ruth waited for Bernard's son with the manicured northern suburbs behind her, the city turbulently ahead. Bernard had lived with his parents not far from here in a two-bedroom flat for which the rent was reduced because his mother was the building's caretaker. To her left were the interchangeable side streets where she'd gone nervously to secret political meetings, in flats in little buildings with corridors oozing the smells of boiled mutton, fish and chips, bacon, above all cabbage, yes, and beets too, concentrated in assertive little puffs hovering in the air above each front door. When she was driving about looking for parking, she found that those buildings had been torn down and replaced by high-rises with marble entries, banana trees, and uniformed armed guards, but for Ruth these were flimsy shadows superimposed upon stuffy buildings with folding metal doors in creaky lifts and clanging slippery steps on the fire escapes, precarious routes for a quick departure.

Nelson was already twenty minutes late. After nine o'clock at night, with the stores closed since five, the smart hotels and restaurants and little cafes and movies filled, Hillbrow was jammed with traffic, choked with tourists mingling among the residents, kids moving in clusters, but she wouldn't have missed Nelson on the well-lit sidewalk. Brittle anxiety, laced by the counterpoint of calculation over whether it was justified or merely the performance of an overheated imagination, had once lodged durably within her. It had departed slowly, eroded by time and the conditioning of measuring her judgments against others' and finding them largely rational. The anxiety had disappeared so slowly that she hadn't noticed it was gone. It sprang back now, full-formed, as if it had never been conquered; Ruth was rationalizing that

Nelson had simply been delayed by a patient at his clinic before she was aware that she was afraid.

Perhaps she'd misunderstood, perhaps he was already waiting impatiently inside. She stepped into the doorway of Doney's. Like everything else, it had changed, but not much. Ruth had known it as a steak house. In its current incarnation it was dedicated to pizza and pasta. But it attracted the same young crowd, it simmered in the same brash din. Where there had been red vinyl booths and imitation Tiffany lamps, there were bamboo benches, high hats slanted against a black ceiling, and a neon cube swiveling, colors shifting like a kaleidoscope. There were a couple of groups of Japanese men, made welcome since their official elevation to the status of honorary whites, which distinguished them from local "Asiatics," who, like Indians and blacks, were not seated or served in most white restaurants. Familiar impotent shame crawled beneath Ruth's skin. Nelson was not inside Doney's. She hesitated. Perhaps he was in trouble. She returned to the sidewalk, positioned herself directly under the entrance light and looked up and down. A police car cruised slowly around the corner of Twist Street, three stout black women in the blue-and-white dresses of maternity nurses walked tired and silent toward a bus stop, white rubber-soled shoes squeaking; a man with a tan, a shaggy mustache, and a rough commanding voice delivered a crude punch line to three others, who sniggered, slapping each other on the back. One of them eyed her. Ruth turned to look in the other direction.

"Missus Harris?"

The soft voice and diffident inflection belonged to a black man. Ruth swung around to a khaki uniform standing behind her. His flat, neutral stare was unreadable. His eyes were small and muddy above fleshy cheeks. He was Ruth's height but seemed taller, with a boxer's shoulders. Khaki meant army. As she hesitated, he said slowly, "Are you Missus Ruth Harris?"

She nodded. She couldn't speak.

"I'm bringing a message from Nelson." His lips barely moved. If she hadn't been so close to him, she would not have been able to see that he was speaking.

"What is the matter?" she managed.

"No, is no trouble."

Now she saw that he was not wearing an army uniform. He was dressed in khaki overalls, with red italic script on the breast pocket. It spelled Levitt's. He wasn't a soldier, just someone who worked for the huge furniture wholesaler. She tried to smile.

"Where is Nelson?"

"He told me to come and get you."

She couldn't think. She wasn't used to this, she'd outgrown the habit. Something had already gone wrong. He stood waiting, hands clasped behind his back. They couldn't go on standing like this, it would attract attention, there were cops on every corner.

"He's supposed to meet me here," she explained.

"Nelson says this place is no good. He's waiting to eat with you. You must follow me. Where is the car?"

She stared at him. She had no choice. No plan was reliable here.

"Down the road, around there, just off Esselyn Street."

"Look, that's my truck." He tilted his head across the road toward the next block where a huge delivery van, the Levitt's logo on the side, was double-parked. "I'll drive round, pick you up on Esselyn, you follow in the car."

"How will you know the car?"

"Nelson told me. Go there now."

He moved into the mob on the sidewalk without waiting for an answer. Ruth watched until he climbed up into the big truck and then walked swiftly back to the car, where she found him waiting, blocking traffic.

It wasn't a long drive. Poised uneasily behind the truck, Ruth stopped recognizing streets after the first couple of turns. She couldn't pick out any landmarks either. Growing up in the big city, she'd known only those neighborhoods that intersected with her life; and that had been long ago. The truck turned from one narrow street into another, led her past darkened row houses where lights flickered faintly and at long intervals; through a square that might have been an abandoned marketplace, shuttered stalls lopsided on meager sidewalks; past a corner grocery store blockaded by an iron grille above three steep entrance steps where a huddle of black men sat smoking. She was thinking it might be Vrededorp when, around another corner, the truck halted suddenly under a sign that had read "Orient" before the O bulbs fused. Ruth drew up behind the truck. Nelson's messenger leaned out of his high window, signaling with his thumb toward the sign. Before she could call out, he drove away, leaving her with the choice of trying to find her way back or going inside to look for Nelson.

Through a small lead-paned window overlooking the street, she saw candles in glass tubs and red-and-white checkered cloths, cane chairs and a waiter in a purple turban decorated with gold stars like those Ken had collected on his workbooks in elementary school. Ruth backed down the road into a parking place, locked Gerald's Fiat and walked swiftly to the entrance, thinking how she would judge anyone who behaved as she was doing. She didn't enjoy being manipulated. Besides, she was ignoring elementary rules of safety. She didn't seem to have an option.

Nelson was there. Across the small room, out of sight of the window, he sat in watery candlelight with a group of five or six people around a huge, bowl-bottomed Chianti bottle. The smell of curry spiked the air. Four or five tables were occupied, mainly by Indians, though there were three conspicuous whites. The hostess, majestic in a mauve-and-green sari, head high above broad shoulders and generous curves, approached just as Nelson noticed Ruth. He jumped up, moving quickly across the room to her, narrow, darkly agile.

"This is my guest," he said. "Mrs. Harris, Mrs. Mahommed."

The tall woman smiled faintly, as if she hadn't needed telling. Although her skin was unlined, smoothly uniform, her shrewd glance and dignified bearing suggested that she was older than Ruth. As graciously as if they were honored guests in her home, she led them to a small table in the corner. She hoped, she said, in the rhythmic speech of educated South African Indians, that Ruth was enjoying her visit. She would serve authentic Indian food, was that acceptable? With practiced ease she made them comfortable, brought them wine, retreated behind a screen and left Ruth, at last, with Bernard's son.

"I'm sorry about changing the plan at the last minute," said Nelson. "Johannes found you all right, I suppose?"

"Yes. Why did you change the plan, Nelson?"

He shrugged.

"Seemed sensible."

Ruth waited, watching him. After a while, he stopped shifting about, looked at her directly.

"I was at a meeting before. I mentioned I'd be seeing you. It was suggested to me that Hillbrow is conspicuous."

She restrained herself from observing that when the same suggestion had come from Gerald it had been angrily ignored. Whom had he met who knew her name? Why had he been discussing her?

"Who is Johannes?"

Nelson shrugged again. Against the open-necked white shirt, his collarbones jutted forward.

"A friend. Part of my . . . group, he was at the same meeting, that's why I asked him to help."

She was determined not to be diverted. The new questions were just red herrings he'd be trying to exploit to avoid the issue; she was going to stick with her plan, it was all she had.

"I'm glad to have the chance to talk to you, Nelson. I've thought about you a lot, for a long time. We should get to know each other."

98

He looked surprised. He turned both hands palms up on the table.

"You know a lot about me. Gerald must have . . ."

A waiter, topped by a green-and-gold turban, appeared from the shadows, setting down steaming bowls of curry, saffron-tinted rice, dishes of coconut, banana, relishes, condiments. In the little interval, Ruth watched Nelson as he pushed dishes into order, rearranged the space, murmured to the waiter. He looked more than a few years older than Ken. In the pale light, his face seemed more finished, as if its planes were nearly settled into their mature mold; it was a less open face, trained in reserve, perhaps even duplicity. Ruth was touched by tenderness for Bernard's child, a longing for what his life might have been, empathy for what it had become. As if he sensed her softening, he leaned forward, piling both their plates with food.

"What's it like, living in America, Ruth?"

"It's different. There are things I don't like — the hype, the fads, the insularity — but they're totally outweighed by the openness. It's an extraordinary feeling for a South African. You can say what you like, write what you like, read what you like. Without fear. It's not only politics. It's part of life there."

Nelson had stopped eating, he was watching her attentively.

"Everything's up for grabs there, Nelson, at least on the two coasts. Everything's out of the closet. One can try for anything one wants. Everyone can. I grew up, perhaps you did too, in a very rigid environment. The rules never held up under scrutiny. But in the States there's a kind of native tolerance, there really is respect for difference. Everyone's not flexible, of course not. But diversity isn't just a platitude, people live it. Lots of them actually like being in a melting pot, they value it."

"It's not how I imagine it," he said quietly.

"You know," Ruth smiled, remembering the last time she had said this, defending her wry patriotism to Ken, "one carries oneself around with one. Wherever we go, we don't escape ourselves. But in the U.S. we do have choices."

"Is that why you went there?" he asked abruptly.

"No, not at all. It took me years to discover what I've been saying to you. No, I went to America to escape, Nelson. My idea of it came from John O'Hara's novels and the self-righteous evil of McCarthyism. Nagasaki. Korea. Commerce and consumerism. Not my choice at all."

"Isn't that all true?"

"Of course it is. But it's not the truth. It's only part of it. It's an imperfect world, Nelson. I went to escape, like tens of thousands of others. I found a refuge that became as near a home as I've known. I guess I'll always be a bit of an alien, but it's better than anywhere else I know. And I've been around."

"Perhaps it's yourself you found?" he suggested, surprising her.

"Perhaps. I value that. This is the only life I have."

"Yes," Nelson said firmly. "That's why my place is here."

"I understand how you feel," she said, as she had planned to do.

They ate in silence for a while; Ruth thought he was less tense than when she had arrived, certainly less so than he had been in the zoo with Gerald. She put down her fork and took a long drink of Chianti.

"Can we speak freely here, Nelson?"

When he smiled, he was Bernard again, Bernard companionable across a table, away from the people who hung demandingly about him, at ease with himself, trusting her.

"Of course. We're among friends. That's why we're here."

"Why is Gerald so frightened for you, Nelson?"

"I can't tell you that. I don't know."

"He's convinced you're in danger. He feels his responsibility to your father very deeply, Nelson. He's not stupid, whatever you think of his politics, you know he's very intelligent. Why's he so afraid?"

"I'd just be speculating." He waved a narrow hand.

"Well, speculate," she said lightly.

She was trying to domesticate it, she wanted to make it theoretical, an abstract conversation that would feel like many he must have had on campus. She was searching for a tone that would set him free to talk to her.

He leaned back, absorbed, frowning enough to mark ridges between the thick, familiar brows.

"He knows I'm involved in the anti-apartheid struggle. I haven't kept it a secret from him. I think, underneath all his academic analysis and rationalizing, he knows there isn't a middle here anymore. There are only two sides left now, however people pretend. Gerald knows that, he must. And in the last year or two the other side has clamped down very hard, in spite of all their screams of reform. I don't expect them to give up, roll over and go away, hand everything over on a platter, no one sane expects that. Gerald must know they'll never yield. A lot of people have been tortured. People get killed all the time now. Gerald's trying to do what he thinks my father wants."

"Is he wrong about that?"

"I just don't know." It was a low wail, as if he were in pain. "How can I know? We can't speak to each other, we've never been able to."

"When you visit . . ."

"Of course it's forbidden to discuss the struggle. But it's not only that. We don't know each other, really, can't you see that?"

Over the relief that she had reached him, she was stabbed by pain for them both; and by her own guilt. Blinking, she tried to collect herself, but Nelson didn't notice, he went on talking as if he were thinking aloud.

"It's not only that Gerald thinks he's got to protect me. There's something else. One thing, I think he's afraid that Derek . . . you know my stepfather?"

Afraid that if she looked at him he'd stop talking, she shook her head, moving rice around her plate. "I've never met him. I've heard of him, of course."

"Everyone's heard of Derek Brand, haven't they?" he said, his voice rising, his words crackling at the edges. "The great patriot.

Inventor of deadly weapons. Self-made multimillionaire. The Man. The one to see if you need a string pulled, a lever tugged, a body buried. Living proof that you can be the son of an illiterate drunk and a Boer peasant and still reach the top. How my mother —"

He stopped, touched his napkin to his lips, shook his head.

"How is your mother?" asked Ruth. "I did meet her, once or twice."

"She's all right." He had turned off.

"Nelson," Ruth said gently, "do you see your grandparents?"

His full lips curled.

"Which ones do you mean? I've got so many. I see my mother's parents very seldom, perhaps slightly more than she does, a ritual visit once a year or so. They are divorced, they live their own lives, they don't approve of my mother. I visit my dad's parents every few weeks, but I make them nervous and they don't know who I am, we don't have much to talk about. No one sees Derek's father, he's been disposed of in an institution up north. And I see Derek's mother all the time, she lives with Derek and my mother, on and off, when she isn't visiting her constituency."

"What?"

"She has relatives and friends and people who want favors from her in every Afrikaans community in the country. She's treated like a dowager queen by all the *tantes*."

It was a long time since she'd heard the phrase. Afrikaners weren't unique in having aging aproned aunts managing the community's business over coffee and doughnuts from rockers on the front porch. They weren't unique in clinging to the comforts of their religion or their money or land either, but she did not make the point. Nelson had no one, no one who cared or understood, no one to share himself with, no one who even wanted to try.

"Gerald's worried about Derek Brand?" She prodded Bernard's boy.

"Ah, who knows." He was sick of it.

"Doesn't he object to your activities?"

Nelson laughed loudly enough for people across the room to turn and smile.

"He doesn't know about them, do you think I'm crazy?"

"And your mother?"

His face darkened, he turned away from her and looked about the room, still spotted with late diners watched over maternally from behind the cash register by the woman in the sari.

"She knows a bit. Not much. She doesn't ask questions, they don't occur to her."

Or she doesn't want to know. Rita hadn't wanted to know about Bernard either, which had been her big attraction. Disliking herself, Ruth thought that the evening with Nelson had already returned the taste of her bitter jealousy of Rita as well as her ruminative anxiety. Like long-dormant viruses, these recurred, poisonous as ever, at the slightest provocation, as if they had never gone.

"Will you tell me what you're doing?" she asked softly.

His narrow dark eyes flicked wider, thick eyebrows jumped, long fingers clenched together on the table between them. Then he leaned back again.

"I'm a medical student. I'll be a doctor soon." His lips curved. He was pleased with himself for finding a way to answer.

"Why did you choose medicine?" She went along with it, lulling him.

"I thought it would be some use. I'd have something to offer."

"Do you like it?"

"That's not the point." He dismissed her, amused.

"I know, but still. Do you like it?"

"Yes. At least, I like it when I get results. But I would do it even if I didn't like it." His eyes burned. "It's worth doing."

"Of course it is."

She couldn't be sure what he was thinking, she knew too much to delude herself that she could read him, but she chanced it anyway.

"And in the struggle, Nelson? What are you doing there?"

He laughed.

"I'm not running weapons or training recruits, don't worry."

She waited.

"I don't throw grenades or make bombs. I'm not even organizing boycotts and strikes. I don't go to the mines. I don't go about stirring up protests on the campus or in the schools. There are lots of people to do all that. When they lock them up and stick bags over their heads and electrodes all over their bodies and interrogate them, there are more people out there waiting to take over."

"What do you do, Nelson?"

She made herself be patient as she watched the little wheels whirl behind his face; she saw them turn, click, and settle.

"Ah, what the hell, your credentials are good, Ruth, the best. They are, aren't they?" he asked, as if he needed confirmation.

"They're not bad," she said, despising herself, thinking of Bernard.

Nelson leaned as far forward across the table as he could.

"I supply drugs."

"What?" She was too shocked to keep her voice down.

"Ssh. It's OK. I forgot, you're an American now. Medications, I mean. Penicillin, sulfur, morphine, whatever they need. Whatever I can get. I told you before, we specialize now, there are enough of us, we don't all do everything the way you people used to."

"You sell medicines?"

He might have been Bernard, smiling at her naiveté.

"No, of course not. I provide them."

"But how?"

"Ruth, I'm a medical student, I'm the right man in the right place. I've got access. The pharmaceutical companies donate free drugs in quantities to Baragwanath and other hospitals, it's good

104

PR for them, all the med students learn whose stuff to prescribe when they go into practice. We run clinics out there for Soweto, it's part of our training. I work in the clinic."

"Where . . . where do you take the stuff?"

"Wherever it's needed. Our networks are all over the country. People get hurt, wounded, sick, they can't get medical help without being exposed."

She was suddenly cold, suddenly jolted by his tone of experienced assurance, suddenly thinking, it's real, it's not a game, this is deadly, I don't know what to do.

"You're breaking about ten different laws, Nelson."

"That's what I get up for every morning," he said gravely.

Ruth shivered. She couldn't help it. That had been Bernard's proud declaration. Nelson had learned it from Bernard, he said it with Bernard's solemn certainty; he would, if she couldn't manage something, end up like Bernard, or worse.

"Aren't there records at Baragwanath?"

"Of course. I'm in charge of them."

"Do you . . . do you deliver the stuff yourself?"

"Sometimes. I can't always. And it depends where. There are others with good cover."

Like Johannes, driving the big furniture truck with the Levitt's logo. Furniture delivered to retailers all the way around the Reef, up to Pretoria and the little villages beyond, close to the border with Zimbabwe. Shipments dropped off along the Garden Route, over a thousand miles to Cape Town, with stops at the Kango Caves, the peacock farms, the wine country. Furniture for the department stores in Port Elizabeth, East London, King William's Town where, in hot dark shacks, union organizers planned the next strike, organized the boycott of white businesses, selected the next collaborator for burning.

"You're delivering supplies to guerrillas who infiltrate over the border, aren't you, Nelson?"

"What you call guerrillas I call freedom fighters," he said briskly.

Ruth nodded.

"Yes," she said.

"And not all of them have gone outside to train. People have spent twenty years building a network across South Africa. And I don't just mean the so-called Bantustans either. I mean all over, in the cities, in the white urban areas. They've been at it since before I was born. Now, it's harvest time."

"What kind of harvest?" she burst out, struck by déjà vu, having the same desperate argument all over again, repeating herself to the same willful, dogmatic, certain face.

"It should never have had to happen," he answered soberly. "But it has. There's no alternative."

She'd heard it all before. She'd had no answers then, she didn't have them now.

"Nelson, do you go outside? Over the borders?"

"Sometimes. There are meetings, you know. Plans. Orders. Lines of communication."

"Nelson, you are defying the law."

"There are higher laws than the apartheid apparatus."

"Nelson, when you are caught . . ."

"If. Not when."

"If they catch you, you won't be able to finish your training. Won't you be more valuable to the struggle when you're qualified?"

"Of course. That's why I'm so careful."

He had told her about his drug-running with barely any prodding. He had revealed his sources, his colleagues, his masters, and his intentions without resistance. Her credentials, one hundred and thirteen days in solitary confinement twenty years ago, were enough for him. That's all it had needed. She could have been turned, couldn't she? She could have been lying in wait all these years to come back and pay the dues the other side would demand. It didn't even occur to him.

But, as if she had spoken aloud, he reminded her, "Ruth, my father told me to talk to you. I trust my father."

It didn't occur to Nelson that his father wasn't in a position to make a judgment about her or anything else. What she could not understand, could not handle, was why Bernard didn't seem to know that. How could Bernard trust her? It wasn't only that he couldn't know the impact of the last twenty years on her loyalties and commitments, though that should have been enough. But what about her betrayal, surely he must know that she had proved she couldn't be trusted? That isn't knowledge it is possible to forget. Had his judgment been whittled away by loneliness, tedium, torture, boredom, worn to nothing by incarceration? She thought she glimpsed him for a second, bending among the plants in the vegetable garden he was allowed, she thought she saw the long fingers extend, grip a throttling vine at the roots, tug, heave it out, carry it away before it could strangle the ripening tomatoes, she thought she could see Bernard, dark head against the sky, arm raised to throw away the murderous vine; and then she remembered that Nelson had said his hair was white now. She couldn't see him at all. Head bent, blinking, she scrambled miserably to recover the strands of her effort to save Nelson.

"Ruth," Nelson was saying as if there had been no interruption in their conversation, "I want you to meet a friend. Come with me."

"I can't . . ."

But he had jumped up, he pulled her chair back, with a wave and jaunty smile for the woman in the sari he led her into the kitchen behind the little restaurant. The turbaned waiters washing dishes nodded, but paid them no other attention. Nelson pushed at a swinging wooden door and started climbing the steep bare steps behind.

"Come on. It's all right. Really," he urged as Ruth hesitated at the foot of the stairs. She followed slowly, muddled by the unexpectedness of Nelson's agenda. She'd lost the initiative somehow and didn't know how to regain it.

At the top, he tapped quietly on an orange door.

"It's me." He sounded flippant, cheerful.

Ruth was behind him on the second step when the door opened. A woman glowed in the entrance. Slanting black eyes above elegant high cheekbones under deep gold skin. Black hair like silk cut above the collar of a tailored shirt that flattered the voluptuous, supple body beneath. Long feminine lines revealed by severe black pants. A smile that lit the dark doorway, a smile of welcome that reached beyond Nelson, beamed expectantly at Ruth herself.

"Vicki," said Nelson, touching her arm, "this is Ruth."

He shifted his glance reluctantly away from her and turned back to Ruth.

"Ruth, this is Vicki Naidoo."

He said it as if she would know the name and she did. Gerald had told her about Victoria Naidoo.

"I'm proud to meet you, Ruth. I told Nelson I'd never forgive him if he didn't bring you up. Please come in."

Vicki led them down a narrow hall to a sitting room with chairs covered in floral chintz arranged on a light green tufted carpet. Against one wall, a glass-fronted cabinet displayed bric-a-brac and on carved wooden tables, china and brass ornaments perched in orderly clutter. It might have been a sitting room in Bournemouth or Wembley.

"You met Vicki's mother downstairs," Nelson told Ruth. "The Mahommeds live above the restaurant."

"But . . . I thought you said Vicki Naidoo?"

"Naidoo was my husband's name," Vicki said softly.

"Not . . . it couldn't be Rajiv Naidoo?" asked Ruth, tugged by memory.

"Yes," Vicki smiled. "Rajiv was my husband."

"Oh, we were at college together, I remember . . ." Her excited voice, charged with vibrant images, tailed off as she absorbed the past tense.

"Was?"

"Rajiv died two years ago. In jail. They said he hanged himself."

"No. No." She was shaking her head from side to side, muttering "No" again and again, pushing it away, the fact of it as well as the utter impossibility of Rajiv taking his own life.

"Of course he didn't hang himself," Nelson said sharply. "Anyone who ever knew him knows that. Besides . . . ." He glanced at Vicki and stopped talking abruptly.

"He'd been tortured. He was badly beaten many times. He was dead before they hanged him." Vicki was matter-of-fact, she'd obviously said this often before.

"I'm so sorry. I'm so sorry about him." Ruth fumbled for a tissue. "I didn't know, it's terrible, I'm so sorry." She rubbed her eyes and blew her nose. "Vicki, I'm sorry to be upsetting you."

She thrust her fingers through her short hair and looked helplessly at the woman sitting opposite. Compassion softened Vicki's jangled eyes; enduring resignation settled upon her face, marking it with a passivity that made it less beautiful than it had been at the doorway.

"We go on. We continue." Vicki spoke as if it were Ruth who needed comfort. "Rajiv told me about you."

Ruth made herself look at Vicki. She knew that the Indian woman was telling her that she knew all about her. Rajiv had been in London at the time she and the others had been arrested at Sandown, otherwise he would almost certainly have been arrested with them. By the time he'd returned, Ruth was in the U.S., the trial was over, Bernard was serving a life sentence. Rajiv would have heard from the underground grapevine what she had done, he would have heard the speculations, the guesses, the half-truths, the gray shading layered onto the few clear facts, the shading and the judgments that depended always on the point of view and personal jeopardy of the viewer. Some time later — it must have been much later, Vicki couldn't be more than thirty — he had married this girl, and told her the stories of his life. Taught her the motives that impelled him. Introduced his friends and identified his enemies. Explained, no doubt, the risks he brought her. And, somewhere along the way, he must have told her the story of Ruth Fredman and Bernard Levine. And what happened to them. And why.

And yet Ruth saw in the expression of Rajiv Naidoo's widow nothing but sympathetic acceptance. There was no hint of judgment in the level gaze; there was no shard of criticism, no glitter of muted rage. Ruth had been punished so badly by her encounters with old South African connections after she had escaped to America that she had taught herself to avoid them; they had all been devastating, always, up to and including the meeting with Max Hepburn in Vienna. And yet Rajiv's widow had wanted to meet her. She had welcomed her, spoken to her as if she were an old friend. She looked at her now as if she were entitled to respect and affection. The ground shifted under Ruth's feet, the air altered.

"You must find things very different here now," Vicki was saying. "It's a long time since you left, isn't it? How does it seem?"

"The same," said Ruth, blinking fast, wiping her eyes again. "The same but worse. It seems there's more of it all."

"I know you get news we never hear," said Vicki. "And your television gives you pictures we only see if we're in the middle of them."

"There's so much I don't know, though," Ruth cried. "What's really happening, how much is spontaneous, who's doing what, what's happened to people I knew. There's so much I want to know." Saying this, she discovered that it was true; for the first time in more than twenty years she really did want to know; unleashed at last, she cared again.

Vicki at once began a dispassionate dissection of the current state of the revolution. Nelson, who had been so quiet that Ruth had forgotten he was there, added a brief sarcasm here and there, his eyes rarely straying from Vicki's face. He sat next to her on a sofa, close, but not touching. In his wife's hothouse Gerald had told Ruth that Nelson's girlfriend was an Indian fifteen years older who had refused nomination to the Indian chamber of

Parliament because she wouldn't participate in phony tinkering with apartheid. But, watching her with Nelson, Ruth did not think she was fifteen years older; and she did not think that she was Nelson's girlfriend. Vicki treated Nelson as if he were a favored young brother, dogmatism and narrow-mindedness tempered by talent and endearing eagerness. Nelson treated Vicki with the homage due a princess, though it was laced perceptibly with the urge to touch, caress, adore, the barely concealed desire to possess; or, perhaps, to be possessed.

Vicki, it quickly emerged, was a doctor. Struggling to hurdle the twenty-year transition, Ruth tried to remember if she had ever heard of an Indian woman doctor in South Africa before; she had been similarly struck the year before, reading reports of a death squad's stabbing murder of a prominent black civil rights lawyer, also a woman. But, though some opportunities had opened, the cycles of repression and resistance had deepened explosively. Why else would this woman and this boy and the driver of the furniture truck and God knew who else be huddled in a conspiracy to supply antibiotics and morphine to guerrillas who were conditioned to equate murder for human rights with breaking eggs for omelets?

Ashamed of herself for the thought, exhausted, miserably aware that she had made no progress toward getting Nelson away, she waited for a lull and said she would have to leave; jet lag and the excitement of her return had taken their toll, she excused herself.

"Could you give me a ride home?" Nelson said. "I had to lend someone my car."

He had simply taken it for granted that she would drive him home. How could he have been certain that she would not refuse? She didn't know if it was nothing but simple self-centeredness or the same ingenuous trust that allowed him to tell her about stealing drugs to distribute to undercover militants. Or was Nelson routinely manipulative? Or all of the above? In any event, his tactic worked. A few minutes later, with promises to meet again, warm farewells, and a firm protracted handshake, they had left Vicki Naidoo and settled into Gerald's Fiat.

"You'll have to direct me or I'll never get out of here," said Ruth.

"Yes. Turn right. Isn't Vicki lovely?"

"She's very beautiful. And warm and pleasant." Ruth was relieved that she had to keep her eyes on the road.

"She's a wonderful woman. What she's been through . . . and she's always ready to help everyone, she'll do anything, always available, reaching out to anyone who wants a piece of her. Everyone loves her."

At a traffic light, she glanced at him. The wisp of resentment in his voice was echoed in the troubled frown, the compressed lips.

"The struggle is her whole life," Nelson muttered. "She doesn't leave anything over for herself."

So Gerald had been wrong. Not about Nelson's desire, which rose off him like steam after a summer storm, but about its fulfillment. If Gerald was wrong about that, he might be wrong about other things too. This had not previously occurred to her; she put it aside to think about later.

Nelson directed her through a series of turns to avoid one-way streets and brought them quickly back to Hillbrow.

"Go round Clarendon Circle," he pointed.

"Yes, I remember." She drove out of the Hillbrow traffic, thinner now at midnight, sweeping around the Circle, the tall apartment buildings surrounding it like sentries. "I don't know where you live, Nelson, I'll take Oxford Road, all right?"

"I'm surprised you remember so much," he said.

"This was my territory." Hundreds of times, crossing from city to suburbs and back along this route, Nelson's father had been beside her.

"I live in Sandton, I'm afraid. I know it's out of your way. You go straight out here, no need to turn for miles." He settled back comfortably.

Ruth welcomed his silence. Driving the broad highway, nearly deserted, she waited for the slight dip, the curve in the road from which you could see the Jewish Orphanage perched high above. Although the bulky brick buildings stood on level ground, the land dropped steeply to the road below over rocky protuberances spattered with weeds and vines, giving it a Gothic look of forbidden isolation. Driving past it in the midst of some diatribe about proper behavior and five-year-old Ruth's disrespect for her elders, her mother had flung an open palm up in the direction of the Orphanage. "Perhaps you'd rather live in the Orphanage than stay with me. I can easily arrange that." Ruth didn't know what an orphanage was then but it became, instantly, a desolate prison; for years, every time she passed it, sometimes several times a day, she wondered if she would be sent to live there with the children who, she discovered, either had no parents or had parents who hated them. Sometimes she thought that she was an orphan and deserved to live there. She was largely cured of these ruminations when, at fourteen, she met a boy who actually did live there. At the invariable Saturday night house party, from which her father would collect her promptly at ten-thirty, one and a half hours before everyone else went home, she met in the kitchen of Joan Furman's house, where she was hiding because no one had asked her to dance, a boy called Saul, who didn't seem to grasp that she looked all wrong, felt all wrong, was, as a matter of fact, all wrong. He didn't even ask, just led her, with pleasing authority, back into the long lounge, cleared of furniture, Louis Armstrong hoarse, mischievous from the record player, kids pressing tentatively against each other in the dim light, watching to see who was watching them. Saul put both his arms around her, leaned down with his chin against her forehead, and moved her around as if she knew how to dance, muttering the words of "Stairway to Paradise" into her hair as if they meant something. He lived in the Orphanage, he was the first boy who kissed her, if you didn't count the twerp Herbert who'd tried the previous year and been slapped for his effort. Saul was, more importantly, the first boy she kissed. When he abandoned her, not long after, her fears about the Orphanage altered; it became the place from which tough, debonair, and fraudulent boys emerged to seduce the innocent.

Slowing to pass it, Ruth saluted her recovery from her vulnerable girlhood with its special terrors. She had recovered, hadn't she? But before she completed the thought, she switched to guilt that she was wasting crucial time with Nelson.

"I want to ask you to think about something," she said.

"I've thought," he snapped out of his silence as if he'd been waiting for the cue. "I'm not leaving South Africa."

"Nelson, let me say something to you. You know your father asked you to listen to me. For the same reason he encouraged Gerald to make arrangements for you. He wants you to leave. It's what he wants for you, Nelson."

"I realize that."

"Well, would you think about doing it for him?"

He swung around to look at her.

"Did he think about me when he got arrested and locked up for life before I was even born, for God's sake?" He was banging a fist on his knee. "Did he think about me when he went ahead and had a baby he wasn't going to be around for? Ever? What did he do for me, leaving me with . . ." his husky voice trailed off. He cleared his throat. "Who thought about me?"

I did, Ruth cried silently. I thought about you. I gave him up for you. Her skin warmed as she remembered. Then the sour overworn effort to track it, to imagine Bernard with Rita, to tame it by putting it into words, giving it a name, overtook her again, as it had not done for years. Calves aching, the nerve behind her neck sending messages to its kin beneath the skin of her cheeks and temples, she reminded herself how little Nelson knew. There were things even the best, the most accessible of parents shouldn't tell their children. It wouldn't help to tell Nelson he was the accident that changed all their lives.

"Nelson, Bernard did what he believed he had to do. He was doing it long before you were conceived."

"I know that. I respect it. He had his priorities." His voice was calmer now, but still thickened. "But still, he didn't keep himself safe for me, did he?"

"Well . . ."

"He didn't. There's no reason why I should do it for him. Our priorities are the same, anyway. That should be obvious to him."

"Nelson, I'm sure he's proud of you for your caring and your courage and for resisting . . . er . . . people around you, I'm sure that means a lot to him."

"How would you know?" No sad tears behind the words now, only the brusque rudeness of his simmering rage.

"I knew him very well. We were very close for a long time, we always knew what the other one thought, we shared everything."

"Yeah? Well, then, perhaps you'd explain how —"

But she stopped him, as she had that afternoon at the zoo. She knew what he wanted to ask. Why had they let her go? Why had they released her and allowed her to leave the country? Why was she free while Bernard was locked up forever? She didn't want to answer him, she couldn't, she had never talked about it, she wouldn't do it now. Besides, answering Nelson would preclude any chance of helping him. There was every reason to evade him.

"Nelson," she interrupted before his question could stain the air, "your father has spent more than twenty years in jail already. Perhaps he regrets his choices now."

"He doesn't. He told me that, at least." Flat dismissal.

"But he's given his life for other people's freedom, Nelson. He wants you to have yours to live. Hasn't he earned that?"

There was a long silence. Nelson sat as still as if he were deeply asleep. Ruth made herself wait, letting her challenge echo in the little space between them. She felt him shift slightly, saw the long fingers clench together on his lap. Then he sighed.

"I don't know what my father's earned," he said softly. "I have to do what I think is right."

Ruth thought that it was hopeless. Nelson had been right all along. How could she accomplish what both Gerald and Bernard had failed to do? She'd owed it to Bernard to try. She'd tried. Her shoulders rose in a little shrug.

"Turn right here," said Nelson. "Be careful, the road curves."

He directed her down a long street bordered by banks of trees and huge shrubs. There were no cars on the road. There was no sign of houses, not even lights blinking beyond the dense bushes. Nelson told her to turn left. "Stop almost at once at the big gate," he muttered. She pulled up in front of a seven-foot-high black wrought-iron double gate with intricate designs. "Just a sec," said Nelson. He jumped out of the car, reached an arm inside the gate, turned a dial, and climbed back into the car as the gates swung open toward a wide brick drive. "Combination lock. Electronic. Security," Bernard's son explained tersely, waving her on.

It was one o'clock in the morning, but Derek Brand's estate was generously lit. There were great sweeping lawns, a pond, a tennis court fence glittering beyond an oval pool set in rock formations, several small buildings and an elaborate formal garden with brick lanes between manicured shrubs; then Ruth drew up at the foot of three marble steps leading to massive double doors, made of carved wood with brass inlays. Tall narrow stained-glass windows bordering the doors revealed lights within. The three-story mansion gleamed white and huge. Wrought-iron balconies dripped flowering plants from the upper floor.

"This is it," said Nelson. He sounded embarrassed. "Do you know how many servants it takes to maintain this place?"

Ruth tried to smile. She was more than exhausted; she was tired of Nelson.

"Nelson, let's talk again. Please."

"There's no point. Surely you realize that?"

"Perhaps you'd think about what I've been saying?" She knew she sounded limp.

"Sure." He shrugged. He was obliging her by going through the formalities. She was tempted to let it go. She had to push herself.

"Could we get together, not tomorrow, the next day?"

"I'm not sure," he said, letting her see how hard he was trying to be patient. "I'll get in touch with you. Through Gerald. Day after tomorrow, if I can."

CHAPTER FIVE

L et's lunch with the lions. At one. I'll provide."

The message was penciled on a page torn from a pocket diary. Ruth folded it back along its original crease and looked at Sara. Sara had handed it to her as soon as she stepped out onto the sunny verandah.

"Gerald Gordon came by on his way to work hoping to speak to you, but he wouldn't let me wake you. He asked me to give you that."

Sara's round, sallow face was stiff above the folds of her maternity dress. Obviously, she'd read the note. She resented being unable to comprehend it. Ruth thought that if she fed her a bit of information, she'd be less hostile.

"Thank you, Sara. It's just an invitation to lunch at a place we used to go, long ago, out of town."

She hadn't planned the lie, it just popped out. Gerald didn't want Sara to know where they were going and she didn't either. She'd been right that Sara could be mollified. It didn't take much for her to recover her assurance.

"Oh, how nice! You go out and have fun. You must be worn out after spending so much time with that boy yesterday. Are you getting anywhere? Of course, you can understand him being really wild, what with his father in jail and all, but still, he's a dangerous kid. Are you taking him back to Philly with you?"

She stopped abruptly, as if she'd suddenly realized that Ruth couldn't tell her anything while she was talking.

"Too soon to tell," Ruth made herself answer. "I'm trying." It wasn't enough, she observed. "I do want to help Gerald," she added, throwing another snack at Sara.

"You must have been very close," Sara smiled at last.

"Yes. I'm very fond of Gerald." That would have to do.

"You know," Sara was awkward now, "I just heard the news. Last night there were more riots right here. Fifty-three killed and a lot more injured. They've sealed off Alexandra Township with tanks. It's unbelievable, isn't it, just a few miles away? It's so peaceful here." She gestured at the sunstruck lawn, the laden fruit trees. "I mean, riots over the border, that's one thing. Or blacks fighting in the mines. But this is right here. It's unbelievable." She shifted to a more comfortable position.

Ruth did not feel obliged to answer, but it didn't matter. Sara wasn't finished.

"They're talking about a nationwide strike. The government says they'll bring out the army to force people back to work. It's tough to know what's right or wrong here, isn't it? I mean, any government has to keep order."

"I'd better get going," said Ruth, who didn't trust herself with Sara any longer. "I must write letters before I drive out to meet Gerald." She turned toward the door, but Sara wasn't finished with her.

"There haven't been any more phone calls, at least. Who do you think it was?"

"Sara, I have no idea. None at all. I'm sorry you were bothered with it. I hate to be such a nuisance."

"It's not really your fault. I did get nervous, but I've learned a lot about this country. I realize there are some fanatics around. Of all kinds." She paused significantly. "But you must be careful. Who could it be? You must have thought about it?"

"Well," said Ruth, who hadn't, "maybe someone who knew me before. Saw me at the airport, maybe. Someone who objects to my democratic ideas."

"Do you think he'll call again? Can he harm us?"

"Sara, I think it was someone from the Special Branch. They enjoy intimidating people. They won't do anything, don't worry."

"Have a good day now."

Bedroom door closed firmly against Sara's inquisitive, slightly protuberant eyes, Ruth pulled a pad of tissue-thin airmail paper from her bag and sat on the chair near the window to write to Ken and Anthony. They both seemed very far away, distant reminders of another life. Two days in South Africa will do that to you, she thought irritably, that's all it takes to loosen your hold on reality. Ken and Anthony were going about their lives as if everything were normal. Ken stretched loose-limbed in class, recovering from a frat party the night before, mildly mocking Aristotle's elitism, distracted by the half-hidden curve of a girl soft across the room. Anthony strode city streets, cameras swinging from big square shoulders, searching behind masks for the faces underneath, separating disguises from feeling for his exhibition. He'd shot enough war pictures for several lifetimes. Now he was searching for internal struggle. Ken and Anthony were oblivious to the danger Nelson defiantly pursued, the hippos and *sjamboks* and fiery roadblocks crisscrossing pitted lanes, the solitary mind tricks to ward off madness in isolation. What could she write to them? She'd sent a cable telling them of her safe arrival, that was all. It wasn't Ken's fault, it wasn't Anthony's that neither of them knew why she was there or what she was trying to do. It was her fault, of course, that they would not understand if she wrote and told them that she had failed. At first, in America, she was unable to talk about what she had done; later, she wouldn't risk exposing herself; and now, after long years of disciplined conditioning, as long as the time Bernard had been in jail, she couldn't soften her failure by sharing it with her son or her lover.

She had failed, of course. She leaned her head against the back of the chair and closed her eyes. She had to face Gerald and tell him she couldn't shift Nelson, not even slightly. She had tried every argument she could summon. So there was no point writing to Ken or Anthony. She would be back in Philadelphia long before letters would reach them. She had not been aware that she'd decided to leave; but, after her punishing ride to Nelson's stepfather's estate and the long drained drive back to the Sterns' at two o'clock in the morning, she had known it was hopeless. She'd given up. She had to get past lunch with Gerald and handle Bob and Sara and then she could pack her bag, board a plane, and go home. There was nothing she could do for Bernard in South Africa. No letters necessary.

Ruth tucked the writing pad away and walked over to stare at the fig tree beyond the window. Its branches, heavy with ripe fruit and abundant deep green leaves, curved down toward the earth. She could see the figs hanging from the lower boughs, fleshy, ripely bursting. In the dense leafy heart of the tree the fruit was hidden, but Ruth knew it was there because a bird fluttered down and disappeared within; and then another, followed by two more, summoned to feast by their inhuman code. She couldn't follow them beyond their descent, but the leaves trembled, a bough dipped and Ruth knew that sharp elongated beaks tore into the succulent green flesh, ripping it from fibrous skin and milky lining. She watched, waiting to see them sated, wishing that she had not failed, that she had been able to convince Nelson to do what Bernard wanted and leave South Africa. She couldn't imagine, she forced herself not to try, how she would feel if she had been able to pull it off. Now, she had to acknowledge that Nelson's freedom was pitifully finite. And jail his best chance for simple survival. As a plump bird flew up through the branches beyond, fluttered and descended again, Ruth was invaded, pierced deeply by an image of Bernard's boy, dark intense face marked already by his inescapable struggle.

He might have been hers. He should have been hers. By all the laws of reason, all the force of human passion, even by the rules of statistical probability, Nelson should have been hers. Bernard's brief flight from her futile efforts to save him had landed him in Rita's ingenuous hero-worshipping arms, deposited him frivolously upon her pale, downy, credulous skin. It was over as it began; but there was Nelson, the innocent one-in-a-thousand chance product of Ben's spasm of rage at the agony of his choice. There was Nelson, who should have been Ruth's. Instead, she had Ken, with choices opened before him limitless as the ocean on a clear day, and with the cool intelligence and sturdiness to make them wisely. The birds flew up in a sudden bunch, rustling leaves, the detritus of their orgy hidden. Ruth knew why Bernard had wanted her to take Nelson away. And why he'd known she would try. He'd had twenty years to think about it; he knew that Nelson should have been hers.

She couldn't read the time on her wristwatch, her eyes were filmed by tears. She hadn't known that she was crying. In the bathroom, patting water on her eyes, her wet cheeks, her damp forehead, she saw that she had stood at the window for too long. She had to dress for this lunch. She'd have to hurry to get to Gerald in time.

Irritated by his insistence on revisiting old haunts, she drove his Fiat across the northern suburbs, cutting around the long side of the zoo with its high spoked iron fence, rounding it, to its front entrance. The war memorial still sat off to one side. Saxonwold was to her left. Down the road and around one corner was the house where Ruth grew up. She didn't want to be there, she had no intention of going near it, she didn't want to spend her last hours in South Africa revisiting her youth. Gerald had devised arrangements where everything she had to pass was a jarring reminder. She made for Oxford Circle, crossed the road and was in Killarney, far grander now than she remembered, its elegant condominiums shining in the sun, velvet lawns punctuated by blazing flower beds, artfully composed. Jaguars and Mercedes, Citroëns and Porsches turned off the avenue to park near the chic boutiques and Continental restaurants, all new to Ruth. Every surface was sleek, every window beckoned prosperous patrons, all was order, patterned serenity. Stopped by a traffic light, she looked ahead, caught by a vision of her grandfather stepping out of his big black Dodge, swinging his walking stick with its carved ivory handle and smoothly polished wood. His chauffeur drove the car away and Grandpa began his constitutional. He'd never learned to drive. Ruth smiled, remembering him strolling on these very blocks, jauntily doffing his hat to acquaintances, taking the sun before his lunch, which was usually borscht and a boiled potato. Cream on the side. Lingering there, she outlasted her light change, infuriating a honking driver behind. Uncertain where to turn, she drove away very slowly.

She needn't have worried about finding the right turn; it was posted on a prominent sign these days, a proud declaration where once restraint was admired. Ruth drove up through the immaculate side streets of Killarney and turned into the broad gravel drive of the Automobile Association Club, past the bowlers in their white flannels, panamas trimly ribboned. Spectators sat prim in lawn chairs, covered by proper hats and gloves, as if they'd never left. They were always there, like the rolled tennis courts and the golf course stretching beyond. Ruth drove straight to the Members' portico in front of the long, low main building, halting at the foot of the steps, where a valet waited crisply to remove her car.

Here were the lions of Gerald's note. It had been Bernard's contemptuous name for the captains of commerce who brought their guests here to transact a little business at oligarchy's watering hole. They sat about the long slate verandah, shaded by clusters of star-shaped white flowers profuse upon climbing vines; they were decorous, in their summer suits and muted neckties, around tables decked in stiffly shining white linen, occasionally accompanied by pastel ladies in broad-brimmed hats to protect pale skin from the sun. Their gin tonics or beer shandies were presented on glass trays by gloved waiters, whose starched white uniforms and caps contrasted nicely with their dark skin.

Gerald was there, among the lions, fully qualified by his family and his wealth and his dispassion and his titled British wife. Gerald waited for her at a table near the balustrade, from which he'd been gazing at the lawn croquet ritually enacted beyond. As soon as she arrived at the table a waiter appeared with drinks Gerald must have ordered in anticipation.

"Still Scotch, I assume?" he said, with a smile that looked a little taut around the edges. "Still insist on the right to differ?"

"Gin makes me queasy and I hate beer, it's not a principle. Why here, for God's sake, Gerald? It's not exactly private. You know, they all look as if they've stayed in place since the last time you dragged me here."

"You've learned how to dress since those days," he said, nodding at the black-and-white suit she'd been relieved to find she'd brought, its tailored geometry pure among the watery prints and pinks. "You look terrific, Ruth."

"Why here, Gerald?"

"It's convenient here," he said vaguely, waving a hand about. "And for our purposes, very private, I should think."

She didn't suppose the AA Club was bugged, and Special Branch Afrikaners would be as jarringly obvious as if a black man sat at one of these tables.

"What happened with Nelson?" Gerald hadn't moved, but she felt as if he had, she felt as if he leaned in closer, prodding and nudging. His soft hair was carefully combed, his light suit perfectly fitted, well pressed, his slim frame erect. But his face was rumpled, sagging around the sharp blue eyes, which were concentrated upon her. He held his gin in one hand; with the other, he held the edge of the table so tight that his knuckles shone.

"I'm sorry, Gerry," Ruth said. "It's not going to work."

"What do you mean?" His voice was very low, his blue gaze unwavering.

"I've really tried, Gerald, we were together for hours last night. I had no impact on him."

Gerald put his drink down, pried himself loose from the table and clasped his hands on his lap.

"You must have made some impression," he said.

"No." She watched color climb into his cheekbones. Thin vertical lines showed on his neck. She hadn't noticed them before. She told him about the previous night. When she got to the part about Victoria Naidoo, he sighed and his mouth curved in a derisive smile.

"I pulled out what I thought was my trump card on the ride to Brand's estate," she went on. "I tried to convince him he owes it to Bernard to free himself."

"How did he react to that?"

"More emotionally than to anything else. But not the way you want. He got quite heated and demanded to know what Bernard had given up for him. That sort of thing."

Gerald's cold blue eyes moved from Ruth to some intricate distance. Then he unclasped his hands and leaned across the table toward her. Speaking very softly, lips hardly moving, he murmured, "There's more to it."

"More to what?"

"To freeing himself."

"What are you saying?"

"There's also a question of freeing Ben."

Ruth drew a sharp breath, clapped a hand over her mouth, felt the tremor begin, moving up all the way through her, to her mouth, where her teeth chattered lightly, as if he'd hurled ice water straight at her face.

"Be careful, Ruth. You don't know who's watching."

She removed her hand from her mouth, pressed her teeth tight together, crossed her legs, folded her arms around herself, and smiled with her lips closed.

"Go on."

"I haven't told you everything."

She waited.

"They're offering a deal. They're prepared to free him if I get rid of Nelson."

There was a very long pause before she could trust herself to speak in a low tone.

"I can't believe . . . The government will let Ben out?"

"Yes."

"But," she pressed forefinger and thumb around her quivering chin, "you know he'll never agree to their conditions."

"No conditions, Ruth. Except sparing them the embarrassment of Nelson."

"Just a minute. Hold it." For more than twenty years Ruth had wished for Bernard's freedom. She had wished for it as a poignant fantasy, wished for it the way a little boy drapes a cloak around himself and jumps from sofa to armchair wishing to fly, wished for it knowing, except for the transitory intensity of belief suspended, that it could never happen. She drained her glass, saw Gerald signal the waiter for another drink, looked away across the green lawn, so perfectly even and unmarred it looked fake, trying to compose herself. They sat silently until the waiter returned, white-gloved hands placing the drinks neatly in front of them.

"But why, Gerald? Why would they" —

"I'm going to try and tell you." He leaned forward. "Try and listen as if I'm telling you a yarn about an old acquaintance."

"That's what you are doing, isn't it?" she said, releasing them both to mild chuckling.

"I was approached and told" —

But she couldn't sit still, she couldn't let it pass.

"Approached? By whom?"

Gerald flicked his hand impatiently. His eyes were paler, frosty with determination.

"A colonel in the Special Branch, if you must know. Just listen, would you, I don't want this to take too long. We must go in to lunch soon or we'll attract attention." He gestured, as if pointing out some amusing byplay on the croquet lawn, then talked quietly on.

"He beat around the bush a bit, the usual cat and mouse, but soon became quite explicit. They want to let him go. They want a sop for the West, the pressure is mounting every day. Holland and France have been pressing for years. Now the U.S. Even some of the business community here. They're thinking of the whole picture, the foreign banks, trade balance, all that. They've taken such a beating, they're looking for gestures. This is one they think they can make without much risk, buy a little time."

"Really no conditions?"

"They're banking on his whiteness." Gerald didn't mask a supercilious smile. "They're reckoning he can't have much impact anymore. Not on the guerrillas outside or the tough teens inside. The formations have shifted so much since they put him away. Now they think they'll gain more than they're risking."

Ruth shivered, pressing fingers against her chin.

"And they've learned from Mandela about the risks of asking for a commitment to nonviolence. They don't want a rejection. They want Ben out, Ruth, that's the point."

As Gerald talked, his expression pleasantly subdued for any observers, his own agitation buried beneath layers of a lifetime's veneer of civility, Ruth was suffused by the possibility that Bernard might, after all, eat strawberries again, lie on a grassy slope above a river, walk barefoot on a beach with the ocean stretching infinitely beyond; he might barbecue *boerewors* again in sunshine, choose a new shirt, play chess, sit on the floor in a circle at a party and sing off-key; he might make love, he might even be loved again. It was too much to absorb, all at once; besides, it might not happen.

"What's it got to do with Nelson?" she whispered behind her glass.

"The kid's a double embarrassment. They know what he's up to, of course." He nodded at her raised eyebrows. "Oh, yes, I'm sure of it." His resigned certainty rolled like a ball slowly inching across grass toward her. "They can't let him go on, obviously. They can't arrest him, because then if they let Bernard out they'll make fools of themselves. Their own right wing will scream for blood. They want to get rid of him."

Ruth put her glass down hard. It made a little bang.

"What do you mean?"

"If I can get him out of the country, that's OK. If not, they'll find another way." He returned her stare grimly.

"This colonel actually told you that? In so many words?"

"I'm afraid so. Actually he said, 'This is war!' "

Ruth surprised them both by a short, harsh laugh. She slapped the edge of the table with the fingers of her right hand, long, narrow fingers that delivered a sharp metallic thud when they hit the iron beneath.

"Let's go in to lunch. Right now." He was standing already.

"But . . ."

"There's more. But not here now. Come on."

Gerald led her down the parquet-floored hall, where gilt-framed portraits of distinguished members looked severely down, into the paneled dining room. Great dripping chandeliers vied with the sunlight and deep carpets muted the clinks and tinkles of silver and glass. Copper bowls of chrysanthemums enlivened the stiff white linen at the round tables. The long room was impeccably decorous. Following the maître d' to a table near the wall, Gerald held her elbow firmly. He must have felt her tremor.

"Let's order at once," he said, as menus were passed.

When the waiter withdrew, Gerald pulled his chair closer to the table, settled upright against its carved back. The flush had mottled his cheekbones, but around them his skin was drained.

"You must behave, Ruth. There are people I know all round. And some I don't know. And some who're wondering why I'm lunching a strange chic lady with huge eyes. I can't tell who might be watching. Be careful."

"One thing I'm wondering," she said, in a smooth conversational tone, "is where all this puts you, Gerald? Isn't the ivory tower a trifle claustrophobic after hearing a threat like that?"

He was alarmed.

"Please, don't. That's not the point now."

"Oh, really?" She heard her voice rise and made a conscious effort to lower it before she went on. "Whose agent are you now, Gerald Gordon, tell me that? Who are you acting for?"

"Ruth, stop it at once."

"Does Ben know about all this?"

"No." He sounded like an angry drillmaster. "Of course not. He knows about the pressures from foreign governments to release him, he gets rumblings, considering what's been going on the last year or two he probably guesses there are some possibilities. That's all."

She didn't know whether to believe him. She had no way to measure any of what he was saying, it was all utterly outside any experience she had. They were interrupted by the waiter. Shellfish basking in delicate sauce dispatching smells of wine, basil, lemon; crisp vegetables bathed in tangy dressing glistening along the edges of their leaves.

"Eat," Gerald commanded. "Eat while I tell you the rest. Try and behave, if you please."

She picked up a fork, speared pink flesh, dipped into the creamy bed of sauce, ate obediently, swallowed with difficulty.

"When were you offered this . . . trade?"

"A few days before your friend Bob Stern tried his discreet interrogation at my dinner table. That was the first time."

"He's been back?"

"Oh, yes, they're pushing. He brought someone else along the other two times."

"Who?"

"A minister's secretary. The point being to convince me it's real, official and so on." Gerald was weary now, his voice limp. "They have another motive, Ruth. Derek Brand is a very powerful man. He's a huge contributor, and a very prominent figure in financial circles. Here and abroad. They don't want to mess with him. They're afraid they'll antagonize him if they arrest Nelson. They're embarrassed."

"Are you seriously telling me they think killing Nelson would antagonize him less than arresting him?"

"Actually, yes. If you think about it, it's not unreasonable for them to think so. Derek stands for the opposite of everything Nelson does. Some . . . accident would be far less . . ." his voice trailed away, leaving harsh strains upon the air between them.

"Anyway," he went on severely, "you understand now why you have to get him away."

"He doesn't know about this, does he?" She abandoned all efforts to eat.

"No."

"Why haven't you told him?"

"I hoped to avoid it. I thought it would be easier if I could get him out without telling him he must buy Bernard's release. I thought you'd succeed. But you've failed so far, Ruth."

"Yes. I've failed."

"Well, now you have the ultimate weapon, you'll succeed."

"I'm not sure of that, Gerald." There were tears behind her eyes, surging in her throat. She swallowed hard. "Why me, anyway? Why don't you tell him?"

His fingers drummed on the tabletop, his eyes locked remorselessly upon her.

"When I told you, the first thing you said was 'Who are you

working for?', wasn't it, Ruth? What do you think he would say to me? I'm afraid he won't even believe me, he'll think it's a trap coming from me, you know he will." He paused, then started tapping again. "The kid is so naive he doesn't even realize they're onto him, Ruth."

"Yes, he claims he's too careful for them."

"Well."

They sat quietly for a while. Questions drifted through Ruth's thoughts, rising and dipping like fireflies on a summer evening, too many to catch and trap in a bottle at once. After a few minutes, one flashed more insistently than the others.

"They know I'm here, I suppose? And why?"

He shrugged. "Of course."

"Why the cloak and dagger, then, Gerald? George sweeping the hothouse for bugs, no talking on the phone, assignations in the zoo? What's the point?"

"Really, Ruth, surely you don't think I want to be overheard discussing all this, do you? I don't work for them, you know, I don't report to them, I will not permit them to spy on me."

She stared at him. She thought he meant it. He saw himself lofty, high above it all, working out of loyalty to a boyhood friend, nothing else. Perched arrogantly in an ivory tower, determined to stay there though even he knew by now that its foundations were eroding a little faster every day.

"Is there a time limit for Nelson?"

"They haven't given a specific date. But there's a lot of urgency. They're tired of waiting for me to convince Nelson, they want to make their big gesture with Bernard, make a drama with the media and get credit abroad. Make the New York banks roll over the loans. I think they expect Nelson to be gone when you go."

A couple of hours before she'd thought she'd fly away tomorrow. No letters to her son because she'd be with him soon. And Anthony also waited for her in Philadelphia while she hung miserably about Johannesburg, unable to separate fact from deception, unable to pass up the chance to give Bernard back the freedom she'd helped him lose. Even if she was being manipulated, spun in a dense web of deceit, pulled on like a puppet in the hands of an anonymous showman, she couldn't run away this time, not if there was the slightest chance. If she didn't take it, she would never know.

"I'll try again," she said quietly, trembling. His shoulders shifted, rose, settled in a little hush of relief. "We arranged he'd contact me tomorrow through you, Gerald. But I got the impression he might not. Shall I phone the Brands' house?"

"No. Don't do that. Keep Rita and Derek out of it. She certainly doesn't know you're here or why. She would make it all even worse. Don't go near them. If Nelson doesn't call me tomorrow I'll find him. I'll get back to you as soon as I do."

On the way out of the dining room he was greeted twice by acquaintances, stopped by a third. He introduced Ruth as Mrs. Harris, chatted courteously, moved on, hand firm on her elbow.

"You're a cool customer, aren't you, Gerald?" Ruth murmured, as they stepped outside into undiluted sunlight, waiting for the valet to bring the cars.

"Not always. I've been living with this for months, don't forget." His forehead was newly furrowed, crumpled pale tissue. "I did try to do this without getting you or Nelson involved in Bernard's release. Now there isn't an alternative. Need I say no one else must know? If they're humiliated, they'll be merciless. Remember that, Ruth."

Gerald looked as he had at the little lake at the zoo, staring at the water, inexplicably agitated, instincts for privacy, discretion, and restraint at war with an obscure imperative. Now her failure to shift Nelson's obduracy had blown away the gray obscurity. Gerald had announced an imperative Ruth could not evade. How many times in one life is a person expected to measure survival for someone else? She couldn't even judge what was true, but she had to behave as if she could make a difference. She'd done it before. And failed.

When she drove the Fiat out along the gravel drive they were all there, the bowlers and the spectators, all doing what they always did in the bright afternoon of the planet they inhabited.

Ruth drove away through the streets of Killarney. Without planning it, she headed unerringly for the back entrance to Daventry Court, which had been her first South African home.

CHAPTER SIX

W hen Ruth first arrived in South Africa she was four years old. The long war-ravaged voyage from Liverpool to Cape Town on the battered *Umgeni* ended within sight of Table Mountain with a score of rowboats rippling over sun-streaked water, filled with nearly naked black men bringing pineapples, melons, huge bunches of glossy grapes to welcome them. When they clambered aboard chanting, waving their offerings, Ruth's mother thought she would be frightened. She had never seen natives before.

"They're just here to give us this lovely fruit," said Mildred. "They won't do us any harm. Don't be afraid."

She said this exactly the way she'd explained, when Ruth first met a puppy, that it wouldn't hurt, it only wanted to kiss her. Ruth was not frightened by the black men, but she was terrified of the fruit. She had never seen anything like it before and refused to taste it in spite of Mildred's insistence.

"Ah, don't badger her, Millie," said a woman with whom her mother had spent a lot of time on the journey. "The children have been through a lot, they need time to get acclimatized."

Ruth's mother, who detested being called Millie, turned away abruptly, with a characteristic shudder and tightening of the shoulders that expressed restrained disgust. The voyage was over, the woman's usefulness with it.

Mildred's parents, who had never met Ruth because of the war, were waiting on the dock to welcome them safely home, armed with chocolates for Ruth and several letters for Mildred. Edward's anxious letters from somewhere in the rubble of Europe had streamed reliably into South Africa during their three-month journey.

Ruth's grandparents gave her things all the time; Granny always had sweets tucked into her handbag, licorice and chocolate and little bright-colored chewy things covered with sugar, and she had jerseys and coloring books and dresses and storybooks and a kaleidoscope waiting at the hotel in Muizenberg where Ruth and her mother were to have a holiday before going to settle in Johannesburg. Mildred had been born there long ago. Grandpa had silver coins and packs of cards all about his person. He wore a pocket watch with a thin gold chain and gold cufflinks with his initials, H.H., cut on them. He taught Ruth to play rummy the very first day she met him. And he told her stories about other lands with funny names like Minsk and Pinsk. Best of all, he made Ruth's mother softer, somehow. If Grandpa didn't like something she was saying to Ruth, he'd turn and gaze at her, shaking his head with its little cap of white fluff, blinking his moist pale eyes.

There was lots more family to welcome them at the train station in Johannesburg, but the one Ruth liked best was waiting at her grandparents' flat in Daventry Court in Killarney, where she and her mother were going to live until Edward was demobilized. Lizzie was waiting on the fifth floor when the lift stopped with a satisfying bounce and Grandpa pushed the door open. Lizzie gave a shriek and grabbed Ruth and folded her against her snowy white apron and said a whole lot of things Ruth couldn't understand because she spoke funny. She wasn't black at all, Ruth discovered quickly. She was a dark brown color with smooth shining skin and very bright eyes and white teeth. She wore a starched white cap over her close-cut wiry black hair. She didn't speak funny either, just different, because her real language wasn't English, it was Sotho. She also spoke a language with a click Ruth couldn't quite master, called Xhosa.

Ruth liked Lizzie for a lot of reasons, especially because she was funny. Ruth went into the kitchen in the evenings to ask what they were having for supper and Lizzie, standing tall and very thin over the stove, would push her full lips together and out, shaped like a kiss, and groan. "Questions," she said. "I can't tell you." Ruth jumped up and down, knowing it would charge her up. "Please, please tell me." Lizzie groaned louder. "No jumping inside." Ruth begged some more. After a while, Lizzie, peering into a pot where food mysteriously steamed under her sturdy hand, said, "Let me look and see." She heaved hugely, a large sigh. "Tell me, tell me." Lizzie turned, wrinkling her stubby nose. "It's *hesse, hesse* and *skapora*," she said lugubriously. "What's that? What is it?" Then Lizzie slapped her own bony hip in delight. "I can't tell you," she shouted, erupting into shrieks of the wild, high laughter that Ruth loved to provoke.

Lizzie was always there. She walked Ruth to her new school in the mornings, listening attentively while Ruth explained that the other children were teasing her because her hair was so short and her nails were so long. All the other girls had pigtails and bit their nails and knew how to play netball. And they laughed at her because she got all her spelling right and no one else did. So she was going to start making mistakes on purpose, then she'd have something to do while the others did their corrections and they wouldn't notice her so much. Lizzie nodded approvingly and held her hand firmly, swinging their arms back and forth. Lizzie told her about her own little girl who lived far away with Lizzie's mother at a place called Thaba 'Nchu in the Orange Free State. Upon questioning, Lizzie was vague about her husband; she had a boyfriend now, who worked for Ruth's Aunt Eva. Aunt Eva often said, with a wink and a slow raising of penciled gray brows, that her most treasured possessions were her perfectly waved blue hair and Charlie Mohali. He was her chauf-

136

feur but he did all kinds of other things for her too. Charlie Mohali was almost as nice as Lizzie. He came to visit Lizzie in the kitchen, sitting on a little stool in his black uniform with gold braid, perching his hat with its shiny brim on his knee. He was a tiny man, half her height and with half the humor, but it was enough. He told stories about Aunt Eva, her afternoon bridge games and little dinners, the big pointy rings she wore on all her fingers, her stately confrontations with children and grandchildren. Charlie Mohali had a broad impish grin and a malicious wit. Ruth knew for a fact that he and Aunt Eva shared a few laughs most days too.

After school in the afternoons, Ruth liked to visit Lizzie in her room during her hour off. She lived in the gray building behind Ruth's grandparents' one, across the drive and behind the covered garages. You had to climb up seven flights of metal steps to get there because there was no lift. The room was very dark because there was no window, but Lizzie had a lamp on a packing crate and a red-patterned Basuto rug on her bed, so it was bright enough. Her friends crowded in there to gossip about their employers and Ruth liked to listen and egg them on. But her mother didn't approve of her visiting so Ruth had to sneak over secretly. Mildred was pretty busy, doing something she called "picking up the threads of her life." Lizzie was always there.

When Edward came home, battered by war, determined to catch up with life and impose order upon it, he bought the house in Saxonwold; when they moved, Lizzie moved too. Ruth's grandparents were going to make their long dream come true and live in Palestine, so Lizzie could be handed over to Mildred. There were three servants' rooms across the cement yard outside the back door of the new house, and Lizzie occupied the largest of them. She recruited Amos, who lived in the second one and tended what Lizzie called the Doctor's garden in the day and served dinner at night. It was just as well there was a third, because when Ruth's little sister Rachel was born a year later, Lizzie sent to Thaba 'Nchu for *her* little sister, Alina, to come and be the new nanny. Ruth still liked to go visiting, especially on Lizzie's days off, "my offs," she called them, Thursdays from noon and every second Sunday, when she dressed in her finery to ride out on the bus to Moroka or Sophiatown or Alex to entertain others. Ruth had never been to any of the townships; she imagined them as villages filled with noise and laughter and camaraderie. Ruth liked to see Lizzie out of her white uniform, her lean strong figure draped in a dress Mildred had handed down to her. It always looked different on Lizzie somehow; taller, thinner, more angular than Mildred, she lent everything a racy grace, and disguised all hint of previous ownership with bright colored bangles and yards of beads and a cheerful print scarf on her head, not like the *doeks* of prim Afrikaner housewives, but flamboyantly twisted into a crown.

By the time Rachel was being walked to kindergarten by Alina, so shyly pretty that she had to fend off the attentions of every gardener and chauffeur along the two-block journey, and Ruth was twelve, starting high school at Parktown, having long mastered nail-biting, netball, and suburban school politics, things had changed. It was imperceptible at first. Lizzie was having trouble with the loyal Charlie Mohali. He was, it seemed, drinking too much. "In his cups," Edward muttered irritably to Mildred after stumbling over a raucous Charlie Mohali sitting on an upturned pail on the back porch. Once, Ruth was wakened late at night by harsh ripping sounds, followed by thuds and shouts and high wails. She crept into the hall outside her bedroom to find her mother hovering at its end, outside the kitchen door. "Don't worry, Ruth, there's nothing wrong." Her mother, in a pink quilted robe, peered anxiously into the kitchen. "Where's Daddy?" Her mother gestured imperiously, palms flung wide. "He's outside. Lizzie has some noisy guests, that's all. Now go to bed at once."

Unmasking this particular distortion of Mildred's gave Ruth no difficulty; she was easily able to piece the facts together over the next few days. Charlie Mohali was drunk, rowdy, and abusive to another man visiting Lizzie, so she had beaten him. She would, she told Ruth, do it again whenever the spirit moved her, no matter what the Doctor said. Lizzie had thickened over the years. Still handsome, but heavy, she moved more deliberately; the shrieks of joyful laughter were less frequent. For a long time, Charlie Mohali didn't return; when he did, he was permanently chastened, nodding dully, subdued forever. But Lizzie, it emerged a year or two later, had turned the tables on him and asserted herself. She had undertaken a private enterprise. She was running a shebeen in the Fredman's backyard. Edward and Mildred had no idea where she obtained the liquor, but she kept it in two huge vats behind the garage. Customers streamed in and out of the yard, day and night, but mostly at night, because Lizzie sometimes shouted at them in daylight. They were all afraid of her, Ruth could see, watching from the kitchen window. Lizzie sat grandly on her wooden stool in the yard, directing traffic toward the minion who poured after she'd pocketed the take. She sat there for hours telling stories, mocking disbelievers, urging on the drinkers with her high wobbly laughter.

On New Year's Eve, the year she turned fifteen, Ruth heard music from the yard and went to investigate. Rachel was asleep. Edward and Mildred were at a New Year's dance. Lizzie and Alina had to alternate nights for "stay-in" with the children and it was Lizzie's night "on." She was supposed to be in the kitchen but she suspended the rules. She was holding her own celebration in the yard beyond, she was dancing wildly in the center of a cheering, stamping crowd, the light from the kitchen and the servants' rooms and the stars glowing gold on their faces. The music came from a small portable gramophone someone had brought and set up on the washing tub, next to the vats of booze. Ruth had never heard the music before. Its heady, rhythmic beat lured the dancers into feverish gyrations, compelling Ruth to disobey what was called a Cardinal Rule and step out to join them. On the point of doing so, however, the door already open, she saw two white men and a black one standing at the gate.

Lizzie saw them too and roared for them to come in. Ruth closed the door quickly and returned to the window, because the men were police. They were definitely wearing navy police uniforms with black boots. The white ones had guns hanging from their belts, the black one sported a *knobkirrie*. She didn't risk going out. But she did watch.

Lizzie disappeared with them into her room and closed the door. All the while the New Year's party went on, music storming the air, bare feet hammering the cement, cups raised and raised again. When the police came out of Lizzie's room, they ignored the party. The black cop bowed to Lizzie and pressed his pink palms together. The white cops each put something in their pockets. When she was quite sure they had gone, Ruth went out to dance, but first she asked Lizzie what she had given them.

"A drink, what you think? *Skokiaan* for New Year," she said, contempt curling the grooves that had come from nowhere to settle like deep ruts down her cheeks. "I mean what were they putting in their pockets?" Ruth insisted. But Lizzie wouldn't answer, she put her hands on her hips and swayed back and forth, producing the old long laugh, more rumble now than shriek.

"She bought them off, I'm afraid," her father explained, when she told him about it the next day. "It's illegal, what she's doing, they come for a share of the take and she gives it to them so they don't arrest her. She's been doing it for years, Ruth. I'm sorry you had anything to do with it. I don't know how much longer we can go on putting up with it. At least she never touches a drop herself."

But that changed too. Lizzie was still always there, but she was becoming very heavy, actually she was hugely fat; her beautiful glowing skin had darkened in patches, her eyes were half-hidden in swollen flesh; she was often sullen, muttering darkly, incomprehensibly; there were days when she was unable to do much more than stagger about, forced to retreat sick to bed, leaving dire quiet behind.

Ruth spent less time with Lizzie by then; she was preoccupied with boys or, more usually, the lack of them; with not getting on the school swim team because she hated to do racing dives; with the nerve-dulling rituals of learning Latin; and with avoiding confrontations with her mother, because she always dragged her father into them for reinforcement. He always took Mildred's side, no matter how distorted. Still, there was never a day without a talk with Lizzie, a joke about some pompous guest in the house or a quick hug and a forbidden morsel. So that when she returned from school late one afternoon, having taken the slow route through the zoo by foot to use up time and avoid her mother and her tea parties, disguised as meetings, she was appalled that Lizzie wasn't there, hanging around, because she'd been fired.

It took Ruth a couple of weeks to find out what had happened. Nothing was the same anymore. It didn't seem right that Lizzie wasn't there to wake Ruth for school in the mornings and urge a hot breakfast upon her before waving her on her way; or that Lizzie wasn't hanging about when she came back, waiting to exchange news; or that Lizzie wasn't hovering late in the kitchen at night, leaning heavily on the sink, scarved head propped up by a massive arm, flesh hiding her once-proud neck, gossiping. Ruth's mother refused to explain why she'd fired her. "She's impossible, that's why. Stop nagging me, Ruth, must you repeat yourself so much?" Ruth sought information from a strained and timid Alina, whose loyalties were stretched; and from taciturn Amos, whom Ruth thought was the most private person she knew, not grasping then that Edward lived in a far more intricately constructed fortress, better disguised, of course, but more deeply solitary.

The explanation came, surprisingly, from Rachel, who led Ruth down to the back of the garden, beyond the hydrangeas and the cherry tree, and pointed to a freshly dug and turned bed of soil, almost hidden by jacaranda branches.

"They made Amos dig it all up," Rachel declared, proud to have more information than Ruth. She was at home more, of course. "They don't know that Amos dug out all the roots and planted them somewhere else," she giggled. "And don't tell them. I promised him I wouldn't say a word." Ruth was mildly startled that Rachel shared a secret with Amos but that was secondary.

"Dug up what?" she demanded. "Ssh. Ssh," said Rachel. "We're not supposed to know. I only know because Amos told me. It's *dagga*. Lizzie made him grow it for her back here. She used to sell it and give it to the cops sometimes also."

Lizzie had been growing marijuana in her parents' backyard? And they hadn't known? Exactly, Rachel assured her; they found out, by accident, when one of Edward's colleagues, who was a farmer as well as a doctor in the Northern Transvaal, came to visit and hilariously identified what they had thought were wild-flowers as marijuana. It was the last straw for the humiliated Mildred. Lizzie had to go.

New cooks and chief domestics came and went. No one stayed long. At first Ruth thought that none of them could satisfy her mother or tolerate her imperious whims, but Edward explained that they didn't stay because Lizzie had put the evil eye on them. Ruth gaped at him.

"Oh, I don't believe in it, of course, but they do," he said. "She's let it be known that this is her job and anyone who tries to take it is risking their life."

Ruth had frequently observed her father's conspiratorial concerns, his formulas of persecution. She dismissed this as one of them. But she discovered Lizzie on the chipped green Non-Europeans Only bench at the native bus stop four blocks away one afternoon, holding court among a group of her familiars. When Lizzie saw Ruth coming, she looked away blinking, hunching huge shoulders to turn her back. Ruth sat down next to her and took her gnarled hand and Lizzie turned and hugged her. Ruth visited her there quite often, when she had time and could manage it without anyone knowing.

By the time Lizzie defeated Mildred and returned, a smidgeon thinner and less frequently stuporous, having, Mildred announced, "turned over a new leaf," Ruth was on the point of entering the University.

Her new activities didn't leave much time for Lizzie, but Ruth was relieved she was there. It wasn't home without her. Ruth was busy choosing courses, enraptured to discover that she could study whatever she liked. She'd never have to look at a trigonometry table again, never memorize a theorem or multiply a fraction or raise anything to the nineteenth power. She asked her parents to explain the topics in the course book that she didn't know. Philosophy, her father declared, was a waste of time, nothing but undergraduate chasing after ideas that couldn't be measured; "waffleosophy" was a better name for it. Political science was even more rigorously attacked, more of the same abstruse theory, an excuse for not doing something real. So Ruth registered for philosophy and politics, shifting the primary focus of battle from her mother to her father, which was OK by her, they always backed each other anyway. She also enrolled for sociology, because it purported to offer a study of society and Ruth knew there had to be more to that than the suburban one she'd grown up in, where everyone valued the same things, scrambled discreetly to acquire them, and vied with each other to demonstrate superiority. Her final choice was history because she loved it, she'd even loved it at Parktown, where she first thrilled to the discovery that history varied according to who was recording it. Sorting it out was fun.

These were not interests that could be shared with Lizzie. Ruth quickly found other companions at Wits. One of the first was Max Hepburn, an intense boy in her politics class who concentrated fiercely in lectures and attached himself to her to discuss them afterward. He had absolutely no sense of humor and became distant and overwrought in the presence of frivolity, but he'd read a lot of the stuff Ruth was only beginning to encounter and he knew a lot of people, like Julia Gordon, whom he introduced to Ruth. Julia was in Ruth's sociology class. She explained she was only there because it was known as a free ride. They actually spent the first three months trying to prove it was a science, then they just muddled on. The reading for the year could be done in an evening and Julia, an aspiring artist, didn't want distractions. Julia had a light, aristocratic voice, soft bronze hair curling bouncily around a square, interesting face, and a brother called Gerald. He was two years older, a third- and final-year student who would get his Bachelor's at the end of the year, majoring in political science, planning graduate studies already. Julia tossed this out nonchalantly. It seemed very remote to Ruth.

She met Gerald Gordon when she tripped over him in the library during a thunderstorm. Carrying a huge pile of thick books she'd dug out for her first history paper, making for an empty table near the window so she could watch the storm, she stumbled over a well-shined brown loafer that should never have been sticking out in the aisle. She fell on one knee, books thudding all over the floor, making such a racket everyone stared at her. Awkwardly grappling for them, she looked up to apologize and found Julia laughing down at her from the table. Julia had claimed she'd never entered the library and never intended to. "I'm only here because it's too darned wet outside," she said. "And to cadge a ride home with Gerald." The brown loafer belonged to Gerald, who was watching Ruth with the same blue gaze as Julia's. His was far more penetrating, though, increasing Ruth's embarrassment.

"I quite realize you couldn't look down for stray feet, with that impressive load you're lifting," he murmured. The words were disarming, but were accompanied by a derisive smile and amused glints from the blue eyes.

Ruth was amazed a few days later when he phoned to invite her to a flick. Not at a regular cinema either, but something foreign and political at a private club. She didn't know what to wear or what was expected of her and she didn't like to ask Julia. But, with the liberated glow that had suffused her from the first minute at Wits, she decided she didn't care what was appropriate, she'd do what she liked. This seemed to work well. She was pleasantly surprised that Gerald didn't make fun of her, what she wore, or what she said. The film, which was shown in the velvet-draped screening room of the annex to a house belonging to an uncle of Gerald's, was in French, which Gerald spoke fluently. Ruth depended on subtitles that didn't match the length of the speeches, but it didn't matter, because she was instantly absorbed. The film was about some aspect of the Nuremberg trials, and raised the possibility that there were good Germans as well as bad ones. This was a novel idea to Ruth, whose father had returned from the devastation of Europe with bitter anguish, about which he spoke very little. Ruth was impressed that there was a discussion after the show, in which people of her own and her parents' generation participated freely. The older ones didn't seem to require the youngsters to be either silent or especially respectful. The concept of national pathology was heatedly argued. Afterward, Gerald took Ruth out for coffee and cheesecake in Hillbrow and asked for her opinion. "It's too new to me still," she said. "I'm going to have to think about it and read some more before I have an opinion." Gerald was delighted. "I could lend you some stuff to read," he offered. She had expected mockery.

It was the first of many evenings together. It was Ruth's introduction to the world of ideas, more stimulating by far than anything she'd heard in her classes. She leapt joyfully into a dappled colony where ideas mattered, history was relevant, moral choices were identified and dissected. Gerald was a guide, sometimes even a proselytizer, in her intriguing exploration.

She was amazed that her parents were so cordial to Gerald. He was only half-Jewish, and that half was substantially smaller than the other. They had both, many times, voiced horror at Jewish girls going out with Gentiles, a word Mildred uttered with disdain. There was also a great deal of hostility to what was contemptuously termed assimilation, in spite of their own refutation of religious practice on scientific grounds. But they both worked hard on committees that supported Israel; that, they explained, was their Jewish identity. Gerald was the ultimate example of what Ruth thought was meant by assimilation, but that didn't cause even a flutter of dismay at home. Although they had never met them, Edward and Mildred knew a great deal about Gerald's family, including his uncle who was a Member of Parliament and his father, who'd inherited a diamond fortune and multiplied it many times over. Mildred and Edward gave every encouragement to Gerald Gordon, in contrast to all the other young men who visited or called for Ruth.

They disliked Max Hepburn on sight, dismissing him as "shifty-eyed." When they discovered he wasn't Jewish, they banned him from the premises. There were others also, because Ruth certainly wasn't limiting herself to Gerald Gordon, however much they liked him. There were a lot of invitations, visits, parties, and Ruth made the most of every one, sometimes having dinner with one boy and then insisting on coming home early so she could get rid of him before another one came to visit. Although her parents had eased her curfew hours since high school, they were still pretty rigorous with everyone except Gerald. Ruth often spent the night with Julia or other girlfriends, so she could stay out late without being grounded for weeks.

There were some new friends she didn't risk bringing home even once. At Wits she became aware that there were Africans (she heard the term and abandoned the word "native" forever on her first day in college) who, unlike Lizzie, could read. There weren't very many of them at Wits. If you counted them and the handful of Indians and so-called Coloreds, they made up about three of every hundred students, which was ridiculous considering that nonwhites outnumbered whites by five to one in the country. Still, they made far more impact than their numbers suggested, because they were all exceptionally bright, they all worked very hard, and most of the time they all hung around together. Max explained that as a group they were obviously much brighter than a random sampling of white students, because it had taken such intense striving and determination to get there. They were really an elite, he said.

Max introduced her to his friend Peter Shabalala, who was supporting himself through college by working as a part-time driver for the printing company where Max's father worked. Ruth felt very daring and uncomfortably conspicuous the first time she sat drinking coffee at a table in the cafeteria with Peter, but the feeling soon passed. It had to, if they were going to be friends, because there was nowhere at all but the college cafeteria where they could sit and have a meal together. A tall, handsome Zulu from Natal, Peter was quite unlike anyone she had ever known. He was studying literature in several languages and wanted to be a poet. He pulled lilting music out of a mouth organ, long fingers delicate on the tiny holes of his bazaar-bought instrument.

Peter told Ruth that the din in the cafeteria made a hush like the ocean crashing on the rocks near Umshlanga. Transported to a stretch of beach where spray rose high and misty off primordial formations, Ruth made him tell her all about growing up there. His father was some kind of tribal dignitary, but Peter dismissed "all the tribal myths" as just another way to "keep black Africans tripping over roots in the jungle, eating weeds and swelling up with kwashiorkor." One day Peter had to pick up a paper in the registrar's office and came out to the hall where Ruth was waiting with his chin jutting forward, a glaze of anger scarring his liquid eyes and a rigid set to his shoulders. He wouldn't explain. All he said to Ruth was "She treats me as if I just crawled out of a shebeen at three in the morning covered with slime and contagious." But Wits was proud of being an open university and making space for the cream of the dispossessed. The Senate bore its share of the white man's burden as a noble responsibility.

Ruth didn't take Peter Shabalala home, of course, or several other new friends either. It occurred to her that Lizzie would be as outraged as her parents if she did and she struggled secretly with this. She started going to political meetings on campus and joined the Students' Liberal Association. Peter and Max were already members. So were a lot of other people she liked. Julia joined the Players' because she said the arty types were more amusing. Gerald had never joined anything and didn't propose to. "I'm an academic, not an activist," he said, with his odd nonchalance. "An ivory-tower voyeur, you mean," Ruth teased. He didn't seem to mind, he tolerated her sharpness with a curved smile.

The president of the Liberal Association was a tall, angular, final-year student named Bernard Levine. He seemed to be all over campus, his crisp, curly black head higher than everyone else's, his narrow face slanted by energy, chocolate eyes busy under heavy brows. Lean and wiry, he moved fast through the halls and seminar rooms of the Great Hall building, always surrounded by people. In her second week at college, Ruth came out of a class onto the sun-drenched bank of long, shallow steps in front of the pillars of Great Hall, to find a couple of hundred students gathered around him. He was calling for a student march to protest Bantu Education, a recent Nationalist Government invention to prevent black Africans from getting even a chance for education. "Let's not wallow in our privilege," he cried. "Let's insist on sharing it. March with me next week and let's show the Nats we won't be silent collaborators." The students roared approval.

Ruth marched the following week. She also watched Bernard Levine whenever she had the chance. She learned that he was the most important liberal on the Students' Representative Council, leader of the majority, running for election as its president. She wasn't the only one who watched him, she noticed; lots of students admired him, girls hung around him, prominent students were respectful to him. There were some, of course, who thought "liberal" was a dirty word.

When Ruth told her parents she'd joined the SLA, Mildred raised her eyebrows high, rolled her eyes heavenward and sighed. Edward asked what the SLA did, besides the usual undergraduate hot air. Ruth explained about keeping the university open, fighting for universal education, taking a stand for tolerance and respect for dissent.

Edward said that Jews ought to be particularly careful not to draw attention to themselves; they were history's permanent scapegoats and would always take the rap for conflicts in any society outside of Israel; that had always been the case. He devoted the entire dinner period to proving this with examples beginning with the Maccabees and continuing all the way through the Warsaw Ghetto. Ruth interrupted once to point out that most of the members were Jews; Edward fixed his gray, slightly pop-eyed stare on her, freezing her into preconditioned panic. That was the point, he snapped, dismissing it. Jews often took the lead in confronting injustice and got whipped for their trouble. They had to look after themselves. No one else would do it for them. He resumed the presentation of supporting evidence. His peroration included the observation that liberals were left-wing troublemakers, seeking power.

Ruth, who felt better equipped to argue with him now that she was a serious student of history, suggested that the British Labour Party would not regard liberalism as left-wing. Edward stared at her grimly and said that this was specious undergraduate hot air. In South Africa, words had different meanings; if she didn't understand that, she'd find out soon enough. Ruth murmured something about Humpty-Dumpty.

"What did you say?" demanded Edward.

"You know," Ruth explained hurriedly, "*Alice in Wonderland.* Words mean what you want them to mean."

Edward froze her again. "Sheer impertinence," he said.

That was the first round. There were many more, but Ruth was a fast study; she offered less information and tried not to supply new ammunition by arguing. She didn't tell them that she'd been asked to become the freshman rep and secretary of the SLA committee, she didn't discuss strategy meetings or election campaigns or protest marches at home. And she didn't talk about Bernard Levine, whose magnetic leadership gave the organization momentum that far outstripped its small membership.

She was surprised to learn that Gerald Gordon and Bernard Levine were friends and had been all through high school. She assumed it was a relationship like those few she retained with old school friends, keeping in vague contact, while drifting apart as new interests displaced the old ties, already strained by boredom and habit. But it wasn't like that between Gerald and Bernard at all, Gerald told her. He and Bernard spent a lot of time together, went out weekends and evenings, even double-dated. They studied together a lot. They were both majoring in politics. He planned graduate work at Wits and then hoped to go on to Oxford. He looked forward to academic life. Bernard was going into law, if he could scrape the money together for law school.

At least twenty-seven questions clamored on the front line of Ruth's mind, but she was unusually diffident about asking them. She was going out with Gerald quite often and Bernard was his friend. There were conventions about these things that Ruth had not examined but felt obliged to respect.

"Your ideas are so different," was all she said.

"We argue a lot," Gerald replied lightly. "Always have. We don't have to agree about everything."

It wasn't Gerald Gordon who introduced Ruth to Bernard Levine. It was Max Hepburn who urged her inclusion on the inner councils of the SLA and introduced her to Bernard at a meeting to plan the contents of a new monthly journal of opinion.

"Glad you can join us," Bernard said. His voice was deep and very smooth. His dark eyes were already roaming the student office, checking who'd turned up. Ruth was intimidated by the wit and composure of the other students, who'd been around and knew what was going on. She didn't say anything while they discussed what topics had priority for the first issue of the magazine. Who should write what. Who should approach which faculty member to contribute. What to charge for space, who would put a sales staff for ads together, how many pages. Whenever they got off the point, quite often, actually, Bernard Levine steered them back again, moving at a heady pace. Energy seemed to spring from his dark curly hair, his high temples and narrow, mobile face, his triangular chin.

The final item to be settled was the name of the journal. Ideas flew around like autumn leaves, falling away quickly when Bernard grimaced, or shook his head, murmuring "Too trite" or "Weak politics," a damning phrase.

"How about *Progressive Student?*" Ruth said, immediately terrified, wishing she'd kept her mouth shut.

"What was that?" Bernard asked.

Ruth chewed the insides of her cheeks.

"Sorry, didn't hear, what did you say?"

Ruth cleared her throat.

"*Progressive Student,*" she said loudly. He was looking at her now, his eyes weren't roving at all. She felt hot, she knew she was blushing.

"That's great, I like that," he said. "*Progressive Student.* Sounds just right. All in favor?"

After that, Ruth saw Bernard quite often at meetings and political rallies and on the late hectic nights when they read proof for *Progressive Student.* There were always people around him, always a sense of pressure, no time to waste, important things needing his attention somewhere else. He was always rushing off to keep an appointment, make a speech, finish a paper, he was abstracted, short on sleep, missing meals. Sometimes he carried a small carton of milk, gulping from it as he persuaded someone to spray-paint a building or hang a forbidden banner high over the wide avenue in front of Great Hall. Max, who seemed to watch Bernard at least as much as Ruth, speculated that he might have an ulcer.

Ruth was pretty busy herself, frenzied actually, she pleasurably informed anyone who wanted to know. She had so much to catch up on, she was always coming from behind. She never had enough time to fully develop her papers and often sat up until three or four in the morning to complete them by the deadline, which was a shame, she really enjoyed her courses. She was devoured by campus politics, racing from demonstrations to the cafeteria to recruit more people, stenciling posters, arguing strategy. And there was so much she didn't know, so much had passed her by during high school; she'd never even known there was a Defiance Campaign, never heard of Mandela, even the concept of passive resistance was new, Gandhi only a name. She heard about American McCarthyism years after the army hearings and the blacklists, years after the South African Government passed the Suppression of Communism Act, which turned every shade of dissent into red treason. Ruth made the connections between these witch-hunts for herself with an archeologist's thrill and moved hungrily to the *Areopagitica* and Mill, to the Cold War and the Bomb, to Sacco and Vanzetti, to the Rosenbergs in America and Maclean and Burgess in Britain; there was Suez and Israel's survival, and there were the Soviet tanks in Hungary. Ruth gobbled voraciously at it all, indiscriminately feasting on an orgy of ideas, gulping them down the way Bernard gulped at his milk. She had so much catching up to do.

She made time for Gerald Gordon, though. One blazing afternoon they cut classes and went to the zoo, driving down Jan Smuts Avenue in Gerald's white Triumph convertible, the sky sun-swept, brilliant steady blue. Gerald knew all the lanes and corners and hidden, intriguing little spots in the zoo as well as if it were his own backyard. He came there often, he explained. He showed her a short cut that took them straight to the lions, stopping only to buy something to eat. Ruth expected peanuts in hairy shells, but Gerald came away from the tea room with a bag of fleshy white litchis, cool and sweet, luscious under their knobby dark coats. You had to remember to be careful of the large dark pits; if one popped down your throat you could choke and die, Edward always warned.

Gerald and Ruth settled down to eat the litchis on a bench in front of the railings that surrounded the high rocky space where the lions lived. Gerald had spent a whole afternoon watching them, long ago, a tumescent high school senior, enthralled by the courtship of an angry lion for a disdainful, sauntering, long-maned lady. She'd rejected him time and again, she taunted him from the highest point of the stone hill, she jumped gracefully to evade him, she kicked her back feet into his straining pelvis until at last he grabbed a secure hold on her haunches and mounted her, panting, tongue dangling wet and red. With a vicarious shiver, Gerald saw her at once subdued, shuddering delicately as he pounded at her, complacently receiving the pleasure she had enhanced by prodding and poking the flaming coals of his lust. The image of the lions coupling in the setting sun had reverberated for Gerald since then, the hot summer light gleaming on their muscles, their manes and tails swirling wildly, subsiding in a hush as they unlocked to sprawl languid on warm rock. He had returned many times hoping to see another lusty chase. Gerald liked to watch.

Today they were dozing on the rocks, barely a tail twitching. Neither of them seemed to need anything. Punchy from sun, they looked almost asleep or numbingly bored. Ruth wasn't interested in them, she kept talking about the Freedom Charter, which she'd only just read. It was a plan for democracy adopted at a mass meeting at Kliptown a couple of years before. Gerald didn't tell her about the lions. He didn't know why he'd wanted her to see them. He made some acid remarks about the Charter's call for the nationalization of the country's resources. Ruth felt inept. She hadn't tampered with economics yet. The afternoon was one of their less successful outings.

One night soon afterward, Ruth went to the door expecting Max Hepburn, who was supposed to pick up an article for the journal she'd been typing during the late afternoon thunder-shower. Edward and Mildred were out at a dinner party, Rachel was pretending to be asleep while reading trash by flashlight under the blankets, and Alina was in the kitchen with the next-door neighbor's new chauffeur, who was enacting an account of his recent sixty days in prison on a pass offense with all the ritual of a slow mating dance. Ruth didn't like to disturb them to answer the front door, so she went to open it herself.

Bernard Levine stood smiling there. Drops of water shimmered under the light on his black hair. She could see the bones in his face, arching under shadowy skin, full lips open above the cleft in the chin.

"Why are you here?" she blurted, trying to comb her hair with her fingers.

"Max couldn't make it, so I came. Do you mind?"

"No, of course not." She realized how she must have sounded. "It's fine. I'm sorry, I was just surprised. Do you want to come in? I've finished the typing, I hope it's all right, perhaps you want to check it, if you . . ." She stopped abruptly, as she heard the sounds of her babbling. He was still standing there, smiling, presumably because she was blocking the doorway. She moved aside and he followed her in, through the mirrored hall and into the lounge, where she waved vaguely at a chair.

"I'll just get it, the article, I mean," she said and ran away. She dashed back down the hall into her room, grabbed the thing off her desk, raced back. Halfway, she had another idea and flung herself around again, reaching for a brush, stopping breathlessly in front of the mirror over the bureau. She pulled the brush over her hair, glancing at the mirror. She was flushed and her eyes were enormous, the deep brown irises large and weirdly shiny. She put the brush down and stared at herself for a second or two and then poked long fingers through the top of her hair, tugging the front bits of hair down over her forehead in wisps. Afraid she was taking too long, she hurried back again down the hall and into the lounge, where Bernard was standing staring at a photograph in a silver frame.

"Who's this?" he asked, as soon as he saw her.

"It's my parents and me, in London just after Dunkirk," she said, offering him the paper. He didn't seem to notice.

"But what uniform's your father wearing?"

"British. That's the Royal Army Medical Corps badge. He was wounded at Dunkirk. This was taken after he recovered, just before he went back to the continent again."

"He's not a South African?" He was still staring at the picture.

"Well, he is now, I suppose. He was British. He was Austrian before that." She tossed the manuscript onto a table. "He was sent away to London to live with his uncle when he was about twelve. That's his uncle's house in the picture."

She was afraid she was talking too much, but Bernard kept asking questions.

"Is your mother English also?"

"Oh, no. She's a South African through and through."

"They look so young," he murmured, taking a step forward to examine them again, Mildred holding Ruth in front of Edward, almost hiding the crutch he'd still needed then.

"Well, they were young, I was just a baby. It's a long time ago."

"But I mean . . . ," his voice faded, he turned to her with a bewildered shrug. "My parents are much older."

"So are mine," Ruth laughed and he did too.

"I mean they were much older when I was born," he said quietly.

Ruth suddenly understood that he wasn't trying to rush off to another errand or an urgent meeting. Without thinking about it, she shifted into herself, followed her instinct, put her hand on his arm.

"Tell me about them," she said. "Let's sit down."

So Bernard told her about being the only child of parents who'd married late and waited till the last possible minute to have him. They worried about him a lot, he said. His father taught history at a school where all the boys were going into the mines, the police, or construction and didn't acknowledge that there had ever been a past, let alone that it mattered. His father was pretty frustrated and spent his spare time teaching himself foreign languages; he was trying to learn Greek at the moment. Bernard's mother gave piano lessons to chubby little girls with sweaty palms and lace-trimmed dresses. And she was the caretaker of the apartment building where they lived, which earned a rent reduction.

Ruth couldn't imagine Bernard's home life at all, but she could tell he wasn't accustomed to talking about it. She wondered what they thought of his achievements at Wits. "Oh, they're proud of me," he said with a small smile. "And they're pleased to raise the money for law school. But I've got to get a job, it's too much for them." Ruth didn't know what to say, so she started chattering about possible jobs, but Bernard's eyes were roving the room, he'd lost interest. "Let's go for a walk outside," he suggested.

She didn't say anything to Alina, she just walked out of the door, leaving it unlocked.

"There's a wonderful smell near your gate," said Bernard. "I noticed it when I came in. What is it?"

"It's these bushes," Ruth said, reaching out to touch the peach and lilac flowers, silvery in the light from the streetlamp beyond. "They're called yesterday, today, and tomorrow."

She put her face close to them, opened her mouth and drew in a deep breath of their heady perfume, feeling it saturate her skin. She turned and looked up at him and found him watching her. His eyes were glazed, the lines of his face softened. His lips brushed her cheek and then fastened warm on her mouth, hands slipping from her shoulders to go around her, pressing her close.

After a while they went over and sat down on the damp earth under the fig tree. Drops of water shimmered like jewels on the plump ripe figs hanging above their heads. A drop fell, dazzled Bernard's cheek. Ruth dried it with two fingers and he caught her hand, bent his head and buried his mouth right in the center of her palm, he kissed her fingers one by one, light as a drifting leaf, he bent and kissed the hollow above her collarbone and she felt him tremble. "You're so lush," he murmured, fingers trailing softly down the white V of her blouse, urging her with melted chocolate eyes.

At first Ruth couldn't believe this was happening; she'd never

156

thought of him this way, she'd never imagined herself possessing the appeal he seemed to find. But, presented with burning signals of his arousal, hearing his short, shuddery breaths, feeling his light tantalizing touch press firmer, his hardness shifting against her, his opulent skin warm under her hands, her perception of herself changed forever. Seeing herself fresh through his inflamed eyes, she abandoned the girl she'd thought she was; limbs and skin and blood unleashed, she opened herself to throbbing pulses, thirst-driven searching, melting fullness. In Bernard's passionate arms, Ruth wasn't an alien anymore, she wasn't alone; her difference became strength.

Ruth didn't see Bernard the next day, but it didn't matter. It was enough. She ambled mesmerized through the day; her skin still glowed and, beneath it, the memories of her senses surged radiant. She didn't expect him to seek her out first thing in the morning, she knew he'd find her soon. She knew already who he was. He was there for her as much as she was for him.

She glimpsed him the following morning, hurrying to a class, surrounded by his usual disciples. She sat through her own class as distracted as if he had touched her. She was determined not to go and look for him. She knew he would come to her. He did, walking over to the table where she sat in the cafeteria with the usual crowd. She couldn't look at him, she was afraid what the others would read in her face. He bantered for a minute with them, then abruptly asked if she could retype something for him. Outside, he jerked his head back toward the friends they'd left behind and shrugged. He looked at her unsmiling, eyes hooded. He touched her cheek with one long finger.

"Look," he said.

She waited. She wanted to touch him but she didn't.

"I hear you know Gerald Gordon," he said awkwardly.

"Yes."

Bernard prodded at a clump of grass with the toe of his sneaker. He shoved his hands in his pockets and looked away over her head. People walked by, staring curiously at them. Ruth's skin remembered him. She lifted her chin and waited. A nerve she hadn't known was there jumped in the back of her neck.

"Gerald is my oldest friend. We grew up together. We're very close." He sounded hoarse.

"There's never been anything between us, if that's what's bothering you," Ruth said. "We're friends, that's all."

Bernard's face unwound, his eyes no longer pinched at the corners.

"Are you sure?"

Ruth laughed.

"Nothing else ever occurred to me, I'm sure of that."

Bernard moved his hand lightly over her head.

"You're very direct, aren't you, Ruth?" he smiled at last.

"Yes," she said. "Do you mind?"

He laughed.

"I'll be in touch soon," he said suddenly and was gone before she could think of anything to say.

She did worry then. Not that he didn't want her, she was sure of that. She worried that his ties to Gerald, deeper than she had understood, would disrupt their discovery of each other. She worried that she might have misunderstood Gerald's interest. She worried that anyone should think she had damaged their long friendship.

Two days later Bernard phoned and asked if he could pick her up in ten minutes. She was waiting on the sidewalk when he drew up in a white Triumph convertible.

"Isn't that Gerald's car?" she asked, as he jumped out and walked around to her.

"Yes," he said, throwing an arm around her shoulder, hugging her close. "It's Gerald's car. I often borrow it. I'm staying there for a few days. Where shall we go? I've been trying to think of somewhere private."

And that was all there was to it. Ruth and Bernard belonged together, in their own eyes and very quickly in everyone else's as well. They did everything together. They unraveled their desires and fears and hopes and longings the way they stripped fleshy leaves from an artichoke, seeking the perfect center. They didn't question their need for each other. Unhampered by any other ties, they mined each other thirstily, there was never enough, yet they lived as if time were infinite, stretching away like the sky on a clear day. Loving each other expanded time so that they both poured greater intensity into campus politics, alliances, and friendships. They continued to see a great deal of Gerald Gordon, together and separately. He was unchanged, nonchalant, the bright blue gleam of his eyes as perceptive, as dispassionate as ever.

By the time Bernard started law school and a job as a part-time reporter for the *Rand Daily Mail* and Ruth began her second year at Wits, they were an established couple. Even the professors kidded them about not being able to keep their hands off each other. They were proud that their relationship didn't impose on their commitments. Bernard had meetings and projects he didn't discuss with Ruth, but she respected that, it wasn't a problem. The only problems they had were finding places to be alone together and struggling against their parents.

Bernard's mother told him that Ruth seemed nice enough, but he was too young to be tied down. His father wondered why he didn't go out with lots of girls as he would only be young once. They treated Ruth quite pleasantly, but she was always conscious of being inspected when she visited there. She felt they were looking for a run in her stocking or a worn heel. It was hard to believe that Bernard was their son. His lean narrow height, his energy, his dark intensity seemed sprung from a different, mysterious source.

Her parents were less restrained than this, but that was no surprise. Restraint was one of many much boosted virtues contradicted by behavior. Watch what they do, not what they say, Bernard said, observing that her parents' pronouncements had something in common with the double-talk of the Nationalist Government. Nothing meant what it said. The Bantu Education

Act was designed to prevent education, not promote it. Home-lands meant exile. Security forces meant police brutality. Extol-ling the virtue of restraint was a cover for Mildred's shrill irritation at the Levines' unsuitable poverty and Edward's rage at Bernard's radical views. Ruth assured him she was acting from her own convictions.

"Nonsense," Edward shouted angrily, throwing a book across the room, the corner of its cover hitting her cheek. "You'd adopt the views of any fellow you think you're in love with."

So when Ruth was invited by Rajiv Naidoo to a secret meeting off campus, she told her parents nothing about it. Nervously obedient to his insistence on secrecy, she didn't even mention it to Bernard. Rajiv wouldn't tell her where the meeting was. He said someone would pick her up, she should be ready at eight, so she was surprised when Bernard arrived in his father's crumpled maroon Austin.

"It wasn't up to me to tell you about it," he explained. "There's a selection committee. They're very careful who they invite, they vet everyone for a long time." He was amused, the cleft in his chin flattened out a bit as he laughed and she leaned over and kissed it. She felt honored to be entering Bernard's private preserve because his colleagues had chosen her independently.

The meeting was at a flat in Hillbrow. Bernard parked several blocks away because, he said, the cops had been at a recent meeting, writing down registration numbers by flashlight, better be sensible. They went up to the eighth floor in a damp creaking lift and then walked down two flights, along a dark open corridor and into a lamp-lit flat filled with books and pictures, a desk piled high with papers, mugs of coffee all over the floor where people sat leaning against bright, hand-embroidered cushions.

They were late, the meeting was in progress, Bernard muttered an apology and they sat down behind the others. Ruth looked around and found that she knew many of the twenty people in the room. There were one or two she would never have expected to meet at a secret political meeting, she had not previously thought them worthy of attention. Perhaps they kept a low profile at Wits because of their outside activities. She was surprised to find four or five much older people there, sprawled on the floor in baggy sweaters, like everyone else.

Rajiv Naidoo, a medical student, was speaking. He had notes in front of him as he reported the desperate needs of the families of the defendants at the Treason Trial. It was almost three years since their arrests, he said, the trial was dragging on interminably, most of them were family breadwinners; their spouses and children were desperate, living in misery, short of food and warm clothing, often without hope. They needed support, he said, and he was pleased that Sid Cohen had been able to come tonight and suggest specific plans for their relief.

Sid Cohen was one of the older men Ruth had noticed. He was her father's age, at least. He had a deceptively relaxed appearance and very quiet voice; as soon as he began speaking it was clear that he was accustomed to command. Everyone paid attention. He was terse, explicit as he issued a list of practical instructions about a drive for canned foods, used clothing in decent condition, fund-raising parties, cake sales, raffles, and competitions. No one applauded when he stopped speaking, but a number of people murmured "Thank you." He left alone, soon afterward, and the rest of them started volunteering for assignments. Rajiv Naidoo reminded them that all functions should be promoted as relief for innocent children, strictly separate from defense fund activity, and that the Congress should not be publicly identified. "Let's play it safe," he said several times.

People left in twos and threes. Max Hepburn stood by the door to the fire escape, handing out bunches of leaflets which were to be placed under doors in pre-assigned neighboring buildings. Rajiv Naidoo was doing the same thing at the door to the corridor. When Ruth and Bernard left, taking their piles of leaflets, Rajiv murmured, "Glad you're one of us, Ruth" and Ruth felt a warm glow of acceptance. Bernard told Ruth which building was hers and where she should meet him an hour later. She must not be observed, he said. The Special Branch jumped out all over the place, they'd arrested people before for disseminating treason. He said this with a wry smile and narrowed eyes and Ruth assumed he was joking, but she was very careful, disposed of most of the leaflets and met him only five minutes later than the appointed time. He had the car moving before her door was closed.

He hadn't been joking, it turned out. He knew people who'd been jailed for distributing material like this. People had been interrogated, beaten, and made to stand for twelve and sixteen hours at a stretch. His tone was neutral, his face dispassionate. Ruth hadn't realized but now that she did, she was invaded by an aftermath of trembling fear. She hadn't even read a leaflet.

Well away from Hillbrow, a few blocks from her parents' house in Saxonwold, Bernard stopped under a streetlight, so she could read it. It was an appeal against forced removals to the Bantustans. It asked people to write to their Members of Parliament protesting mass evacuations of people from their lifelong homes to distant barren pockets of land they had never seen before in their lives. The Bantustan program was just a device for forcing apartheid upon oppressed people who had no way to fight it, the leaflet announced.

"But what's wrong with this?" Ruth was relieved to find she had been distributing material whose validity was unquestionable.

"There's nothing wrong with it, Ruth. The Nats call it seditious, that's all." He ran his fingers through her hair and kissed her ear.

"That's insane."

"No, it's treason. If you don't agree with them, it's treason."

He started the car up and drove about for a while, telling her about the African National Congress and its offshoots. "It's a nonviolent organization working for democracy and a multiracial society," he said. He told her about its leaders, who were on trial for treason.

"Aren't a lot of them communists?" Ruth asked. She knew what Edward and Mildred said about them.

Bernard sighed.

"No, not a lot of them. A few of them, yes."

"But . . ."

"Listen, Ruth, think about it. Is it so terrible? Congress has to take help where it can find it. We don't have many friends, it seems to me that anyone who hates injustice and racism needs to work together for change."

"But the Communist Party is banned."

Bernard stopped the car on a side street.

"Listen to me. I want to live in a country where people are entitled to believe what they like, whether I agree with it or not. Isn't that what we're working for? What's wrong with that? Any time someone is jailed or exiled or killed because of what he thinks, I'm at risk too, aren't I?"

"Yes, I suppose so."

"Besides, Ruth," he was sharp, "communism isn't a communicable disease, you know. Perfectly decent people believe it's a better way to organize society. Sid Cohen is a communist, I think."

"You mean the white man who spoke tonight?"

"Sure. He was a member of the party, I've read about him. He's an advocate, a QC. He lives near Gerald Gordon, I've met him at their house, he plays tennis with Gerald's father. He's just a man who wants to share the wealth."

"He must have plenty if he lives near Gerald."

Bernard laughed.

"He does. You don't have to be poor to be a communist."

"But what about Hungary? What about the Hitler-Stalin Pact? What about the purges? What about —"

"Ruth, Ruth, I'm not a communist. I don't like it any more than you do. Most Congress people aren't communists, they want justice, the right to vote, the right to earn a living, own a business, live where you like, think what you want. That's a big enough program for anyone here these days. Basic rights, that's all. Isms are irrelevant now, they're a luxury."

Ruth leapt into political activity as if it were a desert she had to cross to find water. She had found a home, a family where she belonged, people who used words with objective meaning, burned with the same rage, thrilled to the same small victories. The guilt she'd suffered every time she sat on a crate in Lizzie's narrow dark room, every time she climbed on a Whites Only bus, every time she'd kept silent when someone said, "They can't drive properly, they don't understand machines" or "They're lazy by nature" or "They really hate us, they'd slit our throats if they weren't kept in their place," the self-hatred she'd grown up with as intimately as with her own skin was lessened by her effort to change it all. She fed on her struggle like an addict: the more she did, the more she had to do. Sometimes exhausted, discouraged, frightened by the hostility of the government and its Security Branch, she thought that working for fairness and decency was what held at bay her contempt for herself; in a season of mounting threats, there was always more to do.

Ruth stood, feet and calves aching, on city street corners hunting signatures for petitions against Bantu Education, which limited most blacks to four years of school in shacks without qualified teachers or equipment. She'd been taught that "they" weren't sufficiently educated to be "given" the vote, so that education seemed to Ruth a priority. Bernard wouldn't collect signatures and wouldn't explain why. "You have to go through it yourself to know," he said. Ruth was shaken by the whites on Eloff Street, Commissioner Street, Market Street. Most of them hurried by, well dressed, absorbed, looking intently forward. She'd heard of New Yorkers racing past injured mugging victims crouched in gutters, but she hadn't expected indifference or fear of universal education from Jo'burg's whites. The few who stopped were amused or blatantly contemptuous; occasionally there was one she wanted to hug, one who would add a signature, stop to chat. After dogged weeks, tens of thousands of names were collected from all over the country, blocks of black ones, spots of white. Two women, a nun and a domestic maid, and two teenage boys, stiff in unaccustomed shoes and white shirts, tried to deliver them to the prime minister's offices in Pretoria. They were refused entry to the building. The petitions were mailed, after a little ceremony in Alexandra Township, where Ruth helped to seal the large neat brown package in front of cheering workers. That was the last they heard of it.

Driven, fueled by guilt and shame, Ruth hurled herself into half a dozen more projects that Bernard wouldn't share. She wrote letters, hung posters, designed and delivered appeals for school lunches for starving black children. She marched and sat in, sang and wrote letters to keep the universities open to all races, to resist increases in bus fares, to protest forced relocations of whole communities.

Nothing she did made any difference, the system was impenetrable. The only measurable result was that she learned more, especially about her own futility. The harder she worked, the more she discovered the bleak territory beyond the solid walls enclosing dappled sunlit privilege in the white ghettos. She found the wounds and septic sores of interminable poverty; the legal apparatus to sustain slave labor for the mines while wives and children banished hundreds of miles away scrabbled in rocky dirt to drag out brittle survival and await the wage-earner's annual visit and, nine months later, the next infant hostage; the vicious indignity of the pass laws, convoluting everyone over sixteen into a number, compelled to obey increasing restrictions tied by twisted knots of red tape, glued by the spittle of the enforcers' contempt; the state-supported persecution of laborers abducted to the maize and potato farms, beaten by farmers or their servile "boss-boys," locked up at night to prevent escape, padlocked into filthy, airless, crowded huts, with leaking pails for toilets, bug-infested sacks for bedding, *mielie*-meal for food.

Ruth couldn't endure her own impotence, she wouldn't accept it. Her most searing, most personal agony was black submission. It was Lizzie all over again, twenty-four million times over, it was passive acceptance, automatic obedience, generations of covered heads and servility to keep the poised stocked armories nearly unnecessary. Ruth jolted herself out of miserable futility; she was determined to make a difference, she had to help them discover that they had choices. She abandoned petitions and posters and letters to MPs. Bernard was touring the Reef for the *Mail*, reporting antipass activity. Ruth talked to Peter Shabalala about working in the campaign. He would take her to Orlando, he said, to a recruiting meeting. There was no way they could go out to the "location" together by bus; Ruth had no car. Peter commandeered Max Hepburn and his father's car and they drove ten miles to Orlando. Peter told Max to park at a corner fruit stand, three blocks from the church.

Walking the littered paths of an African township for the first time in her life, Ruth cringed at the fantasy her idea of Lizzie had spun. She saw the sunshine of her reverie, but here it beat hard upon the tiny roofs of hovels with walls of bits of board and rags and jagged metal strips, rusting orange; laughter, yes, but she heard it loud from the squalid yard outside the shebeen where men lolled loose-lipped in the passive afternoon. In the scorched dirt lane ahead, heavy, sweating, barefoot women hauled water from the central faucet to their pitiful shacks, passing mangy dogs sniffing for scraps in mounds of fetid debris. Ruth saw children with noses running, drawing pictures in the dirt with twigs, grave dull-skinned faces above alarming poking bones. She walked past a gleaming bicycle heartbreakingly propped against a warped door; she averted her eyes from a glittering bird cage suspended from a nail driven into a splintering window frame. No bird lived there.

Ruth and Max were the only whites at the church. Ruth was uneasy, and not only because she wasn't sure whether she should have obtained a permit before entering Orlando; she was not accustomed to being in a minority, noticeably different, glaringly white, utterly alien. For a minute, wildly, she wished for a dark disguise, a chimney sweep's charcoal.

The church was less than half-full. Peter said that some people were afraid to come to the meeting, they'd seen men and women chased and beaten and gassed too often; but lots of people didn't come because they didn't have time, it took so long to get home after work in the city, and then they had to get water and cook food and find the children and then it was late and dark and dangerous on the streets.

A small, plump woman perched like a bird behind the podium was speaking calmly in Sotho, of which Ruth understood not one word. Her eyes, huge behind glasses, examined everyone in the room. She raised and lowered her arms as she spoke, gray fabric shifting like dusty feathers lifting and settling.

Peter muttered bits of translation for Ruth and Max: "More than two years now since women also forced to carry passes . . . naming them reference books makes no difference, they are the same passes. . . . Men have always been carrying them, so when they go in the morning you can't know if they'll come home at night. . . . Now, if they take us too, what about the children . . . when we are in jail because the cop put the stamp upside down or you're one day late because your child is sick. . . . Lilian Ngoyi led the women to burn their passes. . . . They went to jail, they rose up everywhere to say no to these passes. . . . We must stop it for once and for all . . ."

People were attentive, though some turned to peer at Ruth and Max. A few nodded all the time the bird lady spoke. There was polite applause when she finished, then a loud roar welcomed the main event, a Reverend Thomas Fourie.

The white Reverend spoke English with the hard consonants and precise inflection of a native Afrikaner. Another fixed assumption of Ruth's crumbled. She turned wide-eyed to Max.

"He's a renegade," he whispered. "He saw one of the predawn raids. The cops smashed everything in sight, beat whole families, cracked heads open after arresting them. Then he went to a peaceful demonstration against bus fare hikes. The police charged with batons and gas. They hit the backs of women's heads and necks as they ran away. He kicked over the traces. He's from the Dutch Reformed Church."

"The Afrikaners must hate him. Isn't he taking a terrible risk?"

Peter nudged her arm, people were glaring at them suspiciously, she turned away from Max and listened to the Reverend. Half a million Africans were convicted under the pass laws in a single year, he was saying. One out of twenty, at a time when eight of every ten urban blacks lived below the breadline. The average black earned twenty-seven pounds a year, the average white five hundred pounds, and the government was raising black taxes by 75 percent.

The Reverend's ashen skin was deeply creased and furrowed, pain seeped from his washed-out eyes, his limp hands clutched the lectern, his thin voice clotted with emotion. People were starving, he said, people had no jobs, while the government spent millions on the pass system to maintain slave labor and keep the cities lily-white. It was time, he said, it was past time to say "No more." Passes must go. On antipass day in a few months, people must go without passes, accept arrest, flood the jails, erode the system until it washed away forever.

As he spoke, he voice rising, cracking, and breaking, the gathering stirred; there was a murmur, then a subdued chant, then a clamor as they caught the rhythm of the Reverend's anguish, repeating his phrases, banging their knees for emphasis, shouting agreement, chanting "Passes must go."

In a second's lull, Ruth heard an engine outside, ignored it, watching the Reverend, who leaned forward over the lectern, face sternly gray, finger pointed at the swaying crowd. No violence, he implored, this is peaceful resistance, we will struggle without violence, we must submit to arrest and stop them with reason, never with violence, resistance only. As the chorus "Resistance only" swelled up, filling the building, Peter grabbed Ruth's arm.

168

"It's a raid," he muttered. "I've got to get you out of here."

He was glancing wildly about. Ruth didn't understand. She noticed Max already pushing his way forward along an outer aisle toward the front of the church. Peter pushed her in front of him, mashing her against Max's back, black hands on the platform held the door open, she heard "Keep still, don't make trouble, don't move or I'll shoot" as Peter shoved her outside. Thuds banged behind her, Peter stepped back inside and Max grabbed her hand and dashed for the car.

"It's not surrounded, we can get away," he breathed, hurling himself behind the wheel, roaring off in a cloud of dust, the cops too busy inside to notice them.

"What about Peter?" Ruth shouted as they hurtled onto a little dirt path, out of sight of the church, littered on either side by rusting cans, foul scraps, heavy hovering black flies.

"Peter's just one of a crowd, Ruth. He knows how to handle it. If they catch us out there, it's big trouble. They can chuck us in the Fort for weeks and then charge us with furthering the aims of communism or something."

"We can't just leave Peter and all those . . ."

"Will you shut up? Let me get us out of here."

She was beside herself. Infested by rancid guilt, she imagined Peter beaten, jailed, tortured, she was responsible, she felt her seams tearing apart, threads dangling, helpless. She ran home from the corner where Max dropped her off, frantic to reach Gerald.

"Could you come here right now? I have to talk to you."

"Ruth, it's after eight, can't it wait? I've got a paper due tomorrow."

"It's an emergency, Gerald, please."

She was at the door when he arrived, she led him outside to walk in the garden. Peter must be in jail, she said, she didn't have the faintest idea how to get him out, who to call, where to go, Gerald must help.

"Where's Bernard? Isn't he on the Reef tonight?"

"He wasn't there. I went with Peter and . . ." she stopped abruptly. "Gerry, please help me get to Peter, I . . ."

Gerald stopped walking, turned and faced her, hands in his pockets, eyes piercing blue in the fading light.

"Are you crazy? This happens all the time, there's nothing special about it. There's nothing we can do and no point trying. I can't believe you dragged me out tonight for something like this."

"Gerald —"

"No, pay attention. Listen to me now. You must have been crazy to go out to the location. This isn't your fight, Ruth, I keep telling you that. Stay out of it. You don't have to take sides. You and Bernard are heading for trouble. It's futile."

Fighting the urge to shut those bright blue eyes with a slap, Ruth cried, "How can you just stand by and watch it all?"

"Ruth, simmer down. Get some rest. You've got to keep out of it. I'm going now."

Ruth hurried to the Bantu languages department early the next morning. Peter wasn't there. She returned several times during the day. Peter's classes were being taught by someone else. No one knew where he was, he hadn't phoned. She couldn't find Max until late afternoon. "There's nothing we can do," he said. "We don't even know where they're holding him. By the time we hire a lawyer, he'll be out." When she persisted, he promised to consult his father, a union official with connections.

Three days later, she found Peter in his cubicle in the prefab building at the back of the campus, where he taught Zulu language and lit. He smiled buoyantly.

"I'm fine, Ruth. You get used to it, you know. We're all out now, except Mrs. Mbane and Reverend Thomas."

"They're still in jail?"

"Don't worry, it's not a big charge, the Reverend is in and out all the time."

A raised purple weal marked his temple. It matched the two

she saw on the back of his hand. Ruth started to ask about them, but Peter shook his head wearily.

"I'm OK, Ruth, forget it."

Ruth hurled herself into the antipass campaign. She learned where she could go without a permit, how to fake an identity if she needed one. She went to townships and factories and the gates outside mines and long bus lines at dusk to persuade people to protest on the appointed day. She explained, urged, exhorted on front steps and maternity clinics, churches and beer halls, corner stores and empty fields, trying to convince people that they had a choice, showing them there was a way to resist.

This time Bernard didn't mock her effort. He said it was realistic. The process of teaching them to reject submission had to be gone through, he said brusquely, but change would only come when they generated their own resistance. He wanted to hasten that day. He was organizing protests himself, taking days away from his last year in law school to cover stories for the *Mail* in other cities, using the travel to build Congress networks.

Ruth often didn't know what he was doing, there was never enough time, they were both stretched out as far as they could go, working in a frenzy; they needed their little time together for respite. Bernard was gulping milk every day, he wouldn't see a doctor, he didn't have time. Locked into webs of lies she wove for her parents, her professors, the cops, even Gerald, Ruth wouldn't waste precious minutes with Bernard to explore the grueling details of his shadowy travels.

They used each other as intensely as they did everything else. Senses sharpened by intervals apart, urgency heightened by time sliding away faster, appetite inflamed as sharpening edges of danger angled closer, Ruth and Bernard eased their aching weariness, soothed nerves tugged between rage and compassion, found a place beyond struggle where they floated together, spent, serene. When they made love, everything was new again, their passion, their innocence and optimism fresh as morning light on a tranquil shore.

Ruth was astounded that their parents and their friends didn't understand what was happening all over the country. Bernard was certain that they understood. But their opinions didn't change by a sliver when charges against all but thirty of the original Treason Trial defendants were withdrawn. They either ignored it or applauded when black leaders like Oliver Tambo, Nokwe, Robert Resha were arrested again, banned, banished. Even when the patriarchal Chief Luthuli, the ultimate voice of respectable reason, was banished for five years to Lower Tugela in Natal, they were unmoved.

Bernard was in Natal, covering the story for the *Mail*, when Luthuli returned to a huge, chanting welcome at Durban Airport; he was in the convoy of crowded cars that escorted Luthuli along the North Coast road as far as the turnoff to a rough dirt lane. Chief Luthuli climbed from the first car, raised his arm in the Congress salute and walked away to exile in Groutville Reserve. Bernard's paper wanted the story; Luthuli was an international hero. But Bernard's editor told him not to bother reporting on Robert Sobukwe, whose new Pan-Africanist movement was in revolt against the multiracial goals of the ANC, rejecting collaboration with other races, demanding a pure Africanist future.

This was the most disruptive of many factional conflicts. Bernard was dismayed. "We're too busy bickering with each other to fight the government," he said bitterly. He started making speeches in the townships along his reporter's route. Rajiv Naidoo told Ruth that in Cato Manor, near Durban, covering a riot that erupted after a baton charge smashed a women's protest gathering, Bernard leapt onto a stepladder, shouting "We're harming ourselves," until there was a lull. "He made power come off him," Rajiv said, "he was like lightning, he made them stop and listen." Bernard told them they should be fighting the government, not each other. He said the same thing in meetings around the country, raging at the energy wasted in fighting over isms; a united antipass campaign could make a difference, everyone should work for it.

Unable to think of any other life where she would have as much time and cover for resistance, Ruth told her parents she wanted to work toward a doctorate after she graduated. She expected a massive wrangle, but they capitulated easily because, Edward explained caustically, she was safer in the ivy-covered walls of unreality at Wits than she would be in the marketplace with her distorted juvenile politics.

So Ruth was safely in her library carrel researching the tangle of Kikuyu and British in Kenya when South African police killed 69 Africans and wounded 180 more outside the police station at Sharpeville near Vereeniging. Gathered to turn in their passes and offer themselves for arrest, the crowd fled when the police charged. Bullets smashed into their backs as they raced away. Ruth was in the library until the usual afternoon thundershower had passed, washing the blood away from the street. She got home in time to hear the reports on government-controlled radio. By then, the number of victims had increased. A thousand miles away near Cape Town, a crowd of 10,000 gathered at Langa to hear the response to their demand for the abolition of passes. There was a warning to disperse, which most people couldn't hear. Three minutes later, the police charged, firing at point-blank range.

Raging riots overtook the bitter mourning and vast funerals. Luthuli burned his pass publicly, followed by thousands; the pass laws were suspended and reinstated a few days later. Furious mobs ran wild, burning schools and public buildings, hurling rocks, shattering glass. State-of-emergency laws brought predawn raids around the country, mass arrests, vindictive terror. In the white suburbs and city centers, everyone went about their normal routines. With leaders of every shade of dissent detained, awaiting charges of incitement and sabotage, Parliament banned the Congress movement, sending underground the remnants of resistance that had not yet been massacred, jailed, or forced to flee.

It was a season of terror. Every day Ruth heard about more acquaintances who'd been arrested. One day Rajiv Naidoo came down the hill from the Medical School to warn her to stay close to home and to burn incriminating papers; the next day, he was gone, locked up without charges. Peter Shabalala disappeared again. No one knew whether he'd been picked up or crossed a border. Ruth didn't believe she was seriously threatened herself; she didn't think her work had been noticeable enough. But she pleaded with Bernard to go into hiding. Every day she expected them to come for him at any minute, guns riding their hips. There were hours at a time when she panted in short, choking spasms of staccato breaths. She couldn't stand the image of Bernard in confinement. Bernard, from whose limbs and burning eyes and supple mind energy leapt, mustn't be locked up.

He wouldn't listen to her. It wasn't going to happen to him, not now, he said. If they wanted him they could have found him easily enough in the first scrambling early raid after Sharpeville. He'd covered his tracks too well. He knew how to take care of himself. Ruth went to Gerald; struggling unsuccessfully to disguise her gasping breathing, she asked for help. Gerald drove Bernard to the zoo and led him to a little lake hidden among stands of trees, where he thought it was safe to talk.

Gerald thought Bernard should leave the country. Others had gone, there were South Africans fanning north all through Africa, to Britain and even the U.S., drumming up support for the resistance, why shouldn't he go too?

"I'm safe here now," Bernard said calmly. "Some of us have to stay behind and pick up the pieces and carry on. There aren't too many of us left, Gerry."

"There's going to be a revolution someday, we both know it." Gerald ground his teeth together. "What difference can you make?"

"The faster it comes, the less suffering there'll be," Bernard said shortly. "I'm going to speed the day."

"I keep telling you, it's not your fight."

"It is my fight. I choose it. I get up every morning for it. I'm not going to sit in an ivory tower and watch it. Write books about it. I'm not made like that."

When Gerald reported his failure to Ruth, he said that he and Bernard had quarreled bitterly, for hours, with no millimeter of change. Bernard was a maniac, out of touch with reality. Gerald was sick of being insulted. Bernard had called him a silent collaborator. There was, he said icily, nothing he could do.

They patched it up, but fought every time they were together. After a while, Bernard began to avoid Gerald. Ruth certainly didn't want him to avoid her. As the pace of arrests slowed and her breathing spasms subsided, she stopped trying to persuade him to hide, she forced herself to accept his judgment that it would all calm down until next time.

They both had to get on with their lives. On the point of becoming a lawyer, Bernard needed a job. He was courted by several firms for his fiery oratory and well-researched arguments. Ruth welcomed the time he spent on preparations and meetings and interviews to begin his legal career; the more time he spent on law, the less there was for illegal resistance. Dissent had become treason; security a straitjacket. A lot of people they knew were in jail or under house arrest, banned from attending gatherings, working for newspapers, speaking publicly. They could not even be quoted in the press. Some were gone forever. The resistance seemed to stumble. Ruth was ashamed of her secret relief: the lull had been bought by failure, but at least Bernard was safe. Lying to her parents had become habitual; now, hiding from Bernard the relief she despised as both selfish and immoral built an extra constraint into her life.

Reluctantly giving way to his parents' pleas, including a sensation of his mother's that there was something clutching at her heart and a series of whispered entreaties from his father at three in the morning, Bernard turned down a job as a junior to Sidney Cohen, whom Ruth had met at her first Congress meeting. Cohen was a brilliant advocate with a distinguished reputation but his politics were so public that even Bernard's parents were aware of them; the notion of their son being smeared by the association appalled them; they were, they insisted, reduced to rubble at the prospect. Ruth wasn't sorry when he joined two advocates with a multiracial practice and a rare record of accepting political cases. She was comforted when he flung himself into preparing cases, overcoming courtroom nerves, battering prosecution witnesses. With his driving energy diverted from the political struggle to getting his clients acquitted, she felt free to work harder herself, discovering she enjoyed research more, not less, as she dug deeper, working for her Master's. She began to resent time taken from archives and writing, though she didn't object to her new teaching assignments, which turned out to be more stimulating than she'd expected. She'd never planned to become an academic but, having fallen into it for convenience, found that she fitted it well. She was turning over half her small stipend to her parents. This was a proper preparation for the real world, Edward explained. Struggling toward financial independence, Ruth and Bernard never discussed their future; they simply assumed that they would always be together.

For almost a year after Sharpeville the resistance seemed to lie like a deeply buried bulb under frozen ground. When it began to sprout tiny shoots, Ruth joined relief groups for families of political prisoners. Bernard went to a conference in Pietermaritzburg and returned electrified, inflamed as he had not been for months. Ruth knew the energy steaming off him, the lively dance of his chocolate eyes, the charged tilt of his agile body were different from the pale shadow his legal work produced.

They hadn't been defeated by Sharpeville, Bernard told her exuberantly. The Nats had captured most of them but not quite all. Free of various banning orders for the first time in nine years, Nelson Mandela was at the conference, able to speak publicly. He was magnetic, he'd inspired them all, blown away the dry defeatism and bitterness. Mandela had been elected leader of a National Action Council. Bernard explained that the other members of the council were secret, as protection against police persecution; Ruth understood that her interval of relieved calm was over. Mandela, Bernard said, would be the public spokesman, he was ready to sacrifice his legal practice and family life for change. He was publicly demanding a national convention; if the government didn't comply, he would call for a three-day stay-at-home. There was something to work for again.

Bernard's excitement was contagious. Ruth began working for the three-day strike while the police searched for Mandela, who had gone underground. She thought that Bernard knew where he was. Police arrested thousands more Africans while whites ambled through business as usual, except that they emptied gun stores all over the country and target practice became the prevailing fad. Ruth had no alternative. She could not submit, she had to act, she couldn't stand by and pretend not to see what was happening. Battling her own fear, swamped in deception, she wrote leaflets, talked to small groups of workers, distributed literature calling for the strike. But the effort was undermined by the opposition of rival factions and the massive mobilization of armed force and official threats. On the first day, tens of thousands of people stayed at home, but the numbers were disappointing. Mandela called the strike off, acknowledging that the intimidation had succeeded.

Ruth took the new failure as a personal blow; working for a decent chance for everyone in South Africa was like pushing boulders up Table Mountain barefoot in high wind.

"I feel like Sisyphus," she said miserably. "And if that's how I feel, what about the people who're giving up their lives for it?"

Bernard didn't answer. He was quieter again, almost morose. He didn't have much time to spend with Ruth anyway, he was suddenly involved with a lot of meetings at night, he went out of town several weekends without explanation, he was sometimes out of touch for days at a time, out of his office, away from a phone. He had sealed himself in an invisible wrap, which locked his preoccupation behind hooded eyes and tense limbs. He didn't explain; Ruth did not permit herself to ask. She had never interrogated him, she wouldn't start now. She knew he wasn't traveling for the *Mail*, he'd given up his reporter's job when he began his practice. She tried not to speculate. She berated herself for her habit of anxiety.

One brilliant Sunday in December, Bernard arrived unexpectedly. He had a surprise, he said, leading her out to admire his first car, a tiny, bright blue Fiat parked cheerfully near the yesterday, today, and tomorrow bushes. It was his first big acquisition, wonderful how beginning a law practice can provide a taste of freedom. He wanted to drive somewhere far away and lie in the sun and look at water. Ruth saw that the pinched creases at the corners of his eyes were smoothed away, his skin glowed, the taut containment in his limbs had melted. She packed a picnic, left a note for her sleeping parents, raced away without another of the scenes that had become routine whenever they saw Bernard. They detested his politics, they disapproved of his way of life, they despised him for doing something called "trifling with Ruth's affections." They'd tried and failed to make her stop seeing him; that didn't mean they wanted him around their house.

Bernard sat behind the wheel of his car like a man released. He drove with the special pleasure of possession. He'd always been short of money, just teetering on decency's side of managing; he was still paying his parents back in installments for the cost of his education, but the hard-earned purchase of the little used car showed him that the days of always being hard up, always pressed for cash, might end some day if he worked hard enough. Ruth caught his optimism and forgot her anxiety, gliding along in the sunshine with the wind in her hair and a day of Bernard to herself ahead. She didn't know where they were going; there were no maps, no directions, no schedules to meet, no arrangements to make. They sang folk songs, freedom songs, college drinking songs.

"It's that freedom train a-coming," Bernard sang like a victory.

"Get on board, oh, get on board," Ruth yelled off-key, exuberant.

Bernard pulled up at the side of a deserted road, green acres of corn shimmering on either side as far as the eye could see.

"Let's get married next year and the hell with the families," he said. "We're free, white, and over twenty-one," he added ironically. "Be nice not to have to hunt places to be together, we can manage a flat by next year. We won't have to creep about like criminals in the early hours. What do you say?"

Ruth, who had been watching his melted chocolate eyes shine as they hadn't done in months, said "Fine with me" and kissed every inch of his face.

He drove for over three hours across the flat smoky cement of the Reef and east beyond Barbeton. When the sun was high above them, he stopped on a slope near a waterfall in the Drakensberg Mountains. They climbed over rocks with flowers nestled in their crevices, stretching out in a mossy curve made by huge slabs of stone to eat their picnic and watch water tumble over the rocks at the apex of the fall and glide silver-streaked down until it disappeared. The sky was evenly blue, gold-shot. Ruth lay back, arms above her head, eyes closed against the sun warming all through her, dissolving chips and tears and knots she hadn't known were lodged inside until she felt them melt away.

"I've got another surprise," Bernard said.

"You mean besides the car and getting married?" she murmured.

"Yes, besides that." His voice was deeper.

Ruth opened her eyes and turned to him. He lay beside her, propped on an elbow. His other hand stroked her cheek; he bent and kissed her softly.

"I've made a big decision," he said. "It's been rough the last few months, I know, but I've been trying to make up my mind. I couldn't talk about it until I knew where I stood."

"I don't know what you're talking about," Ruth said. But the sun burned too harshly on her face, the ground beneath had jagged pebbles hidden below the moss, some twig must have pressed against the nerve in her neck, which throbbed suddenly.

"Everything I'm going to tell you is totally secret, Ruthie, OK? Absolutely between us, never a hint to anyone at all. Ever. I know I can trust you."

She sat up, shielding her eyes from the sun, turned her back to it, and sat opposite him, knees drawn close to her body, arms locked around them.

"After they crushed the stay-at-home, there seemed to be no-where to go. It was the last straw. Peaceful demonstrations just don't work, they never have. These days they only produce more official brutality."

He paused, but Ruth didn't say anything.

"Mandela and a few others got together to decide what to do. It's obvious nonviolent methods will never bring change. They formed a new group to sabotage specific installations. To force the government to reform."

Ruth didn't look at him. She was staring at the ground, patches of yellow were spotted sickly among the green moss.

"The group's called Umkonto we Sizwe," Bernard said. "It means Spear of the Nation. They asked me to join. That's what I've been trying to decide."

She looked at him. The joyful serenity she'd celebrated all day still rested upon him, undiluted by the gravity that carved an angular determination on his face. She waited.

"I've decided," Bernard said quietly. "I told him yesterday I'll work with them."

"Told who?"

"Mandela, I told Mandela."

"How can you?" she burst out, suddenly not caring if he didn't like what she said. "How can you turn violent, blow things up, sneak around like a criminal? It's against everything you've always believed. How can you do it?"

"I can't think of anything else to do," he said sadly. He stretched out his hand but she jerked away.

"You'll be in terrible danger all the time," she heard her voice rise, she felt the knots and tears return and crouch volatile within.

"They'll catch you somehow and lock you up, Ben, you can't do it."

"I must, Ruth. I'll try my damnedest not to get caught, but I can't stand by and watch it, I've got to do something about it. I can't live with myself any other way."

"Why didn't you discuss it with me before you told them you'd do it?" she cried, blinking, clenching her hands together. "Aren't I entitled to an opinion? Don't my views mean anything to you?"

"Ruth, look at me. Listen to me for a minute. You mean more to me than anyone in my life. I know you always will. There's nothing I wouldn't do for you. Except destroy myself, choose to wither away. Because that's the choice, Ruth. I can't be me if I turn away now. I have to do it."

"You didn't tell me a thing. You didn't give me a chance to try and persuade you. You wouldn't share it with me." She cried silently, tears streaming down her cheeks, narrow shoulders shaking. He dabbed her face with a Kleenex and stroked her hair.

"This was something I had to think out for myself, Ruth. I was forbidden to discuss it anyway. I'm not supposed to tell you anything even now. But I don't want to hide my life from you, I know I can trust you."

"You're really going to do it?"

"Yes, Ruth."

"Innocent people will be killed, that doesn't bother you?"

"Ruth, there's an absolutely sacred commitment not to harm people. Sabotage will be directed against government installations with the imperative not to hurt anyone. This isn't desperate terror. It's a valid political statement."

"People will get in the way, can't you see that? Once it starts, things will happen, Ben. How can you risk people's lives?"

"We're going to try not to." He held her shoulders in a firm grip. "Ruth, you're a historian. You know you can't bring about change without some violence, not in a police state like this."

"When will it start?"

"It's started already."

Ruth jerked and looked at him. His eyes blazed with a triumph he couldn't conceal even if he tried.

"There are two groups acting today," he said. "You'll be hearing about it."

"When will you start?"

"Soon. I can't discuss details. I'll have to be away sometimes."

"I'll never know whether you're safe or not," she said resentfully.

"I'm sorry, Ruthie. I wish our lives were different too."

She couldn't believe the same sun still shone, the water tumbled silver over the same rocks, Bernard still sat beside her. Nothing had changed. Nothing, except their precarious lives.

The next day she read that a new militant group called Spear of the Nation had sabotaged electric installations as well as Bantu affairs offices in Johannesburg and Port Elizabeth. The saboteurs had not been caught but one, an unidentified black, had been killed in the explosion he had set off.

Bernard's conversion to violence and sabotage lay like a heavy wool blanket on a hot day over every corner of Ruth's life. She thrashed about, trying to shift its weight and suffocating embrace. Her breathing spasms returned; to conquer them, she submitted to the weighty blanket of fear and retreated into a kind of numbness, coping mechanically with the routine of her life, removed from everything but the most trivial details of existence. After a while, her system adjusted, as if accepting that it was permanently weakened, vulnerable to pervasive anxiety. She tried, in the weeks following Bernard's first nine-day absence after his decision, to identify the precise source of her terror. She had to admit that what obsessed her was Bernard's safety. She crawled through every hour of the day and night afraid that he would be killed by a miscalculation; or injured trying to flee from battalions of contemptuous men in high shiny boots, riding in steel machines from whose every surface guns blazed, grenades erupted; or captured, jailed and tortured until his body and then his mind failed and withered away. More than anything else, it was the threat to Bernard's safety that paralyzed her with terror.

Ruth knew that this was the argument least likely to influence Bernard; persisting with it might drive him away from her. But she had to live with herself also; she couldn't remain silent to avoid irritating him; she had to try to convince him. Every time she did, she sapped his patience further. Every time she searched for the best possible minute to discuss it, or carefully set a favorable scene, or succumbed to her own spontaneous outbursts, they quarreled more fiercely, she wept more convulsively, he became more distant, cool, separate.

"You're ruining our times together," he said icily one evening as he gathered his papers, getting ready to leave her, as he did so often these days. "Is that what you really want?"

"You know it isn't. It's the opposite of what I want."

"I don't agree. That's what you want. That's what your behavior says."

He was gone before she could stop sobbing enough to answer. Bernard left faster than anyone she'd ever known. Once he made up his mind to go, there was no stopping him.

He was often away, sometimes for a week or more; when he was in Johannesburg, he was racing to catch up with the work he'd missed, trying to hold his new practice together, keep the senior advocates satisfied, get his clients a decent chance of acquittal. He knew his legal work was suffering and regretted it, but it was something he had to sacrifice for the sake of the new phase of the struggle. It was months before Ruth accepted that her fear for his safety was damaging their relationship. She stopped talking about it; Bernard slowly relaxed with her again, but she noticed sadly that while he thought they had returned to closeness and trust, she was more tense and brittle than before, trying to hide the anger and fear choked constantly inside.

In these months, punctuated now and then by an act of sabotage in the Cape or the Transvaal, in a little town with an unfamiliar name, or near a bleak border, Ruth searched painfully for ways to convince Bernard to give up violence. Whatever she thought of turned on her own central judgment that it was wrong. You don't, she was certain, fight an immoral enemy by using his own methods. You don't descend to violence to counter violence. You don't risk life and property to fight a life-denying system. You don't abandon values to build them. The end, far from justifying the means, would be corrupted by them.

When she used these arguments on Bernard, he just dismissed them, like so many worn-out light bulbs.

"We've been trying nonviolence since the ANC was formed in 1912. It doesn't work. Things keep getting worse."

"Surely organizing people, stopping the factional bickering and getting everyone together, a real national strike, would be more effective than . . ."

"The whites will never willingly share power. There's going to be a revolution. The only question is when. The longer it takes, the more people will suffer, the more will die, the worse the conflagration. We have to hasten it."

"How can something good come out of something bad?"

"I don't want to go on arguing. I'm tired out. I've got to go anyway. Stuff to do."

Bernard didn't tell Ruth what he was doing anymore. He didn't seem interested in what she was doing, which wasn't surprising, since he regarded academic work as futile in these times. Ruth thought wretchedly that their drive in the new blue car to the Drakensberg had been their last happy time together. When Nelson Mandela went on a secret tour of Africa, addressed a conference, met heads of state and went on to London to meet leaders there, she did share Bernard's jubilation. For the first time in his life Mandela was free of white arrogance. He was received as an important leader. It gave them both a brief sense of vindication, eased their strain with each other.

But Mandela, back in the South African underground, was captured soon after his return. He was sentenced to Robben Island for five years for inciting people to stay at home and for leaving the country illegally.

For Bernard, this was a signal to hit the government harder, step up the sabotage, increase the pressure. For Ruth, it was too great a burden.

"I can't stand it," she told him. "I can't go on like this."

They were sitting in the little car, parked outside her parents' house, where he had driven her after a long evening pretending to enjoy being together. A late afternoon thundershower had left everything shining, the new leaves uncurling in moisture, the grass crisp, seedlings pushing sturdily out of damp earth, all an absurd contradiction in the face of Ruth's misery.

"Are you giving me a choice?" he asked sharply. "You or the Spear of the Nation? Is that it?"

She stared at him. In the dark the bones of his face jutted forward, the cleft in his chin was deeper, his eyes obscure under bushy brows drawn together in a hard line. It had never occurred to her that she was giving him a choice. But the word unlocked an assertion of herself that had been buried during months of agonized doubt and anxiety.

"If you want to put it that way," she said, amazed that her breath didn't falter and choke, amazed that she bothered to notice it now, of all times. She was swept by a gust of reckless release as tangible as the rush of hot water from a brisk shower head on icy skin. "I don't want to live this way, I can't."

"Let's forget it then." Bernard stared straight in front, shifting slightly so that his shoulder was turned away from her. "Let's call it quits."

For a moment she hesitated. There were a hundred things she could say or do to get them past this moment, but she was worn out, she was sick of gluing it all together, exhausted from the diurnal habits of deceit and anxiety.

"Right," she said crisply and climbed out of the car without another word. The car pulled away before she reached the gate.

It was days before she understood what she had done, weeks

before she could try to teach herself to accept it. She had not, beyond the instant, thought their separation would last. Nothing in their past, almost five years together, had prepared her for this. At first, she took it for granted that he would return to her in a day or a week or even in two weeks and that they'd find a compromise. When that didn't happen, it occurred to her that he was waiting for her to go to him; she thought about it, she fell into troubled sleep at night ruminating over it, she woke with a different decision on her mind each morning; once, she even got as far as the front door of the building where he had his office. But she turned away, invaded by rage that he deliberately chose to wreck their lives. Then she endured a period of anguished sadness that it had ended the way it had. They'd loved each other so much, woven themselves so close, so dear to each other, surely their parting should have been kinder, more loving? But then there would have been no need to part. But surely they should at least have acknowledged all that they had meant to each other for so long? She wanted to thank him for everything he'd given her, for the experience of intimacy, for the perception of her own value, for the generosity of his mind, his courage and his energy.

She wrote him a letter saying some of these things, decided it was manipulative and tore it up. Two weeks later, pain at the way they'd parted overwhelming her more than the fact, she wrote another letter and put it in her handbag, intending to mail it. That was the day that, parking her mother's car in the lot behind the Wits library, she saw the little blue Fiat pull up. She thought he was coming to look for her and touched the letter happily. But he called "Sorry I'm late" from the open window and Ruth watched a girl with tawny hair bouncing on her shoulders get up from the grass where she'd been dreaming and run over to the car. She leaned in and kissed him. She stood up, smiling, body straining against her tight skirt and blouse. Bernard reached out and pulled her in to him and they kissed again. For a long time. Then, hair falling brightly back into place, she strolled around the car on heels that flattered long, tanned calves and climbed in next to him.

As Bernard pulled away, Ruth tried to attach a name to the girl. She'd seen her around, but it took a while to place her. Ruth sat motionless until she remembered. The girl was Rita something or other, a couple of years younger than Ruth. She'd hovered on the fringes of Julia Gordon's theatrical group for a time, volunteering for backstage chores and tossing her hair in the direction of the male lead in *Othello*, not realizing at first that, though white, he was also gay; then she targeted Iago. Later, she frequented the crowded corridors outside the offices of the junior psychology professors and was seen about with the previously elusive leader of the anti-Freudian group. She must have taken up radical politics now, Ruth thought desolately, tearing up the letter she had written to Bernard. He was obviously making the adjustment easily.

Ruth tried to make her own through the endless months of spring and summer. In the three months they'd already been apart, their friends, unlike Ruth, had realized their apparently indissoluble bond was broken. Now, as Bernard was seen about with Rita, whose high voice and sumptuous shape left her presence upon the very air, friendships and alliances shifted and reformed. Ruth couldn't disguise from herself the fact that many of their old friends rushed quickly by her, sometimes with a shouted "Hello, Ruth" uttered in a tone of surprise, as if at the fact that she continued to exist at all; or that men were beginning to invite her out, at first occasionally, then frequently enough to draw her parents' attention to the whole mess, and that none of these men was political at all. They were faculty colleagues or historians she'd met and forgotten, or they were young doctors, sons of her parents' friends. Or they were voyeurs who'd heard the gossip or hustlers who wanted to help Ruth recover from abstinence.

She tried very hard. Even her parents' unconcealed delight at the breakup with Bernard barely slowed her effort to reconstruct herself as a separate entity. She tried to make new connections. Uncomfortable now in the company of political friends, she accepted every invitation, even from people she had previously despised; she made herself explore every opportunity; she looked for fresh ones. Everyone was boring, every outing was dull, every conversation trite, every bout of grappling humiliating. Ruth told herself that they couldn't all be inept, illiterate, crude, and tedious, but they were. She had to steel herself against letting them know she thought so. She didn't always succeed.

It was Gerald Gordon's company that made those months tolerable for Ruth. She was sure he still saw Bernard but he didn't mention him. He started dropping in to visit unexpectedly once a week or so, talking with his nonchalant authority about the United States' options in Vietnam or the latest foreign film, or the quality of light in the paintings of Rene Carcan, whose layered oils he'd seen on a recent trip to Europe. Gerald made no demands on her, asked no questions, gave no advice. He didn't talk South African politics either, except once, when he mentioned the sabotage attack on a railroad in the Free State the previous day. A few minutes later he tossed in a phrase about having had dinner with Bernard last night, as if he'd guessed that a part of Ruth's agony was still her terror that Bernard would be captured, and wanted to reassure her that this time he wasn't involved. She leaned over and kissed him on the cheek. "Thank you," she said softly. He looked at her speculatively for a long minute, his blue beam assessing her state of mind. He started to say something, stopped, and then smoothly launched into a description of an elegant new restaurant he was taking her to the following week.

Ruth caught glimpses of Bernard now and then, usually with Rita nubile at his side. The distant image left her with a huge hurting hole deep inside, but at least provided proof that he was alive and free. As the days shortened and the temperatures dropped, she saw him once or twice without Rita. Max Hepburn, who'd been working for the *Mail* for a couple of years already and was one of the former friends who'd been avoiding her, ran into her on Kotze Street in Hillbrow on a gray autumn afternoon and surprised her by stopping to talk. He eyed her openly as, with his usual grim clumsiness, he let her know that Bernard had stopped seeing Rita; that, in fact, she had turned to him for comfort. Getting away from Max as fast as she could, Ruth had an immediate urge to go and find Bernard. But she resisted the leap in her mind, the jolt in her body that Max's news had brought. She'd struggled so hard to live without him, she mustn't damage herself by opening herself up to it all over again.

Two months later, in an unusually cold June, banner headlines in the papers announced a great police coup. Hidden in a dry cleaners' van, police drove to Liliesleaf Farm in the suburb of Rivonia and arrested the leaders of the Spear of the Nation, including Walter Sisulu and Govan Mbeki. They found 250 documents, many relating to the manufacture of explosives, and a record in his own handwriting of Mandela's tour of Africa and plans for freeing South Africa. Mandela would be brought from his prison on Robben Island to stand trial on charges of high treason with the others. The government sought the death penalty.

When Ruth was certain that Bernard was not among those captured at Rivonia, she realized that it was only a matter of time before he would be caught. She was unable to hang on to any illusions that he might evade the security police when she saw the caliber of the Rivonia prisoners, towering names in the struggle. These were three whites, six Africans, and an Indian. Lying in bed, trying to imagine what these men were suffering, she thought that Bernard might have only a little time left. He ought to grab whatever happiness he could. She ought to have him while she could, she would never, she knew, be able to replace him. They'd been wasting time. She was stabbed by the recognition as surely as by the first mature awareness of mortality.

At eight o'clock the next morning she waited outside his office building. She knew it might be watched. She didn't care. She saw the senior advocates arrive, she recognized a secretary who entered the building, she stood with her back to the entrance watching the street in both directions until Bernard came, raincoat flapping about his knees, narrow head high in the breeze, full-lipped mouth firm above the deep cleft. She watched him, waiting to see his face when he saw her. She recognized the pleasure that leapt to his eyes, then saw them blink, then huddle under a frown, though color washed his skin. She smiled as he stopped in front of her.

"I was wrong," she said, feeling the smile sweep through her. "You were right. There is no other way to change. And I can live with it. If I have any choice, that is."

He laughed. His face had become gaunt. His arms went around her and hugged her tight.

"Of course you have a choice. What made you . . . ? Why . . . ?"

She looked about.

"It's a long story," she said.

Bernard pressed his lips together, a long line parallel to the drawn eyebrows.

"Look," he said suddenly, "can you wait here just a few minutes? I'm going to run in and talk myself out of spending the day in here. Then I've got something to show you."

He was back in less than ten minutes. He took her hand and led her to the car parked two blocks away. She didn't want to ask questions. He didn't speak, but his eyes snapped merrily, a glow lay upon the craggy cheekbones, lips curved in a slight smile. He drove out of the city, cut through Hillbrow, turned right past Yeoville and beyond toward a network of quiet streets on a hill, dotted with boxy one-level houses and neat front gardens behind trim hedges. He drew up in front of the only apartment building in sight, opposite a water tower. Then he spoke for the first time since they'd left his office building.

"This is Observatory, I don't know if you've ever been out here," he said. "Come on. Come with me."

He led her into a building so new the white paint was barely dry on smooth walls, up two flights of stairs, along an open corridor to a trimly painted door for which he produced a key. They walked into a large open room, sun pouring in from windows facing both north and east, striking the white walls brilliantly. At one end of the room was a mattress covered with a bright woven throw. At the other, a large battered desk was piled with papers and a garden chair sat with a piece of its canvas seat torn and drooping. Ruth saw a tiny kitchen beyond and another door she assumed was a bathroom.

"Whose apartment is it?"

"It's mine. I only moved in a week ago. As you can see, it needs domesticating, I haven't had a chance to get it organized yet."

How his life had changed, Ruth thought; look at all the things that he'd been doing without her. But there was only a second for regret, because Bernard had thrown his raincoat at the chair, hurled his tie and coat and shirt after it, kicked his shoes away and turned back to her.

Hands on her shoulders, staring down into her eyes which she knew were huger, darker than ever, he whispered, "Let's not talk yet." When he felt her tremor, saw her mouth soften, her head lift toward him, he took off all her clothes, efficient with familiarity, put his arms tightly around her and hugged her to him as if he could imprint the feel of her skin and bones upon his own, mold them together so that they need never be apart again, he buried his face in her neck and shuddered, until she led him to the mattress and drew him deep inside her, cherishing him with her aching tissues, her sun-struck memories, her purest, most irrevocable values. When at last they were still, she lay on her back staring at a photograph he had taped to the wall opposite of searing blue above the Drakensberg. She was washed in contentment, soothed by a certainty she had not experienced since their earliest days together. She turned to look at him. This time, it was Bernard who wept. Ruth kissed his eyes, where the skin fluttered thin and vulnerable.

"I've missed you so much," he whispered after a while. "It's been like a pain inside, always there. And steel bands around my head."

"You won't ever have to have it again," she said. "You were right all along. I know that now."

"Why?"

"It's been hard for me, Ben. I know there won't be change without . . . But it took me a long time to see that you wouldn't be you if you weren't part of it."

He hugged her close again and closed his eyes. They were quiet for a long time. Ruth thought he might be asleep.

"Ruth," he said quietly, pulling away from her. "It's over with Rita, of course."

"I heard." He looked so miserable that she added, "It's all right, Ben."

"I shouldn't have done it." He had a catch in his voice.

"You had every right."

"I don't mean that. The thing is . . ."

"You don't have to put yourself through this."

"I do. I must tell you. She had no idea who I am. Even now, after months, she doesn't know me at all. She can't tell the difference between one thing and another, she won't see things as they are, even if you try to show her."

"She's innocent?" Ruth asked painfully, trying to help.

"No, it's not quite that either. After a while I realized that she isn't obtuse. She just glides around the edges of what she doesn't care to know. She closes what passes for her mind. At first . . . after . . . it was a relief." He stopped abruptly and bit his lip, frowning, terribly embarrassed. "I shouldn't . . . look, I am ashamed. I took advantage of all that. When I understood, I broke it off. I wish it had never happened."

Ruth did too, but thought that it didn't matter anymore. She was relieved that Rita had never been in his new apartment. He had finally persuaded his parents he needed his own place, he explained; he knew that his absences and late hours and phone messages were troubling them unendurably; he couldn't stand being watched and judged anymore. Would Ruth help him get the place fixed up? Would she think about moving in? Could they pick up where they'd left off? They spent the day on the mattress, watching the sun's angles shift beyond the huge windows, sifting through the months they'd been apart, planning their lives together.

He had to go away for a few days, he told her. He had to leave that night. He'd phone her as soon as he came back to Jo'burg and then they'd be together. She accepted it with the serenity her new conviction and his need for her had brought her.

Six days later, he did phone.

"Hello. No names, please. No names. Would you go to a call box and dial four-oh-nine-seven-five-three. Thank you."

From a call box just inside the gates of the zoo, to which she'd raced in four minutes, she called.

"Hello. No names please. Give me that number, I'll return the call."

There was no time to speculate. The nerve in the back of her neck saluted the moment as the call box phone shrilled again.

"I am back in town but I have to lie low for a bit."

She gasped.

"I'm quite safe. Don't worry. I'll get in touch as soon as I can. I love you." He hung up.

Three days later, he phoned and instructed her in a similar ritual, this time with a different phone number.

"Something's happened," he said, talking fast. "I have to see you. Could you come to me?"

"Where?"

"It's a house in Sandown. I think it's safe for you to come here."

She was shivering so much it was difficult to write down the directions.

"It's about half an hour's drive, that's all," he said. "Can you come at once?"

Ruth took her mother's car and left immediately.

The directions were scribbled on thin yellow paper torn from the telephone directory in the call box. It rested beside her, fluttering in the breeze from the open window as she sped north to Sandown. Mind racing with the possibilities, she tried to concentrate on the joyful knowledge that they were together again, she and Ben, she tried to think that they would always be together and that as long as they were, nothing else could really matter.

At the entrance to the driveway of the address in Sandown, huge wooden gates stood reassuringly open. She steered down a long drive that divided in two near a big rambling thatch-roofed house beyond. She took the right section, drove past the front verandah with sprays of golden shower creepers shielding it from view, around to the side and parked. She saw no one at all. She followed Bernard's instructions exactly, jumped out of the car, hurried across a big square courtyard to a stand of evergreens. Beyond, at the front of the stables, Bernard stood waiting, his face marked by lines deep as scars, his eyes bloodshot, his rumpled clothes and unshaved cheeks a reflection of deeper distress.

"Ruth," he said gently, hand on her neck, "I'm glad you could come. Look, there are strawberries growing here. Let's pick some and go down to the water and eat them."

Bewildered, she followed him. She couldn't match the strawberry-picking to his appearance or his manner on the phone. She didn't question him. She trusted him. She held up her long full blue skirt to make a basket and they gathered strawberries, glowing moist and luscious, and walked hand in hand to a little lake beyond. They sat down under the waving fronds of the willows.

"We didn't pick enough," Bernard said mournfully. "They're never enough."

But when she said she'd go back and get some more he grabbed her and pulled her down next to him in the shelter of the willow and they lay there, listening to each other's heart beat, in the warm winter light.

"Ruth," he said after a long time. "I have some things to tell you." He sounded as if it hurt him to speak. She pulled him against her, squeezing as hard as she could. "I love you, Ben," she said. "Tell me why you're here."

"We got word that one of the Rivonia prisoners is singing," he murmured. "It was decided a few of us should hide for a while until we know more."

"But who . . . ?"

"Forget it. It's got to happen sometimes. Sometimes people can't handle what they dish out. We'll have to wait and see."

"There are others here?"

"Oh, yes." He sounded, for the first time, amused.

"I didn't see anyone at all, the place looks deserted."

"Oh, Ruth." He laughed. "We had to work it out that way. You aren't supposed to know who's here."

She hated it, but didn't say so.

"Can they find you here?"

"No. The bird in Marshall Square doesn't have this address. It's a nuisance, though." He sat up suddenly. He looked as troubled as she had ever seen him. "That's not why I had to see you, Ruthie."

"Tell me."

"When I came back to Jo'burg a few days ago I was sent here immediately. I phoned you on the way out here that first time. Yesterday, a . . . messenger picked up my mail and it was . . . brought out here."

"Yes?"

"There was a letter. From Rita."

Ruth could not see his eyes. They were narrowed thin under heavy frowning brows. She could see veins standing out in his neck and another, throbbing along his temple. She waited.

"Rita is four months pregnant, Ruth."

Her body, braced for an assault, took it like the first shock of ice water thrown at the face. The light dimmed. The cold penetrated bleakly, pervasively, burning hot ice. She blinked, rubbed her eyes, pressed her fingers against them. She did not want to look at him.

"I have to marry her, Ruth," he said, as she had known he would.

She thought that she couldn't speak because she couldn't breathe but that it didn't matter because there was nothing to say.

"It's four months, Ruth. It took her a while to realize it." His voice was bent by bitterness. "I've been around it a million times. I have to do it now, in case . . ."

He didn't need to complete the brutal thought. She knew it well. She had tried a thousand times to imagine Bernard in prison and couldn't, but that didn't mean she didn't grasp the threat. She had incorporated it into every cell and fiber of her system long ago.

"Yes," she said at last.

"Ruth," he cried, "one day, later, maybe we can . . ."

"Don't," she said.

She looked at him then, she drew him into her mind so that he would stay there, so that she could pull his image out when she would need it.

"I'd prefer to do it quickly," she said, getting to her feet. "I should leave now."

"We mustn't leave together. Let me go first, I've left it very late, I'll have to see her this afternoon. Follow in fifteen minutes."

She saw that he looked directly into her eyes. He touched her cheek, then wiped his hands across his eyes.

"I love you," Bernard said; and turned and walked away.

She sat down again under the willows, eyes closed, seeing him in sunshine on the bright bed in his apartment.

"Ruth Fredman?" said an unfamiliar harsh accent. She looked up. A man in a tweed coat with a leather wallet waving in her face stood over her. He was smiling. She heard sudden shouts beyond.

"You are under arrest, Miss Fredman."

"For what?" she gasped, scrambling to stand up.

"Treason, that's what," said Detective Piet Fourie of the Special Branch. "Treason and you know it."

CHAPTER SEVEN

R̲uth was afraid to leave the house. She hung around all day waiting for Gerald to call with a message from Nelson. Anticipating Bob's apprehensive speculations and Sara's alarm, she explained that she was waiting to hear from Nelson. Yes, she admitted, it was difficult to convince him to return with her but she hadn't given up. Bob wondered how much of his training Penn Medical School would credit; Sara worried about his living arrangements in Philadelphia, Ruth didn't have room for him, did she? How easy if these were her only concerns! Ruth muttered "One step at a time" and excused herself to go and write letters.

The phone rang twice that morning. Both times, Ruth jumped up and ran to the front hall to find the calls were for Sara. Assuring herself that it was too early for Nelson to have contacted Gerald, she tried to write to Ken. She couldn't risk telling him about her first few days in South Africa, even if he knew what she was supposed to be doing, which he certainly didn't. She managed a few lines about Ken's classes, wished him a happy stay in Boston, where he was to spend a few days with Brian, and then, knowing he would find it odd if she wrote nothing about South Africa, told him that there had been some reforms but their effect was to lock the apartheid structure more firmly into place. There was rioting every day, all over the country. The more people died, the more enraged and frustrated the mobs became. That was surely mild enough. If the letter was opened, it said nothing more than newscasters and even Afrikaans businessmen were saying publicly. Folding the brief air letter, she thought of Ken, sleeping late during the Christmas vacation, wandering with friends around South Street or the campus at night, talking real estate and sailing with Brian in Boston. Her satisfying awareness of his security only sharpened the contrast with Nelson's precarious existence. Pricked by guilt, she wondered if she could ever feel for Nelson the absolute love she carried always for her own child. Ken was her own flesh, that was definitive, she tried to console herself; but didn't succeed because, after all, Ken was Brian's also. Nelson was Bernard's and should have been hers. How would they get along, these almost brothers, if she ever got Nelson away? With a quick warming, she allowed herself a minute's respite; she thought they'd understand each other, Ken would enjoy Nelson's gutsy rebellion, tolerate his naiveté. Whether she got Nelson out or not, she would have to decide what to tell Ken, but it was disgustingly self-indulgent to think of that now.

In the afternoon, the phone rang once. It was Bob, calling from his office at Wits to talk to Sara. Ruth, finding it more difficult now to rationalize excuses for the silence from Nelson, tried to write to Anthony. But Bernard's image obscured Anthony's as if yesterday's news that he had a chance of freedom had deposited him in three-dimensional color at the front of her mind, from which she had worked so hard to banish him. He was firmly implanted there again now, staring down at her with melted chocolate eyes, full lips softened above the cleft in his chin, sunlight chasing shadows across the high cheekbones. She felt uncomfortable trying to summon Anthony's substantial figure, his sense of assurance that grew from having looked long and close at the world and come to terms with it and himself. Not easily, to be sure; Anthony's vision and his camera lenses had penetrated the world's most torrid agonies, from Vietnam and Cambodia to Africa and to the Middle East, most cruelly to Beirut. But Anthony was an observer, after all, his cameras his own ivory tower. Appalled at having allowed this judgment to enter her mind, Ruth scribbled a few innocuous lines. Awkwardly she added, "It needs a lot of history to explain what I'm doing now, I'll try to share it when I get back." She read it several times, steeled herself against crossing it out. "I miss you. Ruth." Who was she betraying now? Which line of truths was she tiptoeing around as if mines lay hidden beneath?

After the miserly letters were finished, there was nothing to do but wait, with rising panic, to hear from Nelson. The urgency of Gerald's disclosures gave her a heightened sense of time and Bernard's chance for freedom racing by. She tried to concentrate on what to tell Nelson when she finally saw him again, how to convince him that he held his father's future as well as his own in his reckless young hands. She was miserably aware of what she would have to reveal to force him to believe her when he wouldn't believe Gerald. Straining for the sound of the telephone ringing, she decided that if Gerald didn't call by seven, she would call him at home, she couldn't wait beyond that.

Gerald called at six-forty-five. Nelson hadn't contacted him. Gerald had been trying for hours, but hadn't been able to reach him. Nothing alarming in that, he said, the words contradicting the irritated bewilderment in his voice, Nelson was often hard to track down. He certainly wasn't at home, the Med School, or Baragwanath, but Gerald had left messages at all these obvious places. If he didn't hear from Nelson that night, he'd search for him the next day. Ruth should sit tight. By the way, he said, his voice guarded, Carolyn and the children had returned that afternoon. Ruth understood that she could not be invited to join his vigil at the phone and that she should not call him.

The dreams returned that night, but with petrifying new contortions. Once, leaning over the *Umgeni* railing, she saw that the fish head in the churning water below had a dark, narrow face and full lips clenched tightly shut. It wasn't Nelson, because the hair streaming out long and knotted on the rolling green surface was white. She woke whimpering, soaked in sweat, panting. She flung herself out of bed, switched on a lamp, paced the room steadily, blinking against the grit in her eyes. When she slept again, men in high-topped black boots spattered in mud and something else marched in and out of a high wire cage from which an invisible man screamed "Last chance, chance, chance" in a high piercing wail. When Ruth struggled awake, she found Bob, flashlight in his hand, standing over her. He looked ridiculous in striped green-and-yellow pajamas billowing around his square chest and protruding belly.

"You were shouting," he said. His face, its salmon color deepened by sleep to scarlet, wavered between pity and irritation. "You must be having a nightmare."

"I'm sorry," Ruth said. "I'm all right now."

She didn't go back to sleep, didn't even stay in bed. She began waiting to hear from Gerald at four o'clock in the morning, rehearsing what pieces of her past she would offer Nelson in return for his compliance with saving his life.

When Sara called her to the phone at almost ten o'clock, she grabbed it and, not even waiting for Sara to leave the hall, said, "Gerald? What's happening?"

"This is not Gerald," said a South African white man whose voice and accent she could not identify. "Am I speaking to Ruth Fredman?"

"Yes."

"Hold on, please, for Mr. Derek Brand."

She moved the phone away from her ear as if it burned. She stretched out her arm to put the receiver down and sever the outrageous unwanted connection; but, both frightened and intrigued, brought it back to her ear just as a deep voice with the careful enunciation of an Afrikaner thoroughly familiar with the nuance and idiom of English, announced, "This is Derek Brand."

"Yes?"

"I'd like to see you immediately."

"Why?"

"I shall explain that when you get here. Do you know where my office is?"

"No. What is this in connection with?"

There was a pause. Ruth gripped the phone with both hands. They were wet.

"It's in connection with Nelson."

"How did you get this number?" she asked suddenly.

"It wasn't difficult. I found it on a scrap of paper tossed in a wastebasket in my stepson's bedroom. Your name and phone number."

"But why do you want to see me?"

"Listen here, Miss Fredman. You listen here. I want to talk about Nelson. Can you understand that or is it too much for you? My office is in the penthouse of the Brand Building, diagonally opposite Carlton Center. I'll expect you within the hour."

The connection was severed with a loud click.

Ruth dropped the telephone directory trying to find Gerald's number and knelt down to turn the pages on the floor, ignoring Sara, who had reappeared, hovering at the kitchen end of the hall, anticipation and fear clouding her face.

Ruth stood up and dialed Gerald's office. He had not arrived yet, she was told. She dialed his home. He had left more than two hours ago, an early meeting at his office, George said quietly. He didn't ask who was speaking. He didn't acknowledge that he recognized her voice. She clenched her hands together, trying to decide.

"What's the trouble now?" Sara asked warily.

"No, nothing, it's all right," Ruth said. "I have to go into the city, I don't know how long I'll be. Would you take a message when Gerry calls?"

She left the way Bernard had taught her, fast. She remembered the Carlton Hotel, she knew it had been rebuilt to provide a sophisticated, glittering haven for international bankers and businessmen, American tourists, and foreign black dignitaries who could no longer be stashed away in primitive hovels in black townships. She drove there as quickly as traffic and her memory of the route allowed. What could Brand want? What could he do to her after all? Maybe he'd persuaded Nelson to leave and wanted her help in the U.S.

The Carlton Center was unmistakable. Its sleek facade, fountains, towering plants in tubs in the adjacent open square, and huge gleaming lobby guarded by elaborately decorated uniformed men could have been picked up and transplanted to Fifth or Park Avenue, where they would have blended well. Diagonally opposite was a striking, tall building of shining steel and stone, broad windows, and the name "Brand Building" cut in a huge slab of onyx in front. Ruth was received in the underground parking lot by a man who asked her name and then directed her to a small, brass-lined elevator which went, he said, straight up to the penthouse where Mr. Brand was expecting her. She chewed the inside of her cheek and stepped out into a lobby equipped with an ornately carved marble sculpture, a huge brass-framed map of the world, and a pert blonde behind a rosewood desk and a battery of multicolored phones. Yes, Mr. Brand was expecting her. She tapped a bell on the floor with the gleaming point of her burgundy shoe and a man emerged from the hall on the left.

"I'm Mr. Brand's executive assistant," he said. "Would you come with me?"

The hall was lined with paintings which Ruth didn't pause to examine. The assistant opened double carved doors, stepped inside and announced, "Miss Ruth Fredman, Mr. Brand," waved her in and retreated, closing the doors silently behind him.

Derek Brand rose from the throne behind his polished desk and stood waiting for her to cross the acre of gold-patterned maroon carpet toward him. He didn't look much like the photographs she dimly remembered. With his imposing height and strapping build, he looked like a well-preserved former rugby forward carefully composed by a slick public relations firm to represent credibly the upper echelons of international mining or banking. He certainly didn't resemble the rednecked son of a dirt-poor farmer and a small-town Afrikaans assistant in a beauty parlor. Brand's tailored charcoal suit, from which snow-white cuffs with big square gold links protruded, his attractively thick, well-groomed iron-gray hair, his well-kept hands with short immaculate nails, looked every inch the powerful Western cosmopolitan. He had a surprisingly short thick neck for such a tall man. Above it, his large head inclined slightly backward, so that the first part of his face Ruth saw was the heavy-boned jawline and square, thrusting chin. His mouth was stern against sun-toughened skin. Pale eyes of indeterminable color neutrally traced her advance. He didn't offer to shake hands.

"Miss Fredman."

"Actually, it's Mrs. Harris," Ruth said firmly.

He didn't blink.

"Would you sit down, Mrs. Harris."

She sat in a carved armchair opposite the desk. She thought a different man might have chosen to move over to the other side of the room, where a sofa and two easy chairs were arranged invitingly, but Derek Brand lowered himself with surprising grace for so bulky a man into the massive chair behind the desk and, leaning back comfortably, examined her without expression across the expanse of polished wood between them.

Ruth couldn't imagine what he wanted with her. She was only there, she reminded herself grimly, because she was afraid that not responding to his summons would increase the havoc he might create. Besides, she had to know how he judged Nelson.

"What is your business with Nelson Levine?"

He spoke with the authority of a man accustomed to command. His voice betrayed no emotion; his accent belonged to a successful white South African at home in the world, barely revealing a trace of his origins.

"Why are you questioning me?" Ruth sat still and straight opposite him.

"I want to know what you are doing with Nelson," he said, exactly as if he were asking a subordinate a routine question.

"Mr. Brand, I don't have to answer your questions." She was telling herself that as much, more than she was telling him. His expression didn't alter. She stared deliberately at him. "Perhaps you should tell me why you're asking?"

"Why are you in South Africa? What are you doing here?"

She didn't answer.

He smiled then, a tight, thin stretching of his lips that left no other alteration on his face. He shifted in his high chair and rested a large hand lightly on the surface of the desk.

"Tell me, how do you find it here now?"

Ruth shrugged. "Much the same."

His head drooped farther down on his left side, bringing his heavy jaw to rest on his dark coat collar. He looked curiously at her.

"I'm surprised. We've made so many changes since you . . . ah, since you left us. Treaties with neighboring states, our own independent homelands, the Ministry of Culture and Cooperation, the new tricameral Parliament. I thought these were the things you . . . ah, wanted. What do you think of the Indian and Colored chambers of Parliament?"

Ruth hesitated. Where do you put your feet when you know live shells are hidden about in the brush? Then, true to form, she said, "The new Parliament hasn't changed anything much, has it, Mr. Brand? The people don't think it has, anyway. There are riots all the time now, all over the country, every day. People are being killed all the time now. The cities are terribly dangerous. I don't think changing the names of things or having these new chambers in Parliament has satisfied people at all."

"On the contrary, most people are . . . ah, very satisfied. Very few are disgruntled, Mrs. Harris. Very few. Only those that take their instructions from outside our beautiful country, you know."

Without any adjustment to his conversational tone, he added, "Where is Nelson getting his instructions from? That is what I am wondering."

Ruth was bewildered. What had Nelson done? What did Brand know? Where would he stand as the system he'd helped to build closed in on his stepson?

"I don't understand," she observed accurately.

"Mrs. Harris, my wife was somewhat concerned when she saw you lunching with Gerald Gordon at the Automobile Club a couple of days ago," he said, raising his head enough to look directly at her. "She thought you were long gone from here. She was surprised to see you. She wondered, as a matter of fact, whether the authorities know that you're here. She mentioned that to me."

Ruth hoped her face was blanker than her mind, in which alarming new questions tumbled. She hadn't seen Rita, Gerald didn't appear to have seen her, yet Rita knew they were there together. Could she possibly have overheard them? Was this tycoon actually threatening her with his casual reference to the authorities? She didn't speak. She was only there to listen. She would give him no ammunition, not even her disquiet. Derek Brand's civilized veneer did nothing to reduce the menace that hovered like murky fog in the air.

"When my wife mentioned that you and Gordon were having a long intense conversation, I told her there was nothing to it. Why shouldn't you and Gordon meet for lunch? But my wife takes a particular interest in Gerald Gordon because he is her son's guardian. Did you know that, Mrs. Harris?"

"I learned it recently. What does it matter?"

"Quite." He nodded. His neck disappeared entirely. His head was planted solidly upon his big sloping shoulders. "Just what I told Mrs. Brand. But I've . . . ah, I've changed my mind. I found your name — the name Ruth Fredman — and the phone number where I reached you this morning, in Nelson's bedroom. That leads to my inquiries now. I want to know why you are in South Africa and what you are doing with Nelson. Why did he have your phone number? What is your purpose here?"

"My brief visit to South Africa needn't concern you at all, Mr. Brand. I am an American now. I'll be returning to the States very soon."

"Do you think I don't know that Nelson is his father's son? I've lived with that. The coconuts fall close to the tree." His even, restrained tone might have been directed at business colleagues, just a rung or two lower on the multinational ladder. "Nelson doesn't understand the white man's problems. He's . . . ah, misguided, Mrs. Harris. Many good people have told me that Nelson Levine is looking for trouble. Has he found it? You tell me that. I'm not going to be made a fool of. I know he's messing in matters that don't concern him."

When he realized that Ruth wasn't going to respond, Derek Brand stood up and crossed the room to the wide window. He stood for a few seconds staring down at the city street, blocked by streams of cars. On the pavements, black men and women, the messenger boys and tea girls of the metropolis, kept their eyes averted from the midday shoppers and office workers out to lunch. Tourists and journalists and cops in disguise and spies and squealers thronged the entrances to the Carlton, hustling or being hustled, looking for the easy opening, poised for opportunity.

Keeping her eyes on Brand, Ruth wondered if he'd stood and watched from this same window five days earlier when several blocks away three hundred blacks had spilled out of a church hall after a memorial service for five murdered adolescents. They'd surged angrily through the streets, collecting hundreds more people on the way, until they thronged across the street between the Brand Building and the Carlton Center, blocked it full so that, from pavement to pavement and for long blocks on either side, a sea of furious black faces heaved and jeered, chanted, sang, jumped up and down, arms raised emphatically until the hippos came. Had Brand heard from up here the commandant shout into a microphone the order to disperse in a few rasping contemptuous words? Had the tear gas wafted high up here, had it penetrated his double-glazed windows? Or did he stand quite still, as he did now, to watch the hippos nudge slowly forward, with ten or fifteen soldiers straddling the top of each one, shooting live ammunition in all directions into the raging crowd? Did he watch while they jerked, writhed and fell? Did he see hundreds turn and run into the firestorm coming from the opposite direction, see them hurl rocks at the plate-glass windows on the street below, smash bottles and race into the stores, holding them aloft to defend themselves? Was he there a couple of hours later, when the bodies had been carted away and the men came with hoses to wash down the street outside the Brand Building?

Blinking as Brand turned back to her, Ruth thought that he looked like a man in total control of himself and of the city spread out intricately below. As if he'd made a decision, he walked back behind his desk and stood squarely, arms folded across his athlete's thick aging chest.

"It's time to stop beating around the bush, Mrs. Harris," he said, his voice level. "Nelson has disappeared."

She couldn't stop her eyes from widening, she couldn't control the sudden clutching of her hands, she barely stifled her little gasp.

"Now we're talking, eh?" he said with the slightest tinge of triumph.

Ruth was furious with herself for permitting him to see her reaction; and with him, for alarming her. Nelson, of course, had not disappeared. She'd spent the evening with him, just two, or was it three nights ago? Trying to work it out, her gaze wavered, she saw a small black cube she had not noticed before on the desk and realized he was recording the conversation. Well, she hadn't told him anything and she wouldn't. She stared defiantly at his pale eyes and waited.

"Listen here, Ruth Fredman," he said, with somewhat more

of the Boer twang than he'd previously revealed, "I'm not in the habit of examining my stepson's wastebasket, eh. I'm trying to find out what has happened. I think you can help me. Let's not make things difficult."

"I have," Ruth said very distinctly, "no idea where Nelson Levine is."

"Well, he slept at home on Tuesday night, Mrs. Harris. The cook made him breakfast very early on Wednesday, about six. She says he drove off in a hurry. We haven't seen or heard from him since. It's Friday. Ah. My wife is upset. Naturally. I don't want to create alarm, Mrs. Harris, but the chappie is missing. He's not at the Medical School and he's not at the hospital where he's supposed to be. I don't know if you're aware of it, though I suspect you know it very well — Nelson Levine is not easy to manage. Not at all. Never has been, which doesn't surprise me. But he's never disappeared for days like this without a word to his mother."

He paused. When Ruth didn't speak, he nodded several times, then let his head jerk forward.

"I went to his room to look for an indication of what he's up to. I found nothing unusual, Mrs. Harris, except your name and phone number on a crumpled piece of paper in the wastebasket. Now. Mrs. Brand wants the boy home. Where is he?"

She stared at the black cube.

"Why are you recording this conversation, Mr. Brand?"

He followed her glance to the cube. He shrugged, shoulders nudging his ears. He touched a button with his index finger.

"There. It's off. Satisfied?"

Ruth stood up.

"I don't like being interrogated, Mr. Brand. I don't like being recorded and I don't understand your intentions."

"Precaution, that's all. You think I don't know your record? How do I know what you might do next?" His tone was as level as it had been all along, but Ruth had the impression of a man determined to maintain his rigid control.

"I don't know where Nelson is. I don't know why he had my phone number."

"Could Gerald Gordon have given it to him?"

"I don't know. Possibly."

"Why would he do that? What do you want with the boy?"

She didn't answer.

"I know you and your kind," he said suddenly, as quiet as ever. "Once a traitor always a traitor. They should never have let you go, they weren't tough enough."

Ruth stood up while he was speaking. When he stopped, she said, "Good day, Mr. Brand," and walked all the way to the door before he said, "They're tougher these days, you know." She opened the doors and left while he stood staring at her back. She restrained herself from running all the way downstairs, all the way until she was safe, all the way to America.

The reaction set upon her in the elevator. Shaking with uncontrollable tremors, perspiration sliding down the back of her neck, she hated herself for obeying Brand's summons. When the elevator stopped smoothly, its door sliding open, she pushed herself away from the brass wall and walked slowly to Gerald's car. She had to find him somewhere. He would have to help her find Nelson. She was afraid that Brand would call the police. She thought Nelson must be on one of his delivery missions, deadly as a suicide run. If Brand dragged the police into this, they'd find him and destroy either him or Bernard's chance of freedom.

"Ruth! Ruth Fredman!" a high, thin voice called. Ruth turned from the car, her hand still holding the key in the lock, to find Rita Brand standing behind her.

The tawny hair was palest gold now. The inner light behind the smooth skin had given way to chiseled perfection. The breasts and hips and thighs straining voluptuously against flimsy cloth were sleekly contained now in elegant raw silk. Diamonds burned from wheels of gold on her earlobes and fingers. But it was Rita all right. When Ruth had sat squashed between two Special Branch detectives in the back of a police car taking her to be booked for treason at Marshall Square, it had been Rita whose image most painfully threatened her. Rita, not the cops and their clumsy error, for surely that was all it could be. It was Rita who was the instrument of her wounded misery.

"I've been wanting to talk to you. Max told me you're stunning and he was right," Rita said, astonishingly.

"Max?" Ruth murmured. "Hello, Rita. Where's Max? When did you see him?"

"Not long after he met you in Vienna. He was here in Jo'burg, you know."

So Max Hepburn went in and out of South Africa at will, free to come and go. He'd never been around when there was trouble; somehow, he'd never been identified with the resistance. He still visited Rita, who had turned to him for consolation after Bernard left her. Had Rita sent him to find her in Vienna?

It occurred to Ruth, leaning against Gerald's car in Brand's underground parking garage, that it was ridiculous to be thinking about Max, shameful to be reviving her poisonous suspicions of Rita. Nelson had disappeared. Brand might be talking to the police at this minute. She had to find Nelson and spirit him away.

"It's not just curiosity that made me come and wait for you here." Rita's voice was still thin, but she'd learned how to modulate its pitch. "I want to talk to you about Nelson." She stepped closer on high-heeled snakeskin pumps. "I knew you were coming to see my husband, so I thought I'd catch you down here. To talk privately." Her voice dropped suddenly to a hush, presumably so that the man at the desk near the elevator wouldn't hear. "Let's go somewhere and talk. I'll buy you a drink."

"I don't have time." The notion of drinking with Rita was both incongruous and offensive.

"But we must talk about Nelson. We must." Rita's pitch rose.

"Go ahead. Speak to me here."

"But . . . I can't. I'm not really supposed to see you. Derek . . . my husband said it would be better if . . ."

"I don't have much time. What did you want to say about Nelson?"

"I haven't seen or heard from him since Tuesday. He always lets me know where he'll be. Nelson is my son, Ruth. Where is he?"

"I've already told your husband that I don't know."

"Oh, I expected that. I understand that. But please tell me. Please, Ruth. If I at least know . . ."

"But I don't know where he is, Rita. Really."

Rita stared at her. After a few seconds, a small smile shifted her mouth. "I promise I'll never let on that you told me," she urged. She was not a practiced conspirator.

"I honestly don't know where he is."

Rita touched her arm.

"Is he in jail?" she whispered.

Ruth moved sideways, discreetly out of range. She thought, not for the first time, that there must be something more to this woman than she recognized. Bernard had found something more.

"I told you, I don't know. What makes you think he's in jail?"

Rita shrugged. She smoothed a strand of pale hair away from her forehead, looked about the garage, stepped closer again.

"Of course, I know Nelson has political ideas. I've told him often, I don't want to hear anything about it. Live and let live, I say. Do what's good for number one, I always tell him. But I try not to interfere, I'm not one of those mothers who thinks she can tell her child what to do, I don't believe in it. I don't know what he's been doing, but I guess it may be dangerous. I don't know," she admitted, "but then I never knew with Bernard either. Who'd think of such things? Look, Ruth," she said suddenly, twisting her handbag strap around and around her fingers, "we're both mothers, aren't we? We went with the same fellow once, didn't we? We've got things in common. Big things. So tell me what he's doing?"

Feeling distaste as sharp as if she'd bathed in foul, slimy water, Ruth turned away to unlock the car door and open it.

"Oh, wait, please wait. I believe you, please wait."

Ruth turned back to her. "I don't have anything to say."

"Wait a minute more. You see, if he's in trouble I might be able to get Derek to help. He's got a lot of influence, you know. He might be very angry, but I could try. I don't know what to do, you see."

"Neither do I."

"Why are you here, Ruth?" Rita demanded suddenly. "Why did you come back? I saw you with Gerald at the Auto Club and I was afraid. You're here because of Nelson, aren't you? To make him do something?"

"I don't know why you should think so," Ruth said, suddenly exhausted.

"You got Bernard back, didn't you? Before he . . . you know. And then you got away. What do you make my fellows do?"

Ruth laughed.

"I'm not a witch, you know." She climbed into the car and slammed the door. Then she thought of something and rolled the window down. "Have you talked to Gerald about Nelson's disappearance?"

"Oh, yes. He's terribly worried too. He's been looking for him."

"Do you know where Gerald is now?"

"Yes, of course. I spoke to him before I drove down here. He's at his office."

"Thank you. Goodbye, Rita."

"Just a minute." She was holding onto the door. She leaned in to the window with a little gush of Chanel. "Are you going to see Bernard? Just tell me that."

Ruth clenched both hands on the steering wheel, blinking.

"No, I'm not going to see him, Rita. I must go now."

Driving away, she saw Rita in the rearview mirror, standing

forlorn, exquisite, exactly where she'd left her, struggling still, no doubt, between her policy of noninterference and her maternal instincts.

Ruth, frantic to go to Wits and Gerald, decided she'd better find out first if there were messages for her at the Sterns'. She pulled up at a call box and called Sara. There had been two calls. Gerald had called to say there was still no news. And Nelson had called, about an hour ago.

"Nelson called?" Ruth asked.

"Yes. I asked him where he was and he said he couldn't be reached," Sara said anxiously.

"There's no message from him?"

"Oh yes, he said he'd try again in a while. He said to tell you that."

"Thank you, Sara. I'm on my way back now."

"What should I say if he calls before you get here?"

"Tell him I'll be there half an hour from now. Ask him to please call right back."

She drove back to Westcliff from the city as fast as she could. Sara was waiting on the verandah when she arrived. She began talking as soon as Ruth stopped the car.

"He called again." She had the air of having been co-opted. "He sounded really pleased when I said you'd be here soon."

"Thank you, Sara. He didn't leave a number?"

"He said he's on the road." Sara looked expectantly at Ruth. She was saved from fabricating an explanation by the telephone. She leapt past Sara into the house and picked it up.

"That's you at last, isn't it, Ruth?" Nelson was in a hurry.

"Nelson? Are you all right?"

"I'm fine. Everything's worked out fine." Before she could ask what he meant, he said, "Look, Ruth, I'm sorry I didn't get back to you sooner. I know I said I would but I've been away. I didn't expect to be, I had to go suddenly."

"Nelson, your mother is terribly worried, she — "

"Yes, don't worry, I've been in touch with Gerald. He'll take care of them," Nelson interrupted, not even reacting to the implication that Ruth had talked to Rita. "I don't have time now. Look, I wanted you to know I've been thinking about what you said. And about my father. I'd like to show you something so you'll . . . well, anyway, can you come out with me this afternoon?"

"Yes, of course. But . . . where?"

"I can't explain now. Look, could you meet me? You've got Gerald's Fiat still, haven't you?"

"Yes, but . . ."

"Do you remember de Villiers Street? The old Drill Hall?"

Ruth laughed.

"I thought you would," said Nelson. "There's a parking lot opposite. I'll meet you there in an hour. So long." He spoke so fast and hung up so quickly that Ruth had no chance to respond. She turned to find Sara just behind her, chin forward, sallow skin shiny with anxiety. She must have heard every word of Ruth's. Uneasily, she tried to remember exactly what she'd said. Not much, not the way Nelson had rushed through the call. She was too distracted to assume a mask for Sara.

"I'm going to meet him, Sara," she said.

"To persuade him to go home with you?"

"Yes, of course. That's what I'm trying to do."

"But where's he been, Ruth? Wasn't he supposed to meet you before?" Sara was monitoring events more closely than Ruth had realized. Maybe Sara had listened in on an extension when she spoke to Gerald. She was sick of it all; it made no difference anyway. Whatever Bob and Sara knew or thought they knew about her didn't seem to matter anymore. She still didn't know what Gerald had told them. She didn't care.

"Nelson's a handful, Sara," Ruth said honestly. Her American personality asserted itself long enough for her to add, "You know these kids, Sara, dates and times and arrangements don't mean anything to them. I've just got to grab him when I can, that's all."

It was good enough for Sara. Ruth was free to walk back to the bedroom and get ready to leave again. She couldn't imagine what Nelson wanted to show her or how long it would take. She took off the suit she'd worn for Derek Brand, munitions tycoon, and replaced it with jeans, a dark shirt, flat shoes, as comfortable, as muted as she could find in her bag. She had the uncomfortable suspicion, based no doubt on standard South African paranoia, that someone might examine her things while she was gone, so she tucked the leather wallet with her papers, Bob's letters, and her passport into her handbag. The only photographs in the wallet were the one of Ken and, tucked under a little fold of leather behind everything else, an old snapshot of Bernard.

"I'm not sure when I'll be back, Sara," she called as she ran out to the car. "I may be late, please don't worry."

CHAPTER EIGHT

Ruth saw the huge van with the red Levitt's logo as soon as she turned into de Villiers Street.

Nelson had assumed she'd know the area because of the old Drill Hall, made famous as the site of preliminary hearings for one hundred and fifty-six people accused of treason. Nelson couldn't know that she'd been in high school then, barely aware of South Africa's first big show trial. Perhaps he knew his father had been there, on the first day of the hearings, at the high spiked iron gates, watching the slow arrival of the police jeeps, their wire cages with prisoners giving the thumbs-up sign, calling "*Maybuye*," shouting "*Amandla*" to the hundreds of people trying to get inside what was supposed to be an open court. Bernard was there when the jittery police suddenly fired in the air and charged the crowd with truncheons and *sjamboks*. His neck was cut by flying shards from broken bottles, his rib was cracked by a flailing *knobkirrie*, his life was committed when he raced away over a bed of shattered glass, down a side street.

Like Nelson, Ruth knew the Drill Hall only by its legend; but she had known Joubert Park, diagonally opposite, as well as her own classroom. She'd spent many solitary hours in its small art museum, searching for answers to questions she hadn't known how to ask.

The Levitt's logo didn't raise a question; she assumed coincidence until, turning into the parking lot, she saw Nelson Levine jump down from the passenger side and wave. At least he was alive, she thought irritably, parked and walked over to him.

"Jump in, Ruth," he said.

"Just a minute, Nelson," she said sharply. "I need to talk to you. It's very urgent."

"We can talk on the way. Come on, it's getting late."

She glanced curiously at the front of the truck. It was too high for her to see inside.

"Where are we going?"

"I want to show you something, Ruth. We'll talk on the way, it's a long ride."

She hesitated. His eyes, narrow under heavy brows, glittered with excitement, his fingers curled and uncurled. She had to find some way to reach this agitated young man and make him understand that his father's life depended on him. She couldn't do it in a parking lot.

She climbed three steep metal steps into the truck. Scrambling into the seat, she found Johannes behind the wheel, hand on the shift, poised to go. She'd thought Nelson was alone. She couldn't discuss the most intimate details of her life in front of this stranger. She turned to climb back down, but Nelson was already on the top step, blocking her exit.

"Nelson, I don't know what you have in mind, but I . . ."

"Move over," he said curtly. "We're in a hurry. We'll talk on the way."

He pushed into the front seat beside her. Johannes had the truck moving before Nelson slammed the heavy door shut.

Ruth drew a deep breath and folded her arms tight.

"Hello, Johannes," she said.

"Missus Harris."

It was the barest token of a greeting. His round face didn't shift by a fraction. His muddy eyes were fixed frontward. He wore the same khaki uniform he'd had on when he brought her Nelson's message in Hillbrow three nights before. The muscles of his

218

shoulder and thigh bulged hard against her. He looked sullen, possibly angry, as if he resented her presence in his delivery truck. Well, he couldn't resent it as much as she did. Nelson might have warned her; he was disgracefully self-centered. Or utterly manipulative. Or both. Wedged between them, she shifted enough to turn and look at Nelson. His long, bare arm rested nonchalantly on the open window edge, fine black hairs lustrous on dark skin. Like Bernard. But not like Bernard.

"Nelson, where are we going?"

"To Soweto."

On her left, Johannes muttered a single word she didn't understand. She had been mistaken. He was furious, but not with her. Nelson must have trapped him also.

"Why are you taking me to Soweto, Nelson? I don't have any reason to go there, I don't even have a permit."

Johannes's shoulder bunched against her own. He raised a fist, then flung his fingers wide in angry agreement.

"Listen, Ruth. You too, Johan, it does make sense, just listen." Nelson jerked awkwardly until his back rested against the door and he could look at them both as he spoke. "I've thought a lot about what you said to me the other night. Especially about my father."

"I have more to tell you," Ruth interrupted. "There — "

"Just a minute," Nelson said. "You've got to understand."

"Understand what?"

"I can't do what you want, what you say he wants. I can't. Especially now." His voice was low and firm, but new needles of alarm shivered under Ruth's skin. "I've thought it out. I owe it to him to make you understand why I have to stay here . . . "

She tried to speak, but he was oblivious. "I cannot leave South Africa. I have to make two stops in Soweto. When you see, you'll understand. Then I hope you'll go back to the States and leave me alone. Leave us all alone to get on with it."

"Nelson, I know about Soweto, I know how terrible conditions . . ."

The interruption was a snort from Johannes.

"You're preaching to the converted, Nelson, I don't question the desperate need for change, I don't have to go into Soweto illegally to support the struggle."

"I'm going to show you exactly why *I* have to stay, Ruth. Then you'll understand. I'm keeping my word to Dad. A fair hearing, he said. Serious consideration. Balancing the values. Well. That's the idea." He awkwardly rearranged his back against the hard plastic seat.

"Nelson, isn't Soweto surrounded by half-tracks and hippos and army and police security?" She tried to keep her voice steady. "I heard they don't let anyone in, no press, no cameras, no whites, no one but residents with papers to prove it."

Another low rumble from Johannes.

"Isn't it a war zone, Nelson, dammit?"

"You might say that," Nelson said, with a curl of his full lips. "But look."

He gestured behind him at a dark frosted window stretching above the top of the seat to the roof of the truck. She couldn't see through it. Nelson's elbow poked into her ribs as he reached up behind her neck, pulled a lever, and got it open.

"We'll get in there in a while." Now he was ebullient. "Johannes and I often go about like that, you wouldn't believe how much room there is in Levitt's cupboards or cabinets or whatever you call them. They never look, you can't even get in from the other end, it's so jammed with furniture."

"And Johannes?"

"What about him?"

"Can he just go in and out at will?"

"My pass shows I live there," Johannes hissed. "And I got the Levitt's driver's authority." He tapped his breast pocket. "But it's blacks get killed every day, blacks get cut and burned."

"Isn't this very dangerous?"

"Nelson's the boss," Johannes spat.

"Nelson," said Ruth loudly, "I don't want to do this. I want to talk to you. I don't want to go to Soweto with you. Please take me back."

Johannes's boot touched the brake, the truck slowed slightly.

"No," Nelson snapped. "Drive on, Johan. There's no time to take you back. We're late enough as it is."

"Then let me out, please. I'm not going to Soweto."

"No." Nelson folded his arms and stared darkly ahead. "I've got things to show you. Besides," he jerked his chin at the racing traffic on the highway, "you'd be stranded here. Drive on, Johan."

Ruth chewed her lower lip and clenched her hands together. Nelson was virtually kidnapping her. Her rage at him was swamped by fury that she had allowed herself to be trapped into a situation she couldn't control; she couldn't even walk away. She was fed up with Nelson, sick and tired of his defiance. She must get away from him, put an end to this futile effort. But, seething, she knew it was not so simple: if she abandoned Nelson, she'd be abandoning Bernard's chance of freedom also. She couldn't discuss Bernard now. She didn't want to talk to Nelson at all.

Johannes had circled Johannesburg's inner city while they argued. He drove now on a broad four-lane highway lined on either side with auto repair and body shops, tire stores, scrap metal markets, parts outlets, and dumping grounds for abandoned wrecks. He passed the turn to Western, the mixed-race township, and then the road to Sophiatown, with neat, uncluttered rows of boxy houses for poor whites. Once it had been Lizzie's territory. The land around was flat, littered by rubble, weed grass, broken bottles, crumpled cans. Traffic was heavy in both directions. It all looked unfamiliar, though not entirely strange, as if she'd somehow imagined this road or dreamed it long ago. The one truly familiar sensation was the blinding effect of the midafternoon summer sun burning against the windshield, white-gold light that made her eyes stream. She hunted for sunglasses in her bag.

They only helped a little. She'd always hated driving south in the afternoon, she'd been terrified of oncoming traffic, so brilliantly distorted that it seemed aimed at her.

After a while the traffic thinned, the drab roadside business was sparse, the debris diminished. Johannes accelerated straight into the sun.

"One stop before Soweto, Ruth," Nelson said gaily. "Remember Bara?"

Johannes slowed to make the left turn into the grounds of Baragwanath Hospital. The chief hospital for a huge population of blacks, it had always been large. But the armed guards at the gates were new, the inspection of Nelson's medical student ID was new. Sprawling low buildings on flat dusty ground spread farther out for miles around. It had once looked like an orderly compound spotting the veld; now it seemed like a military headquarters, uniforms and army vehicles everywhere, long lines of barracks hugging the ground, crude buildings of dull gray cement, sirens shaking the dusty air. Johannes pulled up in a red clay parking area behind what Ruth remembered were once doctors' quarters, ugly rooms lined up off long open verandahs surrounded by scrub. Public bathrooms for the young residents to share, accessible only from outside the structure.

"I'll be quick," Nelson said and jumped out of the truck, disappearing behind the squat slab of rooms.

Ruth shifted to take advantage of the extra space, peeling her thigh away from Johannes's. He grabbed her arm.

"Better stay here," he said gruffly.

"I'm not escaping, Johannes, just stretching."

"You can walk around in Orlando," he ventured.

"That's where we're going?"

He nodded once.

"Unless Nels got some new idea. That's where we s'posed to be."

"Were you away with him the last few days, Johannes?"

He looked directly at her for the first time.

"*Hai khona*," he said, the ubiquitous, derisive "No, no, you're mistaken." Two of his upper teeth were gone, the gap gave his smile a lopsided tilt. It was the first sign that he permitted his face any mobility. "I'm the driver," he said and tucked the smile away.

"Where did you grow up, Johannes?"

"I was born in Sophiatown," he said. "But they broke it down to put houses for poor whites, we had to leave. So, I'm a boy from Soweto."

"Is your family still in Soweto?"

"My mother's mother is there, with my sisters, also their children."

Ruth asked about his parents.

"My ma was here, but she needed work, she went to Vereeniging, near Springs, you know." He turned away. "My father died in the mine when I was *net* a baby, that's why I don't want to work in the mines."

"I hear they have unions now," she said awkwardly. "That's something, I suppose. They weren't allowed to organize when I lived here."

Johannes hooted. The gap in his upper jaw was huge.

"They got unions, and how. But if they try to make a strike, the army comes. Bang bang. They frightened to work, if the *tsotsis* see them they going cut them, if they don't work the army going shoot or maybe send them to Botswana or another place and they can't get money. So it's no good."

Ruth was finding it difficult to keep up her end of this conversation. Whatever she thought of saying threatened a painful dead end.

"Are you married?" she tried.

"What for?"

She swallowed. What the hell was Nelson doing? One last try with Johannes.

"Were you in Soweto in 'seventy-six, Johannes? For the uprising?"

Like hot corn popping in a buttered skillet, he burst lively from his slow sullen shell.

"I was there. I was there, you know. I was in school then, on the students' council in Moroka. I was angry when the blerry government started with us, we must learn in Afrikaans, not Soweto or Xhosa, not even English. And they wanted we must learn woodwork in science class. But we must prepare ourselves and educate ourselves, so we made big trouble in Soweto. We burned many places, all the office buildings and some shops, many beer halls, we smashed things up. Just us, the children. Our parents was frightened of trouble but we finished with that. It was the time of Steve Biko, you know. We made boycotts in all the schools, twenty-eight separate townships in Soweto, we closed down the schools and ran in the streets." He stopped, but only to take a deep breath. "I was here. In Baragwanath. From here I was in jail. The cops took me from here, from the bed."

"You were wounded, Johannes?"

"Bird shot, is nothing." He pulled his khaki overalls away from his neck and shoulder to show her the old pitted scars. "They took it out, nearly all. Is nothing. My friend died."

"I'm sorry. What happened? Who was he?"

"He was Khulu. They killed him here." He put his hand at the base of his neck, pressing·fingers into flesh to show the exact location of Khulu's wound. "We was out pushing boycott papers under doors, after curfew we not s'posed to be in the street. So two came in a van, shooting. When Khulu fell down they drove away."

"Terrible. Awful." She shivered.

"For his funeral, they had to bring the army. They must. After, some of my friends went away, Botswana, Maputo, Zambia sometimes, but I'm staying here."

"Is it the same now in Soweto? Like it was in the children's revolt?"

"Much more dangerous now. More army, more cops everywhere. People are very angry, no more only the children. We used to plan, we tried many things, we ask for our rights. Our rights. But now they too angry to make good plans. *Tsotsis* in every corner. Wild gangs running with knives now. The people are angry and *vreeslik*. You know *vreeslik?*"

"Terrible, yes." Ruth had forgotten the odd insertion of Afrikaans phrases in daily lingo. Everyone did it, black, white, pink, mocha, every shade between.

"Very bad now in Soweto." Johannes produced his unbalanced smile with evident pride. "We make life impossible there, the next thing we make it impossible in white places. All impossible."

Nelson appeared from behind the cement building in time to spare Ruth from finding an acceptable response. While it was a relief to penetrate Johannes's hostility with a subject he enjoyed discussing, everything he said about Soweto confirmed the frenzied, flaming horror she'd been watching on American television for years until they banned television cameras from the townships. Now a foreign journalist could go to jail for ten years for filming Soweto. Here was Nelson, forcing her into Soweto, climbing into the truck next to her, armed with a bulky brown canvas carryall and a huge olive drab duffel bag, which he slung onto the floor in front of them. He had changed his clothes, discarding the blue jeans, T-shirt, and sneaks for a khaki shirt and pants and heavy boots. He had a stethoscope around his neck and his pockets bulged. If he thought he was disguised to look like a genuine Sowetan, he was making another stupid mistake.

"What's in these bags, Nelson?"

He shrugged.

"Deliveries. Let's go, man."

"Wait, Johannes. Wait. Nelson, I can't go with you. You don't understand my . . . past. If I get picked up . . . wait, Johannes!"

But he threw the gear, accelerated and turned toward the main gate.

"There's no danger, Ruth." Nelson was very tense. "It's quiet there now. I have to get this stuff in."

"Nelson. Let me out of this damned furniture truck. Right now."

"I can't." He waved his arms vaguely in the direction of the highway along which Johannes now picked up speed. "It's dangerous out there for you."

"Then take me back. You must."

"There's someone there who has to have antibiotics right now. You want him to die? I'm taking the stuff and you're going to see what has to be done here and that's that, so shut up, will you?"

She pushed her fist into her mouth, biting hard on a knuckle.

"What did you say?" Johannes asked.

"It's Simon. He's hit. I found a message in the pharmacy. I had to decode it, that's why I took so long."

Johannes whistled and accelerated.

"What happen?"

"I don't know. That's the message, they need shots for him fast. Go straight there."

"What about the kids?"

"We'll go after. Change the order, that's all, we'll do the kids, don't worry. Simon's bad."

"Where's Vicki then?"

"No one seems to know. They can't find her."

The truck leapt down the road. Cars ahead changed lanes to avoid it as it menaced their bumpers. Johannes's face regained its former sullen glare, with an added intensity that Ruth thought might be panic.

"Who's Simon?"

Neither of them answered. She felt their tension through the shoulders pressing against her on either side, she saw it in the faces staring darkly forward, blinking against the angles of fierce light smashing against the windshield.

"What's Vicki got to do with this?"

226

Silence.

"Nelson, what's Vicki got to do with this?"

"We cover for each other in emergencies. I've been away, I told you. She should have taken stuff out for Simon hours ago. The message was there since early this morning, when they found him."

"Where?" Johannes and Ruth said simultaneously.

"Behind the privy on the street near Mandiba's house. The Special Branch was cruising. They left him for dead."

"Didn't Mandiba hear anything?"

Nelson shrugged.

"Nelson," Ruth said, shifting her shoulders, sitting very straight, "where were you the last few days?"

"Lusaka." He didn't take his eyes from the road.

Ruth dug her fingernails into her palms. When he did answer her questions, the information was so alarming she was sorry she'd asked.

The sun wasn't bothering her anymore because the sky ahead hung behind a screen of brownish smoke, growing denser with each mile. The highway cut through a ring of low hills. Behind the hills, Soweto stretched away, drab and interminable on barren land. As they drew nearer to the gray-brown sprawl, Ruth's throat burned from the chalky smoke, hovering heavy from tens of thousands of coal-burning stoves. Soweto was less than thirteen miles from Johannesburg, but only a few scattered pockets in the huge two-million-strong satellite had electricity.

Ruth read the sign "Administered by the West Rand Development Board" some distance ahead as Johannes suddenly swerved off the highway into the brush, coming to a bumpy halt.

"Goddam, Nels, we nearly forget. We can't go in like this."

Nelson swore.

"I was thinking about Simon. You're right."

He swung his right arm up above Ruth's head and jerked the lever to open the long window behind the seat. His elbow dug into her neck.

"Climb over, Ruth. Hurry."

She scrambled awkwardly through the opening. There wasn't much space on the other side. It was too dark to see clearly but the truck seemed to be full of furniture piled up high, bureaus backed onto closets, desks on top of tables. Nelson banged into her as he climbed over. He pulled her hand off the ledge just before Johannes slammed the window back down.

"It's too bad," Ruth said. "Once I'm forced to go I'd have liked to see."

"You can see a bit through here. Try. No one can see in, though, we've tested it."

She peered through the dark textured glass. Johannes was slowing to make a turn.

"Not now, Ruth. That's asking for it. He has to show his pass and driver's authority to the army, get down."

Huddled in a crouch on the floor of the truck, Ruth was swept by a sensation of unreality. It wasn't possible, it couldn't be happening, what in hell was she doing in Soweto, surrounded by armored personnel carriers, patrolled by machine-gun-toting security forces, accompanied by two desperate irresponsible young men so brutalized by life they'd already learned to hold it cheap? She couldn't believe it was happening to her, she didn't belong here, her life was back in Philadelphia, orderly, controlled. Open. Well, not exactly open, she supposed. Trying to bury the ugly secrets of her South African past had left anxious scars barely hidden under her disciplined surface. She knew that now. What would she have been like if she'd never been in solitary confinement, never . . . ? She cut the question off nearly as sharply as she'd been doing since she left Bernard behind long ago. She was here to pay a debt, she would get through this crazy trip to Soweto somehow, deal with Nelson straight afterward and get away. Forcing her into Soweto with him like this only hardened her determination to make him leave the country with her. She was going to pull out everything she could. And there was quite a bit.

"Look now," Nelson whispered suddenly.

Ruth peered through the pebbled darkened glass. The afternoon light lay upon the chalky air. A dozen helmeted, rifle-carrying soldiers, escorting three attack dogs, patrolled the pitted asphalt road. When Johannes turned, the street disappeared into a narrow mud track. He drove slowly. The road was alive with children, women clustered together, old men leaning on fences or ambling down the long block, boys sauntering, bouncing tough and street-smart with thumbs in the waistbands of their tight jeans. On either side, rows of identical cement-block huts squatted miserably. Cans and big plastic bottles stood at every door.

"They use them to get their water at the nearest public faucet," Nelson explained. "Also, they keep water available so people can splash their eyes if they've been gassed."

"No streetlights," Ruth murmured.

"There are in a few streets, but they've been smashed. It's not all like this, you'll see."

After another two laborious turns onto mud roads dotted with people, they passed a row of stores surrounding an open market. Vendors hung about carts jumbled with fruit and vegetables, bickering with hagglers. Ruth couldn't identify the produce through the glass but there was no mistaking the burned-out shell that had been a store, the boards tacked across windows lower down the road, the rubble piled about what had been a service station. One pump stood disconsolately in its center. Half a wall remained, a slogan she couldn't read painted on its side.

They drove past burned-out houses and ransacked stores, a security patrol with black and white police walking separately, looking left and right over dark yellowish dirt, more mud tracks weaving among shacks with corrugated-iron roofs, split wood walls patched with wads of paper and scraps of cloth, barefoot children with running noses jumping rope.

"We're nearly there," Nelson said. "We've got to get out of here fast, and get inside. Johannes will pick us up later."

"Where's he going?"

"To the shopping center in Dube. To dump some furniture. He can't park the truck outside Mandiba's house."

Johannes stopped in the middle of a congested road, next to a mound of garbage in which a yellow dog, the ridges of his spine knotted bumpily along his back, sniffed urgently. Nelson climbed out. "Half an hour, no more," Johannes said as Ruth inched through the window. The truck was moving as she slammed the heavy door and ran after Nelson past a wire fence surrounding a cement house. Several men hanging about the yellow clay at the side looked at them speculatively. But Nelson, clutching the brown carryall tight against his chest, ignored them and made straight for the door. It swung open as he approached. He ran inside. Ruth followed.

"Where've you been?" demanded a small bald man with a gnarled face and a rasping voice. "Who's this?" He kicked the door shut. The front room was crowded with several men. A woman who'd been polishing the floor clambered up. Red floor polish stained round patches on her knees. The late afternoon light slanting through a small barred window raised a glow.

"She's a friend, it's all right," Nelson said quickly. "How's Simon?"

"Bad, what you think? We've been waiting all day."

"I was away, Mandiba. I came as soon as I knew."

"Where's Vicki Naidoo, man?"

"I don't know. Let me see Simon."

"What about her?"

"Could she wait with you, Bella?" said Nelson and disappeared with the bald man. Five men and Bella watched Ruth blankly.

Ruth smiled at the woman, gestured at her knees.

"I'm sorry to bother you," she said. "Please don't stop what you're doing."

"No," said Bella, rubbing at her knee with the rag she'd been using on the floor. "You'll drink tea?"

There was a murmur from the men.

"Not you peoples. Come with me," she instructed Ruth and led her into the kitchen. Two pots steamed on the coal stove. Small and buxom, she peered into them, moved one to a crumbling ledge and dumped a tin of water neatly in its place. The spicy sweet smell of pumpkin stroked the air. The other pot held cornmeal.

"Please sit," said Bella.

"I don't want to be a nuisance."

"No. Friend of Nels. Sit."

Ruth sat. The table was covered by a spotless green plastic cloth. Gauze bandages were heaped in its center.

"What happened to Simon?" she asked.

"The SBs shot him. We took out three bullets."

"How do you know it was the Special Branch?"

Inquisitive glints darted from Bella's walnut eyes.

"By the bullets." She shifted the can of water on the stove.

"Why did they shoot him?"

"Are you reporter?"

"No, no. I'm just asking."

"There was trouble in the afternoon and night yesterday. Some gangs of boys were fighting here in the street, throwing rocks and bottles. They were everywhere around in the alley and the yards. The cops came, they sprayed water and a little gas, to chase them. But must be they waited somewhere out there to catch Simon when he was leaving."

"But why . . ."

Bella shrugged sedately.

"You know Simon."

Ruth did not know Simon but didn't think she should say so.

"They hate him. From that time they let him out of solitary and then he gave evidence about the helicopter torture in Muti's trial. From that time."

She put a steaming aluminum cup of strong tea in front of Ruth, who sipped it gratefully. Bella did not sit down. While she stirred her simmering pot, Ruth looked about. A nurse's cap and cloak hung on a hook near the sink.

Nelson appeared suddenly.

"Come with me, Ruth."

He led her back through the knot of murmuring men in front to a windowless room in the back of the house. A gas lamp glimmered feebly on a packing crate. Several mattresses lay about. An unconscious man sprawled on his back on one of them, his heavy breathing shifting the bandages on his neck and abdomen. The little man who'd let them in fussed over the mattress. The gnarled lines on his bald scalp were as rutted as those on his face.

"I've given him intravenous penicillin," Nelson murmured.

"Will he be all right?" Ruth asked.

"I don't know . . . he isn't . . ." Ruth had never heard Nelson sound uncertain. "Mandiba . . . ," he said tentatively.

The bald man, kneeling on the floor next to Simon's mattress, ignored him.

"Mr. Mandiba, you've got to get him to hospital, I don't think all the bullets are out."

Agile as a gymnast, Mandiba bounced to his feet, hands on his fleshless hips.

"Forget about that," he rasped. "You make me tired. If I put him there in Moroka Hospital or even Bara, he's a dead man. They'll take him back to jail. He'll be finished."

"But the bullets . . ."

"Bella took out the bullets. She's got experience."

"The boy's right, Mandiba."

Ruth hadn't noticed that Bella had followed them. She stood in the doorway, the nurse's cap perched pertly on her head.

"The wounds are very bad," she said with assurance. "He might die here, Mandiba. I'm coming with you to the hospital in my uniform. You must get Rathebe's big car."

"They'll get him, Bella."

"While we talking all day, he's going to die here," she announced firmly. "I told you before, now Nels say the same thing. Tell Rathebe to bring his car."

Mandiba wiped his scalp with the palms of both hands. Nelson jerked his head up at a rumbling sound.

"That's Johan. We've got to go."

The ruts on Mandiba's face cracked into deep ridges as he jeered, "Just in time."

"Don't you be a fool, Mandiba, Nels can't take Simon, you crazy or what? Get Rathebe's car, I tell you. Go, Nels." She nodded at Ruth and tugged her arm. "Go on, go straight now, Nels."

"I hope he'll be all right." Nelson stared miserably at Simon.

"Get out of here," said Bella. "You too, Mandiba."

Ruth heard a bubbling sound from the injured man as she ran out after Nelson, eyed by the men in the front room, the gathering at the side, and clusters of children hanging about the Levitt's truck in the road.

"Be quick," Johannes hissed as she scrambled into the front and started climbing through the frosted window. "We're very late." He waited until he'd inched the truck between the curious children and around a corner, slowed by all the people hanging about, made another turn and onto a paved road less heavily populated, before he asked, "How's Simon?"

"Very bad," Nelson said glumly. "I left the morphine supply and the antibiotics with Mandiba for the cell, but Simon . . . I told Mandiba to take him to hospital."

"They'll get him, *domkop*."

"I'm afraid he'll die otherwise," Nelson shouted. "Bella agrees."

Johannes was silent. Nelson wiped his eyes with the sleeve of his khaki shirt.

"Who is Simon?" Ruth asked.

"He's one of the best," said Nelson. "He's the bravest man I know. Absolutely dependable and very well trained. His father's in exile. I just saw him in Lusaka." He sniffed and wiped his eyes again. "Bella knew Dad, by the way. Or at least, she heard him speak. Mandiba too."

Ruth was jolted from her concern for Simon, her terror of being discovered illegally in Soweto, her rage at Nelson's insistence on doing everything his own disorderly way, to a memory of Bernard, standing tall on top of a car, his narrow dark head sharply outlined against a clear sky, urging nonviolence on thousands of people stirring with slow frustration.

Bernard had known it would come to this, sniper's bullets in an alley behind the privy, rocks and bottles to attack armored personnel carriers, starving skeletal dogs to slow the police veterans, the stumbling desperate accumulation of dynamite and petrol to fabricate homemade bombs in answer to tear gas and bird shot and machine-gun fire. He'd known long ago and paid for the prophecy for more than twenty years. She had to penetrate Nelson's despair and make him see that Bernard had paid enough.

"Nelson, I have to talk to you."

"Talk." He settled back against a cabinet, legs drawn up to his chest, arms around them. It was too dark to see his face clearly. Ruth, who had been kneeling at the frosted window, trying to peer out, scrambled down next to him, legs crossed, feet tucked awkwardly beneath her.

"How did you get to Lusaka?" she said, without intending it.

"By car, of course."

"Why were you there?"

"Orders." He sounded limp.

"What were they?"

As if Simon's wounds had drained the defiance out of him, he answered instead of ignoring her.

"They're getting ready for a big push. With occupation armies in the townships, the government's spread pretty thin. Especially now that more people refuse to serve. They think they've got the government's back to the wall. They want to push hard into the cities and have a go at the white suburbs. They've made plans for specific targets and orders are going out."

"Where do you fit in?"

"New lines of supplies. We're going to need much more if these new strikes come off. They've found new sources for me and new supply routes. They need me more than before. You've just seen what I do."

"You say yourself that Simon needs a hospital."

"Besides that. I left a lot of medications for Mandiba's group. Someone has to get it and deliver it. They need me. I wanted you to see for yourself."

He was too self-absorbed and dejected to have intended it, but Ruth heard the unspoken *You left them, you ran away.* Deserter's guilt overtook her like prickly heat. For years she'd writhed to avoid legitimizing the angry contempt of the countrymen she'd left behind. She'd chosen to go, she'd stayed away, although she'd never believed, with Gerald and his kind, that it wasn't her battle. She knew it was. They were all right to condemn her, their harsh judgment was fair. She couldn't buy back the years of her desertion, but there was one service she could render to Bernard. And to the struggle.

"Nelson, more than your safety is at stake here," she began. "The Security Branch wants to make a deal."

"You've talked to them?" He half stood, half crouched above her in the confining space. She pushed him down again.

"No, of course not. Don't be silly. But Gerald . . ."

"Huh!" Nelson sneered.

"No, just listen. Gerald . . ." She stopped because she felt the truck slowing. Nelson lifted himself up to peer through the dark glass.

"We're here," he said. "Follow me and be quick."

He hefted the huge olive drab duffel bag and climbed down. He and Johannes were halfway along the block before she was out of the truck. They were in some sort of shopping center, the truck parked acceptably in front of a furniture store. Ruth ran past a post office and a bank branch, a clothing store and a grocery plastered with joyful posters of young healthy blacks drinking

235

Coca-Cola on a beach, ignoring all the people on the narrow pavement who stared at her white skin. It took her until a block and a half beyond the stores to catch up with Nelson and Johannes. They were standing on the front step of a slightly larger house than Mandiba's. It had a dark red roof. A light came on in the front room. The door opened to a high-pitched din, wails and cries of small children with strong wills. The woman at the door pinched Johannes's cheek and shook hands with Nelson as Ruth ran up to join them.

"This is Queenie, Ruth. Johan's sister."

Queenie's laughing eyes and broad smile disguised any family resemblance. She waved her hand at the room behind her, jammed with children in varying stages of undress, all protesting.

"I'm sorry about the noise," she yelled. "It's time to wash and they don't want to."

There were at least twenty children in the room, all two or three years old. A basin of soapy water and several washcloths were the center of attention. Two gleaming little girls sat in the basin, flicking water at the others, who were engaged in gang warfare for possession of the washcloths.

"I can't talk now," Queenie screamed. "I've got to clean them up. Go in the back, Sindi's there, she'll unload."

Nelson edged himself and his duffel bag through the hordes of jumping, screaming children, Ruth on his heels. She turned at the doorway to the kitchen and saw Johannes sitting on the floor, a baby on each knee and two in his arms.

"Sindi, this is Ruth. Another sister. We've got to get out of here, help me unload."

Sindi was much younger than Johannes and Queenie, a slight, pretty teenager with a shy smile. She helped them unload unmarked sealed boxes from the duffel bag, hundreds of them, all identical.

"What's all this?" Ruth asked. She carried armfuls of small boxes over to a carton waiting in the corner.

"Protein supplements. Queenie and Sindi run a kwashiorkor clinic."

"Those kids don't have kwashiorkor," Ruth protested, looking through the doorway at bright eyes and white teeth, shining skin and flat tummies, falling all over Johannes for a hug and kiss.

"These are the lucky ones," Sindi said quietly. "That's our preschool class, their mothers are working and can pay to put them with us. The clinic is for the sick ones, we go to them at night."

She reached up to the top of the refrigerator, produced another duffel bag, folded it with the one they had just emptied.

"Next week bring both back full," she told Nelson. "More people have heard about it now, they keep asking and we don't have enough for all the kids. Not nearly enough."

"We better get out before it's dark," Nelson said urgently. Johannes stood at the window in the front room, where the children tumbled about.

"Not now," he said. "We must wait."

Ruth peered over his shoulder. Four policemen strode down the block, all business. Six more followed a few paces behind. A whirring hum throbbed, growing louder as an army helicopter flew low over the road. Someone inside it waved at the police on the ground, then made a right-turn sign with an outstretched arm.

"Trouble. Looking for trouble," growled Johannes.

Cold fingers tapped the back of Ruth's neck, crept icy down her spine, lodged in her calves. She clenched her jaws together, blinking rapidly. Arms wrapped tight around her body, she dug fingertips between her ribs. She heard footsteps coming closer on hard cement, she heard the clang of a heavy steel door, she heard muted thuds, raw scrapes, a muffled sob, a cough. Blinking didn't shut out the gray cement walls with messages scratched jagged across them, the rough gray blanket on the iron cot, the five black funneled bars on the high window. Blinking didn't block them out, so she closed her eyes. A hand on her shoulder, a quick shake.

"All clear, let's go," Johannes said.

Ruth opened her eyes, shook the dizziness from her head and followed them out.

The light was fading, yielding to gritty chalk. Thick gray haze clung to the road, the shuttered stores, the loitering stragglers taking notice as Ruth hurled herself back into the truck and through the window to the back. There was a little more space to spread out in now that Johannes had delivered a few bulky pieces. Looking behind, she could make out the handle jutting from the metal doors far away at the other end. The truck lurched suddenly forward and Nelson fell into the back next to her. A heavy boot poked her stomach as he jiggled himself down in the swaying truck.

"Lots of kids, huh? You should see the ones we took the protein for, they don't exactly laugh and jump about."

Ruth felt hollow inside. She still trembled from her moment of terrified memory at the window. She understood that she was supposed to applaud Nelson's provisions for malnourished children but her mind and body were fiercely concentrated on getting out of Soweto. Head thrust forward, he glared at her in the near dark. She gathered enough control to respond.

"Where do you get the supplies?"

"Buy them. I've worked a special arrangement with two or three pharmacies. It's imported, highly concentrated."

"It must be very expensive. How do you raise the cash?"

Nelson settled back cozily. This was the question he'd been wanting to answer.

"Two ways, mainly. The students' council collects . . . er . . . donations and gives me a share for the kwashiorkor kids."

"Isn't the council banned?"

"Yes. So?"

Ruth sighed. Nelson was exasperating. The truck shuddered

alarmingly. This road seemed rougher than any of the others.

"And donations, you say? Come on , Nelson. People here give money?"

"Some do. Honestly. And the students slap levies on others. They make the Putco drivers give, otherwise they stone them. The beer hall managers donate to buy time against fires. You know."

"I know." Reluctantly she asked, "What's the other source?"

"Derek Brand." Nelson laughed gleefully.

"Derek Brand? I can't believe he . . ."

"He doesn't know, of course, but he's contributed enormous sums to keep these kids alive."

"How do you get the money from him?"

"Any way I can. I live in the same countinghouse he does, I take what I find. I'm awfully good at it. I think of it as taxes," he gloated.

Ruth pressed fingertips to her distracted temples. They were on their way out of Soweto at last. She had to summon enough coherence to talk to Nelson about Bernard. She'd waited for this moment, endured Soweto for this chance. She had to grab the time of the long ride back. Trying to concentrate, she ignored Nelson when he scrambled to his knees to peer out of the dark window.

There was a loud thud somewhere in front of her. Then another. A screeching crack against the side of the truck behind her threw her against the back of the front seat. Nelson tapped on the window. The truck moved slowly forward. Ruth saw the outline of Johannes's head ducking and lifting, ducking, lifting again.

"Nelson? What is it?"

"They're throwing rocks at us, I think. Open, Johan."

But Johannes didn't turn. He sank lower behind the wheel, head ducking and lifting. The truck picked up speed. Clanging knocks hit both sides of the truck, along its length.

Ruth strained to see through the window. The light had drained from the sky. In the gathering dark, the truck's headlights cast pale circles, picking out holes and ruts on the dirt road. A huge rock thumped the driver's door, crunching metal. The truck shook convulsively. Ruth saw tall shapes jerking around the headlights, eight or ten on both sides of the heaving hood.

Slowed by the jumping figures, the truck crept slowly, shakily forward. Spatters of stones smashed against the sides. Rocks cracked metal.

"Shit! He can't get through, there must be dozens of them," Nelson panted. "Open, Johannes."

Nelson slammed his fists against the window. He jerked back screaming. A rock hurled through the windshield smashed a jagged hole in the glass in front of them. Hands over her face, Ruth ducked. Shards and bubbles of frosted glass hit her hands and hair.

Johannes accelerated suddenly, driving between the jumping black shapes. Ruth could hear shouts now, rage and hatred screeched above the banging. A tall gaunt young man hanging onto the passenger door hurled himself heavily onto the hood of the truck in front of Johannes, near the gaping hole in the windshield.

Ruth and Nelson huddled close to the floor. This furious mob was inflamed enough without the poison of white skin.

"Scum," the man on the hood screamed. "Filthy stooge! You drive for blerry whitey."

He reached an arm through the window, as Johannes, head bent, slammed his foot on the gas. Two thin streams of blood trickled down from his face to the side of his neck. The truck hurtled ahead.

There was an explosive roar, the acrid stench of burning rubber, broad shafts of smoke. Another explosion. The truck heaved, rattled. And halted.

"What . . . ?"

"They blew out the front tires. We've got to get out."

Johannes roared. Twisting in the front seat, his face drenched, slick, he tried to lever the remains of the window open. Glass clattered. Both doors ripped open. Chanting men jumped onto the front seat. On the road, hammering feet, raised arms wielding sticks and bottles, jeering cries of "Pig," "Fink," "Traitor."

They tore Johannes, screaming, out the passenger door. Fierce chanting thundered. Nelson lifted himself up, apparently trying to get to Johannes. Ruth grabbed his belt from behind, pulled him back down, struggling against the jerking of his lean body.

"You can't help him now. Look."

Twenty men or more surrounded Johannes. They pushed and kicked him over to the side of the road, chanting, jeering, cursing. There were no houses in sight, no flicker of life on the deserted road and veld. Johannes held his hands up near his face, palms out, as if he could push the men away. They clustered around and for an instant Ruth lost sight of him.

There was a roaring chorus, heady anticipation. They formed a crude circle, stepped back. Johannes threw himself on the ground, sobbing, banging his head on the unyielding earth. Two men stepped forward, bent down and pulled him up from behind. A third threw a tire over his head to ring his shoulders. From the circle of men, taunting laughter showed teeth like stripped bone in the dark. Johannes shrieked, high, piercing, hideous, again and again.

Johannes's knees buckled, he stumbled, pulled himself upright. He pressed his hands over his face as the chanting dropped to a menacing murmur. Quick snaky movement, the silver flash of a can, a stream of liquid. The tiny light of twenty matches struck in unison. Johannes screamed raw and high above the rhythmic chanting, heaving up to a huge growl. Flames burst suddenly from the tire. Johannes's head wrapped in fire, thin screams high, fading. Flames licking, spurting over his body. He crumbled in fire in the center of the crazed circle.

Blood trickled from Ruth's lower lip where she had bitten it, fighting nausea, swallowing horror. Ice cold, she pressed herself against the back of the seat, shaking, teeth chattering.

"How could they . . ." Nelson gagged. He clutched his throat. "They'll come back here as soon as he's . . . ," he sobbed. His shoulders heaved. He crouched helpless beside her. "They'll come and loot the truck and burn it."

They'd be seen if they tried to climb through the smashed window. Burning Johannes alive would be a snack before dinner for the beasts out there. Ruth looked back down the length of the truck. It was their only chance. No time to waste before the end of the celebration over the scorched stump that had been Johannes. Odors of petrol, burnt rubber, smoldering flesh devoured the air, billowed into the truck.

"We're going out the back."

She bent over Nelson, shaking him.

"We've got a chance, come on. Go first."

She dragged him to a crouch, pushed him in front of her under desks, between bureaus, shoving at the heavy furniture to make a path, climbing over tables, smashing into cabinets in total dark, urged forward by the raucous triumph beyond, shifting bulky structures an inch here, a gap there, until Nelson stumbled gasping against the closed steel doors. Ruth fell against his back.

"Open the door. Jump out. Now."

He pressed his body against the door. He didn't move.

"Nelson, open it. Go. Hurry."

"They might be out there."

"It's our only chance."

"I can't, they might be waiting." He clung to the metal.

Ruth clenched her arms around him from behind and tugged him slightly to one side.

"No, don't."

"Follow me."

She lifted her eyes for a second from the door handle. She reached up and quickly kissed the cheek of Bernard's son. Then she lowered the metal handle, opened the door a terrifying inch. Only darkness beyond. Lowered the handle to expose a larger aperture. And jumped.

She heard Nelson behind her as she raced, hidden by the long body of the truck, to the other side of the road. The mob roared wild in the poisoned air.

Across the road, there was only bare, flat scrub. Ruth ran, bending low, back the way they'd come, raced desperately until she saw tin cans shining against moldy debris in a high mound of garbage. She flung herself breathlessly down on the ground behind it, flat on her stomach, chin lifted to peer around at the gyrating mob stamping around the flaming fire.

Nelson gasped for breath. He lay curled up behind her, arms hugged around him, knees drawn up close, cheek pressed hard against the rotten ground. She heard a choking gurgle, jerked to look as he vomited. Hand on his shoulder, she peeped around to see the flames sink lower, the vicious dancing feet beat harder. Nelson retched again and again. His head dropped back to the ground.

"Nelson," she leaned close to him to whisper. "We've got to keep quiet and still. They're going back to the truck, don't move."

"Johannes . . . ," he began.

"Hush."

Head on the foul ground, laced rigid with terror, she heard metal shriek. Shouts and heavy thuds as furniture was torn from the van, hurled to the ground. Running feet. Hoarse commands. She lifted her head an inch, looked around the side of the garbage heap. A dozen or more men were lined up along the truck, backs toward Ruth and Nelson. Others lumbered farther up the road, hauling furniture on their backs. The man in front of the truck bellowed a command, they heaved, they forced their weight against it in unison and flung it on its side.

The tumultuous crash rocked the veld. Ruth leaned close to Nelson's ear to whisper.

"I think they're going to burn it. There'll be a huge blaze, one of those damned helicopters will spot it and we'll be caught between the army and these maniacs. We've got to get away while they're busy."

Nelson pressed closer to the ground.

"Nelson, we've got to get away."

"Where?"

"Don't you know anyone near here?"

He gagged and whimpered.

"Nelson, think. You must know someone who'll hide us for a while. Think." She shook him. The din from the road beyond enclosed them.

"I don't know how to find the way."

"We have to go the way we came. That's the only chance they won't see us."

"I can only think of Mandiba."

"Can you find the way?"

He didn't answer.

"Nelson. We can't stay here another minute. I'm going to crouch down and run back across there. Follow me. When we're out of sight we'll work out how to get to Mandiba."

She waited only long enough to feel his body shift. Then she hurled herself across the dry scrub, bending low, racing away. Angry shouts seemed to penetrate her back, she couldn't tell if they had seen her, she kept running, Nelson panting behind her, until the sounds grew fainter. The outline of a clump of bushes farther on drew her forward, kept her charging until she fell on the ground behind them. Nelson crouched beside her, looking back toward the truck. As he watched, a huge explosion smashed the night, the truck burst into flames, the men around it dancing feverishly, roaring. Nelson looked the other way and saw headlights.

"I think I know where we are," he said. "I know the road that car's on. Let's go that way."

"Can we get to Mandiba?" Ruth breathed heavily.

"We'll try. Are you ready?"

The flames behind them scorched spirals against the sky, but before they reached the road, the fevered noise subsided. At the edge of the road, lined with shacks, Ruth turned back and saw only flat ground and darkness beyond, heard only the creak of a twig under her foot, the hum of a car farther down the road, the catch of Nelson's breath, the hammering of her pulses.

"It's not far to Mandiba." Nelson peered about, rubbing his hands on his hips, shifting his shoulders up and down.

"I'm afraid of the road. There might be a patrol. Or if people see us . . ." She didn't finish the thought. White skin was the unmistakable badge of the mortal enemy here. "Can we go behind the houses?"

"We'll go through the alleys," he said, "but we'll have to watch out, there's people around."

Nelson led Ruth on a stealthy path around the backs of shanties, down twisted alleys, across bare yards, detouring to avoid open front doors, people walking to visit neighbors, a boy carrying a bicycle inside. Her foot banged into a large can in an alley, it rolled clattering away. They dropped to their knees, shaking with fright. A cat with a thin swishing tail and glass-green eyes rubbed whining against Nelson's leg; two women taking washing off a line called greetings as they rushed out of sight behind the next house; a dog barked far away; a man stood in his open doorway watching them dive and dip between huts, pressing against walls; a child cried out shrill through a window above Ruth's head as she leaned against boards. She leapt mindlessly after Nelson, goaded forward toward a hiding place, every particle of her being riveted on finding safety. For the hundredth time Nelson stumbled, pressed against a building, paused to look around. Then he pointed ahead. "That's Mandiba's house," he whispered. "Let's go." Ruth gathered her last remnants of energy into hurtling straight down the road, across it, and around a corner to the back of Mandiba's dark box. Several voices threaded by the sound of sobs came through the thin wall. Nelson looked at her questioningly. "We've got no choice," she shrugged, and tapped on the window.

Mandiba's bald, rutted head was briefly outlined in the light from the gas lamp behind him. Then he opened the door.

"Johannes was murdered," Nelson cried and pushed Ruth inside the crowded kitchen.

CHAPTER NINE

Grim faces stared intently. While
Nelson told them in jerky bursts what had happened to Johannes,
Ruth slumped down on the floor, leaning against the powdery
wall, breathing raggedly, battered by raw scrapes and bangs all
over her body. Nelson covered his face with his hands; his shoulders shook with sobs after he told them how he and Ruth had
escaped from the mob. There was murmuring, teeth clicking,
solemn outrage, but Ruth was too overwhelmed to attend to the
people in the room. Overtaken by the horror of Johannes's death,
the residue of nerve-destroying fear, exhaustion, cuts, bruises,
filth all over her, she sagged wearily on the floor until Bella bent
over her.

"Let me help you up," she said kindly. "I put water to boil,
I'll help you wash, you'll drink tea." Arm around Ruth's shoulder,
she nudged her to her feet and over to a chair, on which another
woman had been sitting, weeping, when they came in.

"This is Mary," Bella put her hand on the other woman's arm.
"Simon's big sister."

"You was lucky to find us all here," Mary told Ruth and began
to weep again.

"Sit, sit," Bella instructed a bewildered Ruth.

"What's wrong with Mary?" Nelson asked sharply.

Mandiba, four other men, Mary and Ruth all looked at Bella.

"There's two tragedies here tonight," Bella said softly. "Simon died while we carried him in to Bara."

Nelson cried out, swayed and fell, caught by Mandiba and another man just before he hit the floor.

"Take Nels to the back, Mandiba," Bella instructed. "Take off those dirty clothes and cover him, I'm bringing soap and water. And tea. He must rest, go and put him down."

Half-stumbling, half-carried, Nelson left the kitchen.

"I'm so sorry about Simon," Ruth said.

"Terrible night here," Bella agreed and busied Mary with preparations for tea and basins of water for washing.

Ruth, from whom all energy, thought, and emotion had drained, leaned against the wall behind her chair, holding a mug of strong sweet tea. She felt the quiet as a soothing blanket, the clinks of mugs and sounds of water faint reminders of life around her. She sipped tea, then closed her eyes and rested blankly until Mandiba returned.

"I've cleaned the boy," he told Bella. "He threw up the tea, we had to start again. I've sent the others away now, too many people looks like trouble. We don't want the cops."

"It's true," Bella declared roundly.

"The boy is crying now, he can't stop," Mandiba announced in a tone that made Ruth open her eyes and straighten herself. "I told him about the doctor."

Bella sighed and shrugged.

"What doctor?" Ruth asked.

"He's talking about Vicki Naidoo," Bella said. "You know her?"

"Yes."

"She's in John Vorster Square," Bella said. "They took her last night. That's why we couldn't reach her today for Simon's wounds."

"Vicki's been arrested?" Ruth said faintly, bending at the waist against tearing cramps knifing through her stomach.

"We heard this when we took Simon to Baragwanath," Mandiba explained. "She's there more than a day and a night already, the Indian doctor."

"But . . . why did they . . . what charge?"

"No charge," said Bella, as Mandiba emitted a harsh laugh. "No charge. They holding her with the security laws, no one can see her, no lawyer, no one. They going make her talk."

In a daze, Ruth felt them lift her and carry her to the back bedroom, deposit her on a mattress, draw a cover over her. It was too dark to see much, but she heard Nelson sniff nearby.

"You better rest now," Bella murmured next to her ear. "Mandiba and me, we make a plan for the morning. You sleep."

She tried to thank them, she tried to explain that she couldn't sleep, she tried to get up and go to Nelson, weeping nearby, but her hold on herself slipped away, her mind submitted somehow.

Later, waking in dark silence, her first image behind a blue haze under her eyelids was Bernard, Bernard smiling in sunshine at the edge of a calm ocean, rippling blue, gold-streaked, his white hair curled close to his head against dark silky skin. Eyes closed, she clung to the vision but it dimmed and faded; in its place, the spiky cage took shape, the pounding march of young men in high shiny boots reverberated, green slime slick on the wires in the dull gray light; within, a tortured form writhed, bleeding in rubble. "Last chance, chance, chance" echoed pitifully. When flames and billowing smoke rose above the cage, Ruth forced her eyes open, licked blood from her lower lip, urged her body from its familiar curled position to lie straight, flat on her back, arms at her sides, fingers stretched out stiff beside her. She ached all over. Eyes dry and wide, lips and tongue stinging as if they had been scorched, reaching for the rituals of her incarceration, she summoned the poetry that had fended off despair. "Had we but world enough and time . . . ," she couldn't remember, she couldn't go on; ". . . never chaste, except you ravish me," but she'd lost what came before; "Oh, the mind, mind has mountains . . . ," but the rest was gone. "I am the enemy you killed, my friend." Fragments spurted incoherently, not enough to make the rhythm. It didn't work anymore. There was no screen left to cheat the memories.

After the horror of Soweto and then the news of Vicki Naidoo's arrest, there was no longer any way to stand at a distance and separate herself from what had been done to her. And from what she had done.

When the Security Branch detectives directed her into the back of the unmarked car parked next to her mother's at the side of the Sandown house, she saw four men herded from the door. She recognized them all. Bernard was not among them.

The security officers ignored her in the car, talking to each other in Afrikaans about rugby. Assuring herself her arrest was nothing more than the usual bureaucratic error, Ruth tried to put Rita out of her mind and think of a lawyer to call. Bernard would be a good father, she thought. As they drove into the city, a detective turned to her. "We know everything," he said. "You've got yourself to blame." She stared ahead.

It was after six in the evening when they pulled up to Marshall Square. At the entrance marked "Europeans Only," Detective Fourie looked up and waved. "Cheerio, blue sky," he said triumphantly and nudged Ruth into the charge office.

"Ninety days," he announced cheerfully to the policeman behind the counter.

"Wait a minute," Ruth gasped. "I haven't done anything, you can't just hold me, I want to call my lawyer."

Laughter. A hand on her arm. Tight. She jerked. Someone holding the other arm.

"Now listen here, Miss Fredman," said Detective Fourie. "We're holding you for interrogation under the ninety-day law. You have no rights. You cannot talk to a lawyer. You better cooperate."

"Why don't you charge me?" She sounded defiant.

"We'll see what to do with you after interrogation. It depends how nicely you cooperate, then we'll decide how to charge you."

"You can't . . . ."

"We can, Miss Fredman. You know that. Under the law, we

can hold you in solitary until eternity. Until hell freezes over. That's what the Minister said, you know."

Laughter.

"I have nothing with me, I . . ."

"The sergeant will contact your family. You can have a bag of necessities, they can deliver it here. No belts, plastic bags, scissors, pencils, paper, books. No bottles. The sergeant will give the orders to your family."

Her legs were shaking. Tears sprang suddenly to her eyes. She blinked fast, she didn't want them to notice. Arms gripped tight on either side, she was steered into a dim passage, along gray corridors, across courtyards, stumbling, clattering, under bare bulbs, into a murky gray cell. The door slammed shut. Two more doors slammed. Then Ruth was alone.

She stood there for a long time in her swingy blue skirt with the strawberry stains. Thoughts hurtled, slithered like mercury, too fast to grasp. Although she had a blue sweater over her blouse, she was shivering cold, cold inside, cold a physical invader that hurt. After a while she walked three steps from the door and sat on the bed. So cold her teeth chattered, her hands shook, she crawled under the fibrous gray blanket, huddled in a tight ball. There were no sheets. A moldy stench of rotting vegetables seeped from the blanket. She shifted to fit herself between bumps in the mattress. The clanging of steel doors echoed. Ruth's face was wet, her nose blocked. She couldn't blow it, they had taken her pocketbook, she had no tissues.

From the incoherent slipping strands of thoughts, one became insistent enough to grasp. It couldn't be happening to her. But it was. Of course, they'd have to contact her family to bring her clothes and necessities, as they put it. Once they did, her father would know what to do. At least he'd get a lawyer who'd know what to do. They couldn't keep her here, she'd done nothing. She'd tell them that, of course, and they'd have to let her go.

Ruth rolled onto her back and stretched out straight, hands at her sides. It was very important not to let her head touch the wall behind her. There was just enough room from the top of her head to the tips of her toes on the bed. When she fitted her narrow frame in its exact center, she could lie with her arms at her sides, just off the edges. A tight fit. The overhead bulb was bilious yellow, irritating her eyes. The walls were painted black two-thirds up. Over the upper part, which had been white, layers of grimy dust clung to the concrete. There was an empty shelf on the wall opposite. A high window with five thick black bars and a mesh screen over it. An eye glared from the door. Ruth stared at it. It was a peephole. They could look at her whenever they wanted to, she wouldn't even know. She must remember that she was on display, they mustn't think she had anything to hide. There was nothing to hide. They couldn't just leave her locked up in there, they'd have to come and talk to her, then she would tell them she had done nothing.

She might have dozed. With a start she realized she was suspended in noise. She heard engines rumbling outside, the throb of motors idling, the squeak of brakes. There were voices of authority, raised in brisk command. Shouts and curses. Wild shrieks, screams, pleas for water. Loud unintelligible babbling. Trying to identify the sounds, Ruth thought they must be arresting drunks. Threaded through all the clamor, the clash of steel doors, echoes repeating, doubled, trebled. Assaulted by noise, she lay still, hand shielding her eyes. Bernard, she thought, would tell her father whom to call. At least they hadn't caught Bernard.

She was woken, bathed in sweat, by the clash of keys against steel. A wardress threw open the door and held out a tin dish with a hard-boiled egg and two thick slices of damp white bread. In her other hand was a jeily jar with pale coffee.

Ruth sat upright, reached for the food. She was starving. She asked about a bathroom.

"Later. Not now."

She asked when they would question her.

"Not yet."

Had they phoned her family?

"We're not allowed to talk to you."

She left, with a resounding clang.

Ruth wolfed down the food, not caring if someone watched through the peephole. She hadn't eaten since the strawberries. She finished it amazingly quickly. She was still ravenous. She got off the bed and looked around the cell. A gray early sky hung above the little window. Scrawls and scratches were carved into the walls. "I'm here for killing John," "Bets is innocent," "*Maybuye*," "Daisy loves M.N."

Ruth heard the voices of African women talking, the rough commands of wardresses, the slurping sounds of water. The women must be regular prisoners, she thought, not politicals in solitary, forbidden from conversation. They'd let her keep her watch. It was ten o'clock when a different wardress arrived, keys clashing, and let her out along a gray corridor to a deserted communal cell, from which bathroom facilities were divided by a dented partition. There was a cold-water sink and a seatless toilet. Ruth had no soap, no towel. When she asked, the wardress, dressed in a navy uniform with a leather belt from which heavy keys dangled, rattling, said her things hadn't been delivered yet. Ruth asked when she could·talk to an officer and the wardress smirked.

"They'll let you sweat for a while," she said.

"Are there any other women in on ninety days?" Ruth asked.

"We're not supposed to talk to you. Hurry up now, I have to get the *kaffirs* in the exercise yard."

Hours later, the first wardress brought a small suitcase. Ruth knew she was coming, because she recognized the clash of keys, then another, then a third, then thirteen or fourteen paces leading to her isolated cell.

The woman deposited a small red suitcase on the bed next to Ruth.

"Your people brought this. We gave back what you can't have."

Ruth stared at her. The woman's face seamed with a smirk.

"Scissors. Tweezers. Belt. Needle and thread. Bottles. No glass allowed, see. We gave all that back. The rest you can have."

Ruth opened the case and looked through the clothing, slacks and sweaters, underwear, a warm nightgown, toilet articles, a towel.

"That's all?"

"That's it."

"No books?"

"I've brought you a Bible. Read it. It will help you. You're not supposed to read anything else, you're supposed to be thinking about your sins in here."

"I don't even know why I'm here," Ruth said, and suddenly began to cry.

"That's what you must think about."

Ruth drifted through the day and night in a bewildered numbness. It was hard to concentrate on anything. She felt as if she were waiting for something to happen, compelled to gray neutrality until it did. She slept a lot. Her dreams were jigsaw puzzles made up of stories her mind wove out of the noises and screams in the background. The next day, the station commandant was led into the room by a wardress Ruth hadn't seen before. The commandant was a tall thin man, slightly stooped, with sandy hair and a bristly, drooping mustache that muffled his speech.

"Any complaints," he asked ritually, holding a pen and notepad.

She shook herself from her apathy.

"Yes. I don't know why I'm here, there's no reason for me to be in jail."

He flipped over a page or two.

"Ninety days." The ends of the ginger mustache shivered.

"I've done nothing. I must talk to the Security Branch."

"In due time. In due time. Is that all?"

"No." She was defiant. "I need to take a shower. I need hot water. Isn't there a law about exercise?"

"This isn't a resort, you know, Miss . . . er . . . this isn't a resort. I'll see about exercise. Good morning."

The next day, the third of her imprisonment, Ruth was led outside to an exercise yard. She was told she could spend an hour alone in the sandy yard each day. When she walked out, she was photographed by a security officer who made her back up against a brick wall and look straight at his camera. The yard was surrounded on all sides by fourteen-foot-high brick walls. Ruth stared at the square of brilliant noontime blue above. There was a world beyond these walls, she told herself, and looked up at the windows of the tall buildings surrounding the square. From one, high up to her left, a shirt-sleeved man standing at the window waved to her. He turned away and in a minute was back with another man who laughed and thrust up his middle finger.

The obscene gesture jolted Ruth from her torpor and she set herself to figuring out exactly where she was. As she paced the yard, striding steadily, some of the stiffness melted from her legs. Marshall Square was in the center of the mining and finance conglomerates of Africa's largest metropolis. She could identify the new Chamber of Mines building from which the amused executive had just given her the finger. On Main Street, paces away from where she walked, were Anglo American's famous headquarters, numbers 41 and 42. The Stock Exchange was one block away. Ruth nodded thoughtfully, pleased to establish the geography of her isolation. Then she turned to examine the names scratched into the flaking green paint on the door. Most of them were unfamiliar. The ninety-day law had been passed a year before and the first detainees had scratched their names and sometimes dates among the hearts and slogans that ordinary prisoners scrawled to mark their presence. Here and there, scattered about the door, was a roll call of ninety-day prisoners of the previous year. She was startled by the name of Ruth First, a banned journalist, mother of three, former treason trial defendant. She'd been arrested in a blaze of publicity just after the raid on the farm in Rivonia; Ruth wondered if she was still in Marshall Square, if she could talk to her, if she could ask advice.

There were other names she knew: Wolf Kodesh, Leon Levy, Lilian Ngoyi, Dhlamini, Arthur and Hazel Goldreich, Harold Wolpe.

Ruth stepped away from the door, heart hammering, and made herself walk steadily around the square. She had ambivalent feelings about those names. She did not belong in that group and she knew it and knew she had to convince the Special Branch of it. She had not been part of that tight inner circle of resistance leaders, never one of them, though it seemed that perhaps Bernard had. She didn't want to be identified with them. That would be several different kinds of lying, difficult to define. But her certainty of this was undermined by a small but quite discernible comfort: these courageous people had been through this and survived, she was not in undistinguished company. If misguided. Or were they? She no longer knew; weeping, she no longer cared. She found a patch of sun near the brick wall and sat down miserably, too exhausted to walk, too drained to try to think.

Back in the confines of the cell, where the walls seemed to have shifted, moved in closer to her body, she lay on the bed, reciting the names to herself. This had the effect of making her realize that she should prepare for the interrogation they'd threatened. She'd been hanging about in a daze, irrational, assuming that all she had to do was tell the truth and they'd let her out of there. But now she grasped that they would ask her questions, lots of questions, and that telling the truth might not be as productive as she'd foolishly been assuming. Not as simple either.

They would ask, she thought, what she had been doing at the house in Sandown. Mouth so dry it burned, nerves racing as if propelled by an electrical charge, Ruth tried to formulate an acceptable answer to that question and to the others that now popped into her mind with the impact of darts hurled at a crumbling cork dart board. When would They come? How could she be ready for Them? They might come at any minute.

But They made her sweat for eleven days. While she wrestled with possible questions, tentative answers, convoluted invented dialogues, more complex, infinitely more dangerous than planning four or five moves ahead on a chess board, she learned the routines of life in isolation at Marshall Square.

They came on inspections four times a day, keys clanging in bouts of three assaults on steel doors; at other times they stared through the peephole, she could see the glaze of moisture on a human eye; or she peered out through it and if they caught her, they shouted abuse. The wardresses searched her room every day, a simple task since there was nowhere to hide anything and nothing to hide. The wardresses were all fiercely committed to keeping the floor of her cell clean. *"Gaan haal my 'n kaffir,"* "Go get me a *kaffir*," one of them would yell, and Ruth would sit cross-legged on the bed while an African man scrubbed the concrete floor with thick bright red polish, rags tied around his knees, wadded in his hands, buffing until the floor looked evenly covered by congealed blood. The regular prisoners had to do their own waxing every day; evidently politicals, at least white women in solitary, were regarded as incapable of maintaining the required garish perfection. Straining to hear what the other women were saying, women who didn't get treated like lepers, because they were uncontaminated by politics, Ruth learned that they were mostly prostitutes and drunks, thieves and minor assault prisoners. She could sometimes detect the brawling installation of a *sherry-ganger*, a decrepit aging hobo who carried her possessions about her person or in shopping bags, shuffling from park bench to street corner, settling on the steps of public buildings to sleep, staggering drunkenly up, trailing disreputable debris. Ruth heard them come and, a day or two later, wished them good luck silently when she heard them go.

She had to wash in a bucket. She had to shout again and again to attract a wardress if she needed the toilet. They resented requests to take her there and kept the excursions to a minimum. They searched her cell every day, brought her food, ignored her attempts to talk to them. But they forgot the rules occasionally or perhaps just felt an illicit stab of pity, so she did pick up a few scraps of information, particularly from the one who brought her stewed dinner in the late afternoon, the one with a gray hair net stretched over thin yellow curls, a long nose, and a sweet smile. Ruth secretly called her Sugarcane because she was long, thin, and oddly sweet. It was from Sugarcane that Ruth learned they were all police widows, all Afrikaners, all matter-of-fact about doing their jobs, untroubled by speculation or ethical confusion. She also learned that there had been a sensational jailbreak within a day or two of her own arrest; two Rivonia prisoners had bribed a warden and escaped. A massive manhunt was in progress and prison security was being tightened remorselessly. The news suffused her alternately with jubilant excitement and despair. They wouldn't tell her the names of the escaped men and she ruminated for hours each day about who they might have been.

If she stood on the bed on tiptoes, she could hold onto the bars at the window and look out at the city life beyond. The bars were sealed in grimy dirt. She hung on them every day, hands shielded by tissues she'd found in the red suitcase. It was a precious diversion, she allocated special times to the entertainment, learning just how long her arms could strain. The window was on the corner of Market and Sauer streets, diagonally opposite a Danish restaurant, where solemn businessmen with briefcases lunched. A newspaper vendor set up a stand on the street below the window, but angled the papers to the fortunate pedestrians on the sidewalk so that, although she craned, twisted, and stretched, she could never read the headlines.

Aside from the wardresses and a magistrate who arrived every few days to inquire if she had any complaints and listened patiently to her torrent of fantastic demands, she spoke to no one for eleven days. Her major preoccupation was preparing herself for the interrogation, which would have to come eventually.

Nothing prepared her for the hot steaming panic when a wardress announced that They wanted her. She'd waited for it, demanded it, anticipated it, but now that it had come, she was clutched by fear, she stumbled slowly along the gray corridor in front of the wardress, incoherent fragments of her strategy cluttering her thoughts like shells pelted onto sand at high tide in a storm, terrified that she would lose control, terrified above all that she would say too much, tell Them what she mustn't.

They were waiting in a small interview room. They both stared at her as the wardress showed her in, then went away, closing the door with a firm click.

"Good morning, Miss Fredman." She'd heard the voice before. She made herself look at the man standing behind a small table and saw the detective who'd arrested her at Sandown.

"I'm Detective Piet Fourie." He was tall, broad-shouldered, impeccable in a dark gray suit. Smooth brown hair, brown eyes, pale brown even skin, faint upward lines at the corners of eyes and firm mouth enhancing the look of mild amusement, strong jaw in a square face, controlled set of the head, an image of authority so entrenched it need never be defined. "This is Sergeant Uys," he nodded at the burly uniformed cop who slouched expressionlessly at the wall near the small barred window. "Please sit down."

There were two straight wooden chairs on either side of the table. Ruth and Detective Piet Fourie sat down. The sergeant perched stolidly on the windowsill, blocking the sun. The bare overhead bulb lit the table but the room around it was shadowy gray.

"Are you prepared to answer some questions?" His accent, close to her own, told her that he was educated, traveled, and at ease in a multilingual society, the raw drone of his native Afrikaans long refined.

"I have questions too," she said, clinging to her plan. She leaned against the back of her chair, crossed her right leg over her left, clasped her hands on her lap. She remembered her determination to appear relaxed. "I want to know why I am here."

"Now Miss Fredman, let's not waste time." He had an engaging smile. "You're here for interrogation under the ninety-day law."

"But I've done nothing. Nothing at all."

"That's what we're here to find out, isn't it?"

He rested his forearms on the table, leaned forward and smiled again. It didn't help that he was such a handsome man.

"I'm going to ask you some questions and then perhaps we'll be able to get a written statement from you. Now tell me, Miss Fredman, are you a member of the Congress of Democrats?"

The question came so quickly and surprised her so much that she couldn't conceal her dismay. Her strictest injunction to herself had been to say nothing unless she was certain it was safe to do so. She fumbled for the threads of her plan.

"I can't answer questions without the advice of a lawyer," she said.

"Miss Fredman, I see that you don't understand. Listen carefully now." He was gazing steadily at her across the table. She glanced at the sergeant and saw a contemptuous grin. "You are not entitled under the law to have an attorney. We are going to hold you until we get answers to our questions. You know we can hold you for ninety days here, don't you?"

"And then another ninety," her voice rose furiously.

"And another. And another. However long it takes. Why put yourself through that for nothing, eh?"

"Will you let me go if I answer your questions?"

He smiled again, a model of kindly tolerance.

"It depends on the answers, doesn't it? We may decide to charge you. We may not. We'll never know until you answer."

She'd endured eleven solitary, boring, uncomfortable days knotted with fear. She might as well stop skirmishing, God knew how long They'd make her wait for the next encounter otherwise. At least she'd gained enough time to become familiar with the surroundings and the inquisitor.

"I have nothing to hide," she said proudly.

"Well, the innocent never object to answering questions. Are you a member of the Congress of Democrats?"

"Of course not. It's a banned organization."

He leaned a little farther forward.

"Were you ever a member?"

"Yes."

Without expression, Fourie made a note on the pad in front of him.

"Have you written articles for *Fighting Talk?*"

She was bewildered.

"What's that?"

"Have you written articles for *New Age?*"

"Of course not. Isn't it banned?" She felt much more relaxed. This was quite easy, really. They had nothing on her, of course.

"Did you participate in the organization of the so-called stay-at-home strike?"

"No," she lied easily. She'd been over and over it. They could prove nothing.

"Were you at a meeting in Pietermaritzburg where Nelson Mandela called for a national convention?"

"No," she said comfortably.

"Do you know Nelson Mandela?"

"No."

"Do you know Walter Sisulu or Govan Mbeki?"

"No."

The men arrested at Rivonia. They couldn't link her to them. There was no link.

"Do you know Harold Wolpe or Arthur Goldreich?"

"No. Not personally."

"But you know them?" he asked mildly.

"No. I know of them, I've heard the names. Hasn't everyone?"

"Now they have," he muttered. The sergeant nodded, grinning. It occurred to Ruth that Wolpe and Goldreich must be the ones who escaped. She saluted them mentally, distracted from the next question.

"Where is Rajiv Naidoo?"

"In London, I think," she answered at once.

"So you do know Rajiv Naidoo?"

Damn, he'd caught her, she wasn't concentrating. Well, it didn't really matter, Rajiv was out of the country.

"You do know Naidoo?"

"We were students together at Wits."

"You studied history. He was up the hill at the Medical School," the detective commented.

Ruth hated the confirmation that he knew anything about her life. How much could he know? She crossed her legs. She must concentrate.

"Do you know Peter Shabalala?"

Ah. Here it came.

"We were students together also."

Peter Shabalala was one of the four men she'd seen herded from the house at Sandown as They directed her into the car outside.

"Do you know Amos Lithane?"

"No."

He was another.

"Do you know Selwyn Kagan?"

"I've met him. I don't know him."

"Why were you at Sandown, Miss Fredman?"

"I went to see someone," she said, as she had planned.

"But you say you don't know these people. Lithane, Motswane, Selwyn Kagan. You don't know them. So you didn't go to see them. Was it Shabalala you went for?"

She didn't answer. He'd come at it from the back door, she couldn't quite sort it out, she couldn't think fast enough, she couldn't remember what answer had seemed foolproof on the cot in her cell.

"Which one of them did you go to see?"

She couldn't answer. All the alternatives were dangerous, all led along unknown paths strewn with explosives. But her mind recorded the impression that all this must mean Bernard was still free. They didn't have him. Perhaps They didn't know he was there.

"Or was there someone else there, Miss Fredman?"

Maybe they did know he was there. She must not speak. At all costs she must not speak.

"Why won't you answer?"

She was silent, brain racing.

Detective Fourie stood up suddenly. His chair, skittering across the green linoleum, made an ugly scratching sound. He turned away from her, walked about the room, handsome head bent in thought. The sergeant drummed thick fingers on the heavy blue stuff of his uniformed knee.

From behind her, Fourie said softly, "We know all about it, Miss Fredman."

Ruth turned, startled. His voice was menacing. His face bore no trace of his former nonchalant amusement; instead it was frozen in severity, jaw and mouth long firm lines. He stared at her until she dropped her eyes and turned away. He walked back to the table.

"We know what was going on at Sandown. We know exactly what was going on."

"Well, I don't." She knew she sounded flippant, careless. "I have no idea. I only went to see someone there."

"What about?" he barked suddenly, but she had prepared for this.

"It was personal," she said, with the assurance of honesty.

"Then you won't mind telling me about it. So you can leave here someday."

"You don't understand. It's private. Personal. Nothing to do with the struggle."

He sat down. He folded his arms.

"So you do know the so-called struggle was the purpose of the gathering at Sandown?"

She was sick of it. Every simple statement was contorted, every observation a springboard for a devious new assault, hidden traps everywhere with steel wires ready to pierce. She was angry.

"Rubbish. I know the ninety-day law is intended to trap political dissidents, that's all. You're holding me under that law. It's not all that difficult to assume there was a political purpose."

"And what was that purpose, Miss Fredman?" he inquired silkily.

"I don't know. I don't know anything about it. I told you, I was there for something personal."

"There's nothing personal where state security is concerned. Who did you go to see? What were you doing there?"

She didn't answer. Detective Fourie attempted several versions of the same question. Ruth remained silent.

"Well," he said suddenly, "that's it for today." He nodded to the sergeant, who walked over to the door, opened it and murmured.

"But . . . is that all? Can I go?"

"Back to the cell," the detective said crisply. "We'll try again when you've had more time to think."

"But . . ." The wardress held her arm tight, jerked her up from the chair. "When will you . . ."

"Good day, Miss Fredman."

Back in the cell, she sank exhausted onto the bed. She must review it all, see what information she could piece together, what did They know, what had she given away, what should she do next time. But she was light-headed, her limbs weighted with tiredness, her skin ice cold. She slept.

She had plenty of time to analyze the interrogation, plenty of time to rehearse for the next round. They left her alone for six more days. She slept a great deal. She planned how to handle Them. She lay for long, numb hours, on her back on the bed, devising ways to keep awake so that she could sleep through the clamorous din at night. She tried reciting poetry to keep awake, to fend off dreams until she was too tired to force her eyes open. When she couldn't remember phrases from poems that threaded her childhood and youth, she made them up. Amazing, though, how much she remembered. She read the Bible, very slowly, a chapter a day. She made plans. Next time she would make Them let her go.

Sugarcane woke her for the next round. The sky above the barred window was dark, she groped for her watch. Eight o'clock at night. They'd changed their tactics. Sugarcane let her visit the bathroom on the way to the interview. This time she didn't feel panic, she welcomed the challenge, she looked forward to conversation, she walked along briskly.

But in the interview room she was jarred to find that Detective Fourie had a new companion. This one was also dressed in a business suit. Thin, slightly stooped, gray, face crumpled like tissue paper, he shook hands with her and introduced himself as Detective Potgieter. This time there were three chairs at the table. The change made her uneasy.

Detective Fourie led her through many of the same questions again, adding a few here and there, trying to slip them in to catch her off guard, she thought contemptuously. Had she collected signatures for the petition against Bantu Education? Yes. Had she distributed material protesting the homelands policy? Yes. She was sticking to her plan to tell the truth wherever possible, but she wondered apprehensively how they knew so much about her. Had she been at a meeting to plan a boycott of white-owned stores last February? No. No. Certainly not. And had she, the stooping gray Potgieter suddenly asked, in a thin, shivery voice, ever gone with Peter Shabalala to an antipass protest meeting in Moroka Township?

Ruth bit her lower lip, mind racing. He'd woven the question in so delicately he'd almost caught her. But she was onto Them, she was ready for Them all right, she'd taught herself that They had Peter, They'd have questioned him, she must be careful. If she contradicted Peter, she'd give Them something on him. She couldn't be sure what he might have said. She thought he'd have said no, but perhaps he also tried to tell the truth wherever possible. She couldn't risk answering.

"I repeat, did you go with Peter Shabalala to a meeting to plan measures against the pass laws?" This voice had the monotonous, heavily inflected consonants of careful English superimposed upon the lifelong habit of Afrikaans; its thin, high pitch carried a creepy threat.

"Come now, Miss Fredman," Fourie said pleasantly, "we know the answer. The meeting took place years ago, where's the harm in answering? You don't want to prolong your visit with us, do you?"

Who was the chief here? she wondered. Who made the rules? Fourie seemed so much nicer, she wished They hadn't sent the bleached, hostile Potgieter.

"I have done nothing illegal," she said defiantly, to interrupt their questioning. "You have no right to hold me. I'm innocent, I demand to see my lawyer. I demand a visit from my parents."

"Tell me if you went with Shabalala to Orlando." Potgieter's voice made her skin crawl.

"Yes." What did it matter? It was trivial, it was long ago.

"Good, Miss Fredman, thank you," said handsome Fourie and she felt a small tug of pleasure, instantly discarded in disgust. Fourie leaned forward over the table toward her with a warm smile and went on asking questions, going over ground they'd already covered. Potgieter leaned back, away from the table, his body curved, head tucked like an old bird's on his chest. She tried to ignore him.

"Do you know Bernard Levine?" Fourie asked suddenly.

"Yes," Ruth said. She'd worked it out a thousand times in advance. They must know this. They knew so much else.

"In fact, wasn't he your . . . er . . . your boyfriend?" said Fourie, with a friendly smile.

Wasn't he? Was? It answered what she'd burned to know back in the cell.

"Yes, he was. Long ago. Not anymore." She stopped herself. Don't talk too much.

"How long ago?" The high thin question came from Potgieter.

266

"Oh, a year ago, more than a year."

Fourie nodded approvingly.

"Now, why were you at Sandown?"

"I told you before, I went to see someone. On a personal matter."

"What was the personal matter?"

She'd rehearsed for this, she'd practiced a hundred times. The gray folded bird made it much more difficult, but she'd try it anyway.

"Look, Detective Fourie," she leaned across the table toward him for the first time, she tried to smile, to look directly into his eyes, "we're both human beings, aren't we, we have feelings, you know what it's like. I just went to see a man, to be with him, you can understand that, can't you?"

Detective Fourie looked back at her with all the warm speculative amusement she'd tried to arouse; but Potgieter lifted his gray head from his chest and, with emphasis on every syllable, intoned the question.

"Whom did you go to see?"

She felt harassed, she lost the thread of the connection she was trying to establish with Fourie, the gray one came at her like a bird, wings flapping, swooping.

"Who, I am asking you, who?"

"I don't have to tell you that. It's personal." She was crying, she realized with rage.

"You need more time," said Detective Fourie as he opened the door and waved the wardress back in.

"No, no, I must . . ."

But she was led away. She heard Them talking behind her, but her Afrikaans wasn't good enough to understand what They said.

The next day, fighting a new lethargy interspersed with spells of weeping, she lay on her back raising one leg and lowering it slowly, then the other, again and again, thirty-seven, forty-two times each. Exercise, she told herself dully, keeping fit and distracting herself, concentrating on one small accomplishment, bending her will to increasing the number of lifts each day. The clash of keys on steel warned her someone was coming. Hoping for Sugarcane and a word or two, she let her legs fall wearily to the bed and counted the paces to the door. It was not Sugarcane. It was Detective Piet Fourie. He was carrying a small plastic chair, which he set against the wall near the end of the bed.

"How are you today?" He sat on the chair. He was wearing jeans and a battered tweed sport coat with worn leather elbow patches. He had an open-air look about him, the casual carelessness of a man off duty. He was more handsome than ever.

"I'm taking my children out to row at the Vaal Dam later," he said, as if they were old acquaintances who'd met by pleasant chance. "I thought I'd stop by and see you first."

Ruth stopped herself from saying that it was a treat to have someone to talk to.

"I'm sorry about yesterday," he said earnestly.

"What do you mean?" Ruth sat up, cross-legged on the bed. She ran long fingers through her dark hair to comb it, remembering to pull the wisps down over her forehead.

"I thought Detective Potgieter upset you," he said.

"He's nasty," Ruth burst out. "I bet when he was a little boy he pulled the wings off butterflies, trapped rabbits. He probably shot birds. He hates me."

"Well, I don't know about that," said Fourie, leaning back cozily against the wall.

"I suppose you think he was just doing his job," Ruth went on. "But I can tell he enjoys intimidating people, he likes his bits and pieces of power."

"Mm." There was a hush. Something stirred in the stale air between them. Then he said, "There's only so much I can do, of course, but I'd like to help you."

"Thank you," Ruth said eagerly. "I could use some help."

"You started telling me yesterday about this personal matter, going to Sandown to see someone, a man, you said. I remember, when I found you there, you were lying under a willow tree near the water. Your eyes were closed. You looked . . . well, you looked beautiful. You'd been crying, I could see that. But you looked beautiful like one of those French paintings, as if you were miles away. Peaceful."

Her eyes filled again as she listened. She was returned poignantly to the moment before he'd arrived, the moment when she'd summoned Bernard into her vision, Bernard laughing in sunshine on the bright bed in Observatory.

"Why were you down there, Ruth? Near the water under the willow?"

"For privacy." She blinked rapidly. "We were talking there."

"What about?"

"About . . . about our future," she whispered. Only a few hours before that, she'd thought they had one, she'd thought they'd always be together and that nothing else mattered. And then he said he had to marry Rita.

"Who was it, Ruth?"

She stared at him. She clenched her hands together.

"Don't try to trap me," she spat furiously. "I'm not stupid, even if you . . . you can't . . . that's a cheap trick."

He sighed. He shook his head.

"It's a pity. It's really a shame. I want to help, you know."

"That's a lie."

"No, it's true. Really. Look, you're protecting someone . . ."

"Lies. All lies."

"Well then," he said reasonably, "If that's not it, then why can't you tell me? If he's innocent, there's no problem, we never harm innocent people. If he's not innocent, why should you suffer for him? You could be out, it's a lovely day out there, you could have a picnic near a river."

Ruth swung her legs over the edge of the bed, turned away from him and folded her arms tightly around herself. She would not say another word, no matter how he provoked her. He'd got her guard down and tried to deceive her, he wouldn't get another chance. She heard his shoes on the floor, the little rustle of his clothes.

"You're making it harder for yourself, Ruth," he said, and she could have sworn he sounded sorry for her. Then the door clanged and he was gone.

Over the damp white bread the following morning, Sugarcane muttered, "You're having an important visitor today." For several hours Ruth braced herself. They would come, she thought, and charge her formally with treason. At least she'd see a lawyer then, she wouldn't be in solitary anymore. She rose when the door opened. A trim man in a beribboned uniform took one step inside the cell, leaving the door open behind him. She waited to be charged.

"I'm Colonel van Rensburg. From the Grays."

Headquarters. Big Chief. Supervisor of detectives. Dispenser of privileges. Autocrat of punishment. She waited, trembling, teeth grinding.

"You're being moved today. To more permanent quarters."

She felt as if a blanket had been thrown over her head, as if it was being tied snugly around her neck.

"Why?"

"We're going to have to hold you longer than we'd hoped. You're uncooperative. Very. You're in for a long stay, it can't be here. You're going to Pretoria Central. I think you'll come to your senses there. We'll see."

"But you can't just . . ."

"Oh, yes, we can. We will do whatever is necessary. Pack your things." He looked superciliously around the cell.

"Can my parents visit me there?"

"If you want to request a visit from there, you can try. Offer us something in return, that's what I suggest."

"But . . . no one will know where I am."

"Now look here, Miss Fredman, this is not a police state. We'll notify your family of your whereabouts, of course we will. Wardress!"

Sugarcane appeared behind him.

"Get on with it," he snapped. He spun on his heel and left.

"They say the cells are better there," Sugarcane whispered, standing over Ruth as she jammed her few possessions into the small suitcase.

Two plainclothes detectives sat on either side of her in the car. She didn't recognize them or the uniformed driver. From the windows she saw people in the streets, going about their normal lives as if she didn't exist, as if none of it existed. They passed cars on the road. Did the people inside them wonder who she was? None of them knew, none of them cared, not them, not her family, not her colleagues at Wits, her friends, not even . . . she clicked a switch in her mind, she could not think of Bernard now.

They swept past gates boldly marked "Department of Prisons," toward groups of concrete double-story buildings with huge doors and ugly imitation towers. The formalities were very brief, she walked ahead of a wardress up a long flight of steps, a door slammed with an unfamiliar clatter and Ruth looked around her new quarters. She might have to spend the rest of her life there, better get used to it, she thought bitterly.

The cell was twice the size of the one at Marshall Square. It was bright and felt deceptively open because of two windows; one overlooked the front of the prison, the other gave an excellent view of the stairs. A wardress dressed in a khaki skirt, starched pale pink blouse, and lacquered tinsel hair arrived with a water jug, a china cup and saucer, and a starched white linen table-cloth. She pointed to something she called a *po*, a large covered enamel bucket that fitted neatly under the bed. Ruth would be allowed out for a shower each morning, an hour of exercise each midday and the toilet block each evening. Otherwise she would remain in the cell.

It didn't take long to become familiar with her new surround-ings. Ruth discovered that she was the only prisoner on her floor. From the window over the stairwell she saw wardresses approaching or leaving her cell, nothing more. But if she stood on tiptoes on the bed, she could see from the larger window the main road leading to the prison. Beyond, the sparkling blue of a swimming pool, trim sweeping lawns and flower beds, two bowling greens and several tennis courts taunted her. They were the recreation grounds for the white employees of the prison system. Barefoot African convicts manicured the grass and shrubs, weeded the flower beds, pruned the trees and swept the pool; on weekends, tanned young men and girls in bikinis sunbathed and flirted. None of them ever raised their eyes to Ruth's barred window. The scene might have been a travel poster. Most of the time it didn't seem real, which was just as well; when she perceived it as real, it was such a painful reminder of normal life in South Africa that it brought cramps to her stomach, throbbing aches to her calves.

Ruth learned that Pretoria Central was reserved for blacks serving sentences of six months or longer. Whites were transferred to other prisons at Pietersburg or Ermelo. She learned to identify the isolated building that served as a punishment block, from which screams, long and bloodcurdling, sometimes pierced the sunny air. "I've been long at this game," a wardress she privately called Pineapple muttered darkly when Ruth asked about the screams. "Them screams shows someone's been wicked." Through the open mesh-screened windows, Ruth heard the wardresses abusing the prisoners. *"Kaffir-meid"* and *"swart-gat"* or "black hole," were common forms of address.

Ruth was visited by a major every few days. He inquired whether she had any complaints, shifted impatiently from one foot to another when she heaped shrill demands upon him, left hastily. She had been in solitary confinement for nineteen days at Marshall Square and ten more at Pretoria Central when she realized that it might actually go on for a very long time. It wasn't that she hadn't been aware until then of the threat of remaining in prison "until eternity"; she just hadn't quite absorbed that it could happen to her. When she did, she struggled against subdued apathy, trying to devise ways to pass the time. She decided she must make every small task count, every action meaningful, every movement valuable.

She started the Bible from the beginning again, rationing herself to a few pages every day, pausing to learn passages by heart, dwelling on relevant aphorisms. "A fool's mouth is his destruction and his lips are the snare of his soul" might have been a warning especially for her. She manufactured housekeeping routines, dragging out the meticulous making of the bed, folding and refolding her clothes, scrubbing every inch of her cell with tissues. She kept a record of her days in captivity by turning down the top right-hand corner of a page of the Bible every day; every day she counted and recounted the folded corners, checking, rechecking. She fabricated arithmetic problems and struggled with them in her head, she who could not divide or multiply a simple fraction. She made mental lists of all the writers, musicians, artists, architects, doctors, lawyers, actors whose names began with A. Their family names. Then their first names. Then all those whose names began with B, each day a new letter for the list. She exercised for an hour every morning and every afternoon in her cell, in addition to her hour outside. She worked up increasingly demanding routines, testing her muscles at the beginning and end of every session, forcing herself to maintain her futile schedule even when she was almost too lethargic to care.

No matter how she tried to fill it, time crawled. Suspended from the world, excluded like an alien, a freak from another planet, her obsessive routines anesthetized her. Folding down corners of pages, doggedly doing an extra sit-up on the concrete floor, became more important than the questions they asked, more important, even, than whether Bernard still went free.

Sometimes, waking at night from shadowy half-remembered dreams, she grasped that she was disassociated from reality, she thought she was conspiring with Them in their drive to undermine her. Sometimes she counted the number of words she had spoken during the day. Eight. Fourteen. She recited poetry, sometimes aloud. She collected fruit pits and played with them on the floor like marbles in a school yard. Her routines were seldom disrupted; when they were, by a change in wardress shifts, an oddly timed check for pointless complaints, she was annoyed, disoriented for hours.

The Special Branch interrogated her every nine or ten days. The detectives were always the same, Grof and van Tonder. She never saw Piet Fourie anymore. Grof asked the questions, always the same, droning on over the same ground, repeating the questions, reciting them in the same sequence. He seemed bored. He didn't care. He didn't expect change and neither did she. Only once, when she made the routine demand that her parents be permitted to visit her, there was a change.

"No, your parents can't come here, you don't deserve it," said Grof as usual. But the air quickened, he stirred. "If there's someone else . . . a man, perhaps . . . you want to make a formal request?"

Ruth wasn't too vague, too out of touch, to laugh.

Ruth had been at Pretoria Central Prison for sixty-nine days when Pineapple made a surprise appearance and told her she was going back to Marshall Square. She didn't know why, Ruth must pack her things. Ruth's first reaction was irritation that her exercise period had been interrupted. Then mild anticipation. She might meet Detective Piet Fourie again. Then, carefully folding her little store of clothes into the red suitcase, she slowly pieced the connection together: she had been in solitary confinement for eighty-eight days. Two more to ninety.

In the car, swept with light-headed pleasure at being in movement, she was assaulted by questions, conjectures, speculations that her numbed mind had made dormant. Perhaps they would let her go now, after all, they had nothing on her, she'd served a ninety-day term, she was a good example for other Enemies of the State, perhaps she would soon walk about on the street out there like other people. It was a great deal to cope with all at once. Her thoughts skittered and tumbled faster than the fruit pits. She arrived at Marshall Square exhausted, but buoyed by a feverish anticipation.

She thought Fourie might be waiting for her. But it was Sugarcane who welcomed her back with a tired smile. She'd changed her hair net, it was orange now. She wouldn't talk or answer questions. She installed Ruth in her old cell and left, the door clanging familiarly. Ruth didn't care. She was delighted to be back. She unpacked her things with a comfortable sense of homecoming. She saluted the night sounds, the engines of the police vans humming, the turbulent shrieks of new prisoners, the clanging din of echoing doors.

They left her alone all the next day. Disappointed but not alarmed, she waited Them out. They'd come, she knew. He'd send for her.

When he did, on the morning of the ninetieth day of her captivity, she walked briskly ahead of Sugarcane to the interview room, proud of her taut new muscles, her straight back and flat stomach. Fourie stood waiting behind the table. Potgieter sat folded in upon himself, a stooped gray bird of prey. The hell with him, she thought and smiled.

"Well, I see you're back," said Fourie.

She waited expectantly.

"Like it better here, eh?"

"Are you going to let me go?" she challenged him.

"Yes," he said.

She couldn't believe it. It was fantastic. She hadn't really anticipated . . . and so quick, just like that . . . she couldn't absorb it. But he was smiling, a friendly, confident smile. Even Potgieter was standing, stretching out his hand to congratulate her. It was evidently true. They were letting her go.

Five minutes later she was hurling things into the suitcase. Ten minutes later a uniformed cop she didn't know led her out along the corridor, through the charge room, toward the Marshall Street entrance. Exit. The door out. She hadn't even thought about calling anyone to come and get her. Never mind, she'd call when she was out. Out on the street. Outside. Swinging the suitcase, she stepped onto the street, looked up and down. There weren't many people about. The sun was high. She hesitated. She must find a phone. There was a call box a block away. She took a few steps to her right, going toward it.

"Ruth! Ruth!"

She knew the voice. She turned. Max Hepburn hurried along the sidewalk toward her.

"How are you? Welcome to the world." He hugged her. For an instant she buried her face, wet with sudden tears, on his thick shoulder.

"I counted the days, I thought I'd hang about today in case . . . I thought they might let you out today," he burbled enthusiastically.

Ruth was touched. She hadn't thought about Max Hepburn for so long, but he'd been thinking about her. Old friend.

"Max, tell me the news. What's been happening?" she asked, standing on the sidewalk, suitcase at her feet. She touched his arm to make sure he was there.

"There's a story about that one of the Rivonia prisoners is singing," he said gravely. "Really shooting off at the mouth, telling everything."

She felt a quick chill; she couldn't think about it then, in the first lovely flush of freedom. She put it aside for later.

"And Ben?" she had to ask, bracing herself.

"Bernard . . . well." He shifted awkwardly, looked solemnly at her. "He married Rita, you know. Just after you were picked up."

"Yes, I know." Of course she knew. No need to hear it like a savage blow. "And now? Is he . . . ?"

"Now, well, Bernard is in . . ." He jerked and turned. She followed his gaze. Detective Piet Fourie and a uniformed cop walked briskly toward them.

"Ruth Fredman," said Fourie, as the cop grabbed her arm fiercely, "you are under arrest."

"You can't take her back," Max shouted.

"Yes, I'm taking her. Ninety days." He moved to her other side and they led her back between them, back to the entrance, back inside, back to the dark gray cell where the bare bulb burned.

She should have known, of course. She should have been prepared. They'd done it to others, why not to her? The law provided for solitary confinement without charge for ninety days, to be repeated if the results were unsatisfactory. The law had been refined many times since then, but those were the early days, that's how they did it then.

Remembering, her stomach clenched with the old burning pain, the tissues, the lining of her insides seared as if they'd been pummeled repeatedly. In the dark bedroom of Mandiba's house, she cried out as the pain knifed again, turned clumsily onto her stomach. Sometimes pressing down hard was soothing.

"Ruth, are you all right?" Nelson said sharply. "Are you hurt?"

She'd forgotten all about him. Hurled back upon the buried days of her confinement, she'd forgotten Bernard's son, lying near her in their hiding place after Johannes's murder.

"I'm all right."

She propped herself on her elbows and peered into the darkness. She could make out a bulky shape rising above the floor nearby. That must be Nelson, drawn up into a ball.

"How are you feeling?" she asked. "I thought you were asleep."

"I was, for a while. But, I've been thinking . . ."

"Yes?"

"About Johannes." His low voice cracked. There was a long silence. "What they did . . . they call it the necklace. I can't understand how they could . . . how anyone . . . but they're driven to it, you can't blame them, they've been reduced to this barbarism by the system." His voice rose defiantly. He'd spent hours looking for code words to rationalize the savagery. Now he was talking to himself, naming it, saying it aloud. She sighed.

"Nels," she said softly, "there are bad black men as well as good ones, you know. Whites too. Good people and bad ones. That's all."

"I never thought they'd attack him if they didn't see me with him. He didn't want to come, you know. He thought it was dangerous. But that was because of you. I shouldn't have . . ."

There were a lot of things he shouldn't have done. At least his bravado was pierced enough to recognize some of them. There was only so much a person could handle at a time.

"You've got to remember they didn't see me. Or you. They thought he was alone driving a white man's truck, and they went for him anyway. Remember that."

He was quiet. She lurched away from her memories and tried to concentrate. She was there to get him out of the country. For him and for Bernard. And, perhaps, for Bernard's freedom. First, she'd have to get them out of Soweto.

"And Simon!" He blew his nose loudly, a whistling noise.

"You did what you could."

"I should have got here sooner. I wasted all that time calling you and waiting for you. I could have been here sooner."

Yes, she thought, but didn't say.

"But I thought Vicki was there, Vicki was covering . . . ," he explained to himself, twisting, turning, clutching about for a defense. The huddled shape heaved. He sat up. She could see his head thrown back against the wall. It was too dark to tell if his eyes were open or closed.

After a long silence, he said hoarsely, "I can't imagine her in jail. I can't picture it at all, Vicki in solitary."

Ruth's eyes burned. She turned again and lay on her side, resting on her bent arm, facing Nelson's shape.

"What will happen to Vicki?" he said brokenly.

In her mind, she waved to Bernard where he walked free along the edge of the ocean, white head high against the sky.

"They'll make her talk."

The shape jerked forward.

"Vicki? Never." A snort.

"I think that's what will happen, Nels."

"You don't know Vicki. She's very strong. Tough. A wonderful lady, very special. They'll never get a thing out of her. Never. Not Vicki." He was so certain, his contempt for the idea sparked the air. "She's lovely, isn't she?"

"Yes, Nels."

"Vicki will never sing. Never."

Coming so soon after the news of Vicki Naidoo's arrest had forced her back into her own past, this exchange gave Ruth the first shreds of a half-formed idea. She didn't dwell upon it, she knew that if she did, she wouldn't be able to do it. She chose, instead, to take a flying intuitive leap. In the dark, wedged between bumps on the mattress, she told Bernard's child the story of her own term in prison. She'd never told anyone before, ever; but the memories were vivid now, the words poured out easily, smoothly; she re-created the interrogations, the slow crawling hours, the view from the window, the games with the fruit pits, the numbed acquiescence, the leap of joy at her release; she told him how they took her away from Max Hepburn on the sidewalk, for a second term.

"Swines!" Nelson exclaimed. It was his first comment since she'd begun. "Evil cruel sadists, that's what they are." He coughed, shifted. "Ah, those people would . . . but what happened? You weren't there another full ninety days, were you? I thought a hundred and . . ."

"One hundred and thirteen days," Ruth said.

"How did you make them let you go? Why did they let you out?"

"After they took me back was the worst time for me," she said slowly.

She was still not sure that she could do it. She pushed herself on.

"I cried all the time. I was desperate, I felt as if everything were crumbling away and I had no control over anything. None of my compulsive rituals worked anymore, they'd all been tailored

279

to Pretoria Central, you see, and I didn't have the energy to adapt them to Marshall Square." She was silent, then added, "The poetry did still work then. For a while."

No one talked to her at all. Sugarcane disappeared. Even the wardress who led her out to exercise knotted her lips in grim silence. After a few days, Ruth thought her mind had come out of her body and hung suspended just above the floor. She touched herself all over to investigate. She couldn't feel herself. Something was there, under her fingers, but it wasn't her flesh. She ran the palms of her hands over her body, over the skin that had once surged to Bernard's lightest touch, faintest breath. She felt nothing. There was no substance. Her nerves were dead. She thought vaguely of killing herself, but couldn't pursue the idea long enough to make a plan.

"I spent most of the time lying on the cot," she told Nelson. "Crying a lot. Sleeping. Even when I wasn't sleeping, I might as well have been. I felt empty. I couldn't think." She abandoned the poetry. There was no point, it was futile like everything else. No one cared about her anyway. It didn't matter if she lived or died.

Occasionally she thought about her brief conversation with Max Hepburn, the old friend who'd come to meet her when she was released. She did try to reconstruct the conversation, piece by piece.

"I couldn't hold onto it all at once," she explained to Nelson. "Sometimes I remembered he'd said that someone was cooperating with the police, someone was telling everything he knew. I realized that meant they would know about Bernard, if someone was talking about the Sandown group he must have told them Bernard was there. Then my mind would glance off, I'd fall asleep or weep. Other times I remembered Max saying 'Bernard is in . . .' and I wondered if he was in jail, in England, in trouble, in outer space. In jail? Bernard in jail? I wasn't sure if Max had been about to tell me that when they . . . took me back."

They left her utterly alone for twenty-three more days. When a wardress came to tell her They wanted her, she barely glanced at her.

She stumbled down the corridor to the interview room without curiosity. Shoulders slumped, hair hanging in limp strands, hands grubby, she sank onto the little chair opposite Detective Fourie, barely registering that she was alone with him.

"You realize we know everything now, of course."

They had so much power, They could do anything. Her life was hemorrhaging away.

"You can't save him, Ruth. He's had his last chance."

Last chance, chance. The words bounced eerily off the shadows around the lit table. She moistened her lips.

"You know?"

"Everything." He stared at her. He didn't move. "Who was it at Sandown?"

"You know it was Ben."

"Bernard Levine."

Head bent, fingers knotted in her lap, she waited.

"I think it's time for you to make a statement, Ruth."

They took her to the Grays. Colonel van Rensburg put a typewritten page in front of her. She read it. She did read it. It wasn't very long. She signed it.

"I imagine you'll be wanting to leave the country soon, Miss Fredman." She heard the colonel's voice through a howling wind. It was too foggy to see him clearly. "Within seventy-two hours, I should think."

Her parents waited, grim-faced portraits of injured dignity, at the entrance to Marshall Square. Two days later, Gerald Gordon drove her to Jan Smuts Airport. This would, her father explained, be less painful. After Gerald parked the car, she looked at him directly for the first time.

"Gerry," she said, "will you do one more thing for me? Give Ben a message?"

Color rushed his cheeks, staining the pale skin. He turned away.

"Gerry?"

He lifted his head, pushed back shiny strands of auburn hair, drummed white fingers on the steering wheel.

"Ruth, Bernard was arrested early yesterday."

Her voice fell away. She tasted blood, licked it from the cut on her lower lip.

"Ruth, would you mind if I light the lamp?" Nelson asked softly.

He struck a match, found the lamp, pulled it closer. Another match. The lamp hissed, spurted, settled, a small glow at its center, pale light softly stealing space from shadow. Ruth wiped her drenched cheeks with the cuffs of her navy shirt. Then she looked up, blinking, Nelson was watching her, full lips above the triangular chin with its little indentation, dark curly head bent toward her.

"Thank you," said Bernard's son. "Thank you for telling me. I understand better now."

"I've never known, you see . . ." she began, but found she didn't need to go on. Not for herself. And not, apparently, for Nelson, who raised both hands in a stop sign, smiling.

"You must have loved my father very much."

"I still do. I always will. If you love someone that way you don't stop. Even if you have to go on separately."

Ruth lay back on the mattress, watching the lamp light flicker faint on the low uneven ceiling. After a long time she turned back to Nelson.

"One reason I had to tell you what I did is because of Vicki," she said gently. "They have so much power, there are so many things they can do to you. They didn't abuse me physically, I wasn't beaten or tortured like so many people have been over the years. But they invaded my mind, Nels, they reduced me to rubble. And they've had a lot of practice since then, over twenty years. So many people. I'm saying if they want Vicki to talk, they'll make her talk, and God knows we shouldn't judge her for it."

"And if they make her talk?" he challenged.

"They'll make her identify you, your role in the struggle, they'll have evidence against you, you must see that."

"I have to take that chance."

"Oh, Nelson, there isn't any chance. Can't you see? There's no way they'll leave you alone. They'll have to take you now."

"I'm needed here. I brought you here to show you. You shouldn't have had to go through all this, but I had to show you, I have a job to do. Even now, even after . . . Johannes and . . . ," he gulped, "even after Simon, there's work I can do that matters, the antibiotics, the morphine, the protein for the kids, there's things I can do to help. They need me. It's going to keep on, it's going to get worse and worse here in South Africa."

"I know it is. It's hard to imagine, but it's spiraling down, it'll all be flaming horror before it's over. But they won't let you go on, Nels, they're going to get you, one way or another, you're caught, you must see that."

He didn't answer for a long time. His face, in shadow, was closed to her, his thoughts remote. She waited. When he did speak, it was with effort, but his voice was clear and firm.

"I can't abandon them all," he said. "Vicki. Bella and Mandiba. And Johan's sisters. And the kids. My people in Lusaka. All the ghosts. My father. I can't abandon them all."

She closed her eyes. Bernard was in a cell, white-crowned head bent over a Greek primer, he knelt beside a vegetable patch, melted chocolate eyes searching out weeds, he paced a dry dusty yard, stopping after every fifty paces to count out ten knee bends. He might still stroll the water's edge, gazing out to a limitless horizon, he might clamber up a rocky slope on the side of a hill to a ledge where wildflowers sprang from mossy ground at the high point of a streaming waterfall, he might sprawl, dark silky skin warm over angular bones, on a bright spread in sunshine and make love again.

"Nelson," Ruth said. She sat up, cross-legged, pressed her hands together. "There's something else you'll have to think about. You can't make a decision without knowing it."

Bushy eyebrows raised, skeptical dark eyes returned her stare.

"The Special Branch has known about you for months, Nelson. They know about the medications, the trips to Lusaka, the deliveries to the underground."

She saw him smile and shake his head, but she ignored it.

"They haven't picked you up for two reasons. First, they don't want to offend Derek Brand. He's important to them, they think he'd be furious if they took you."

"Furious?" He was amused. "The most he'd be is embarrassed. He'd agree with them." He shook his head again, a model of weary tolerance. "What's the rest of your theory? What's the second reason?"

"It's not a theory," she said patiently. "It's fact. They went to Gerald, they've been to him several times."

"I can't believe that. It's ridiculous."

"Nelson, Gerald told me about the drug-running himself. Before I ever saw you. He only knew because they told him."

That did reach him, she saw. He looked disconcerted at last, as if he'd been caught peeking at exam papers in advance.

"Well, what's the second reason?"

"Your father. They told Gerald they want to let him go. As a sop to the West. To get the U.S. off their backs, persuade them they're really going to reform. They want to get their bank loans back on track."

"I don't believe it," Nelson snapped. "It's simply impossible." His Adam's apple jerked up and down. "Anyway, what's that got to do with arresting me?"

"They told Gerald they can't arrest you and then let your father go, they'd make a laughingstock of themselves, their right wing would crucify them. They want . . .," she hesitated, but went quickly on, "to get rid of you. One way or the other. You're a nuisance. They gave Gerald the chance to get you out of the country."

He gaped at her, eyes wide. The color of his skin deepened, mottled. He stood up, walked three steps to the wall, walked back and dropped to the mattress. He was shaking. She heard footsteps, then a splash of water somewhere in the house beyond.

"Ruth, do you believe this?" It was a ragged cry.

"I don't know. I'm not sure. Nelson, listen to me. I don't know whether to believe it but I can't afford to take the chance. Do you understand? I can't afford not to believe it in case it's true."

"You're saying they've offered Gerald a deal? Getting rid of me, one way or another, as you put it, for my father's freedom?"

"Yes."

"But even if you believe Gerald . . ."

"I do believe Gerald. So will you, after a while. It makes perfect sense."

"But do you think they'd keep their side of the deal?"

"I don't know. I only know they might."

He stared at the little lamp. Light flickered faintly on his high temples. They both jerked, startled, when the door opened with a whine. Mandiba stood there, gnarled and creased, gray trousers sagging over his thin hips, buckling a belt.

"It's five o'clock," he said. "Time to go, you must be gone from my house. The light is coming."

Anxiety had deepened the ruts in his skin, hunched his shoulders farther forward, alarmed his dignity.

"Bella's gone," he announced single-mindedly. "To get the ambulance."

"What?" Nelson gasped.

"Her cousin James is the driver of an ambulance. She's fetching him, James must bring ambulance here, you can hide in the back. He drives out from here. To Baragwanath."

"Oh, not Bara," Ruth said quickly.

"You talk to James," Mandiba said. "Get ready now." He threw

Nelson's shirt and socks across to him and went away. Looking dazed, Nelson pulled the clothes on. Ruth straightened her hair, tugged her shirt down under her jeans, settled back to wait for the ambulance.

"Nelson," she said after a few minutes. "I'm going to ask James to take us to Gerald's car. Where we left it yesterday, near the old Drill Hall."

He nodded abstractedly. He didn't look at her.

"And then, Nels? Where then?"

He sighed. He rubbed his eyes. His face was dark, closed.

"Wherever you say, Ruth. I'll go with you."

CHAPTER TEN

Ruth sat waiting for Gerald. Civil war and revolution had not altered the seedy colonial air of the long shaded verandah in front of the King George Hotel in the sedate center of Harare. Turbaned black waiters still smiled over the tea and crumpets, the scones and silver-topped jars of gooseberry and plum preserves. There were more blacks than whites on the streets beyond, but then there always had been. The transfer of power was barely visible; soldiers had strolled these drowsy provincial sidewalks under clear blue African skies for a long time, shaded by jacarandas, bearded palm trees spiky in the clear light, bougainvillea bursting brilliant.

It would be easier to talk to Gerald on this neutral, though dimly familiar ground than it had been in his wife's damp, eerie hothouse or under stuffy inspection at the Automobile Club; certainly easier than under grim scrutiny by mustached authorities, their plainclothes disguise belied by bulging armpits.

They'd been watching the morning before at Jan Smuts Airport, when Gerald thrust the papers, rubber-stamped, official, hastily into her hands, along with an envelope stuffed with cash. There hadn't been any time to talk.

"Go through security right now," he'd said, blue gaze fixed intently on the three men staring openly at them across the hall. "Gate Four. You're going to Zimbabwe. Go to the King George Hotel. I'll be there tomorrow afternoon."

"Gerald . . ."

"If I can't make it, I'll phone. Good luck. Go now. It's all right."

The decision to do it this way had been made in the ambulance, where she and Nelson had huddled under blankets on two stretchers in the back, terrified that the shrieking siren James insisted upon would draw attention rather than deflect it. After a lot of argument, during which Bella and Mandiba grew increasingly agitated about the delay, he'd reluctantly agreed not to go to Baragwanath where, Ruth was sure, Nelson would be arrested immediately. He would take them to the parking lot where she'd left Gerald's car. But they must hurry. As soon as they'd scrambled onto the stretchers, the ambulance rolling, he cut on the siren, swerving around corners, racing the engine. When he slowed, Ruth knew he must be approaching the guarded exit from Soweto. She pulled the blanket over her head and waited tensely, rigid with fear when the siren whined to a stuttering halt. James's story of desperate urgency must have been impressive, because in a minute or two the ambulance speeded forward again, this time without the siren. When they heard his roar of triumphant laughter from the front, they emerged pink-faced from the blankets. They were out at last, hurtling along the main Soweto Motorway toward Johannesburg.

"We can drive straight up to Rustenburg," Nelson said. "Go round Pretoria to Botswana. I've got connections there. That's the way I usually go. It's close to the border. They'll help us cross into Botswana tonight."

When Ruth didn't answer, he added, "They use wire cutters at night. They know how to spot the patrols, both sides, of course."

She looked at him.

"I know South Africa's got agents all over Botswana," he said irritably. "But we can do it. I know the route. We'll drive like hell tomorrow, maybe change cars somewhere, and get into Zambia, go straight to Lusaka."

She didn't say anything. She was thinking about Max Hepburn.

"There are Congress people near the border. The ANC will send us into Zambia on citrus trucks," Nelson said eagerly. "It always gives me a charge to cross the border hidden under sacks of South African oranges. Enemy territory, but the trading never stops."

Was it possible that Max's comments on the sidewalk outside Marshall Square long ago were not a chance coincidence, after all? She'd never confronted the question before. She'd never admitted any alternative explanation than that, driven to hopeless despair, she'd betrayed Bernard. Recounting her ordeal for the first time made it impossible to avoid the question: had Max set her up? Was he their errand boy? Had her meeting with Max in Vienna a few months before been accidental? She would never know. But it was possible. And if she'd been manipulated into a setup before, it could happen again. If she took Nelson straight to Jan Smuts Airport and tried to leave the country with him, they might be waiting. They might be ready to take him now. Arrest him, shoot him, whatever. They would do whatever they wanted to do. She certainly couldn't trust them to keep a deal.

"Ruth? Isn't that why you were asking me how I got into Lusaka a few days ago? To see if I knew the route?"

"Yes," she said abstractedly. "That's what I was trying to find out. Just a minute, Nels. Let me think."

If she didn't do it their way, if she deprived them of their victory, they might punish her. If they thought she'd tricked them, evaded them, embarrassed them by chasing over a border with a fugitive, they'd take their revenge. Assuming she and Nelson even made it past all the agents and informers along the route. Then the only way for them to take revenge was to have an excuse to keep Bernard in jail. She rubbed her hands over her face, licked blood off her lip.

"I think we should phone Gerald after we pick up the car," she said quietly. "Get him to help us out at Jan Smuts."

"You're crazy," he muttered. "That's looking for trouble, they'll

get us there at the airport. Anyway, how can you trust Gerald?"
"I think we can." She was calm. "I think we have to."

Nelson, she thought, would have to take his chances. This was the best chance for Bernard. This was the way it would have to be.

Gerald had made them wait three hours, then call him back from a different phone box. They argued in angry spasms while they waited, driving around, stopping for Ruth to buy coffee and doughnuts at a take-out stand on the road to Krugersdorp, turning back. Ruth saw that Nelson relished the idea of the dangerous dash across the borders, the triumphant arrival in Lusaka, the heroic meeting with his leaders. She wouldn't do it, she wouldn't jeopardize Bernard's last chance.

"It's OK," Gerald said when she called back. "I've got a plan, it's worked out. Meet me at the airport in an hour."

The papers he stuffed into her hands were a visa into Zimbabwe for Nelson, his passport, officially stamped, even the routinely required police release. Gerald's connections were apparently holding, Ruth thought grimly. The envelope of cash was just to tide them over, he'd muttered. He'd see them in Harare.

Waiting for him now, in a clean new cotton dress she'd bought that morning, feeling as if she were acting a role of normality, it was a relief to be away from Nelson. His mood fluctuated from sullen regret and self-contempt to wild exuberance. She'd tried to tell him about Ken, but he'd barely listened. She felt compelled to prepare him for Anthony. Dreading his reaction, she told him, but was met with an outburst of anxiety about how many of his medical courses he would be forced to repeat. It was going to take a while for him to discover who he was, she thought; and braced herself for the challenge of coping with him.

"Ruth, my dear," Gerald called behind her.

She turned, flustered. She'd expected him to come up the steps of the verandah. Sandy-tipped strands of hair moved lightly on his pale forehead as he stepped briskly toward her, spare shoulders

trim in his dark blazer with the brass club buttons, eyes piercing
blue. Ruth thought he looked tired.

"You look wonderful," he smiled. "How you do bounce back!
You're a resilient girl, aren't you?"

Sitting next to her, he leaned forward, touched her hand.

"Thank you, Ruth Fredman," he said and kissed her cheek.

"For what exactly, Gerald?"

"For taking Nelson Levine off my back, for one thing."

"I see what you mean." She smiled ruefully. "He's not un-
demanding. And what's the other thing, Gerald?"

"Getting the Special Branch out of my life. No more of their
deals, no more intimidation. Back to normal life."

She stared at him. Color washed high on his cheeks but he
looked back steadily. Didn't he know there wasn't going to be
any more normal life, not for him, not for any of them? Didn't
he understand they'd reached him at last, tapped nerve endings
he'd thought were hidden, found pulses to pound? They'd used
him and they'd use him again and again. Didn't he know that
after just a little while longer there'd be no chink of space for
brokers, no ground for middlemen, only two sides, each moving
headlong to the outer extreme?

"I've left the bags in the lobby."

Startled out of her contemplation of Gerald's future, she asked,
"The bags?"

"For you and Nelson."

"Gerald, how kind of you."

"My pleasure. Sara Stern got your things together for me and
I just picked the bag up."

"How . . . er . . . how are the Sterns taking it all?" She was
uncomfortable.

Gerald's mouth curved, a small mocking twist.

"As you'd expect. Bob is literally rubbing his hands together
with satisfaction that you got the kid out and he was able to
provide a safe house for your headquarters. His patriotism is

shining, he made a stand for freedom. And I think there's considerable relief that he didn't have to cope with the authorities or defend his position. He was very apprehensive about that, you know."

"And Sara?" As if she stood there, Ruth saw her round inquisitive face, her devouring appetite for other people's secrets, the gleam in the voyeur's eyes.

"Well, I think Sara is rather disappointed to have missed the high points of the drama. But she's bearing up. She said to tell you she can't wait to see you at home and hear all the details. She says she's dying to meet Nelson."

She had never asked Gerald what he'd told Bob about her. She'd never found out how much they knew about her past, what they would tell her friends in Philadelphia, how much of her closely guarded fortress had been eroded. It didn't seem to matter anymore.

"You brought clothes for Nelson? How is Derek taking it? And Rita?"

"I'd been in touch with both of them when Nelson disappeared, you know. I'd collected his passport then, just in case. Rita was very upset, didn't want to give it to me. She didn't want her only child living so far away from her, she said. But Derek overruled her. He told her Nelson would be arrested or killed before I found him, but if he wasn't, then the U.S. was a damn sight easier for her to visit than prison for the rest of his life. I thought he was pretty brutal myself, but it worked like a charm. She'd have carried on for weeks if he hadn't put it to her like that."

Gerald pulled a long white envelope out of his breast pocket.

"This is for Nelson." He handed it to her. "There's a check from Derek to open a bank account in the U.S. He says he'll send quarterly amounts when Nelson lets him know his needs. He says, by the way, that he undertook to provide for Nelson when he married Rita and he'll see him through medical school. He says he's an honorable man and would rather honor his commitments to Nelson at long range. There's also a letter from

Rita for Nelson in there. I collected all this after you left yesterday. Where is Nelson, anyway?"

She shifted awkwardly and avoided his eyes.

"He's somewhere about. I think he went to look at the stores."

"He doesn't want to see me?"

His stare was magnetic, blue probes forcing her eyes to meet his own.

"Well, actually no, I think not, Gerald."

The slightest shrug. A small resigned lift of his left hand.

"I'm sure that'll change, Gerry. When he's put some distance between himself and . . . all this."

"Perhaps." Another envelope from another pocket. "His American visa."

She gasped.

"Gerald, how did you manage it so fast?"

"Not difficult." He dismissed it modestly. "I've been talking to the Embassy for a while about it. I had things in motion before you came. When I called them yesterday, they hustled, even had it delivered to me."

"You thought we'd succeed?"

"I thought there was a good chance you'd succeed, Ruth," he said gravely.

She couldn't wait any longer.

"Did I succeed, Gerry?"

He leaned back, folded his arms, gazed away at the birds strutting on the lawn among banks of fiery poppies. In profile, his thin face was drawn. The merest pouch of flesh made a shadow under his jaw.

"What about Bernard?"

He turned back slowly. He clenched his hands, crossed his legs and leaned toward her.

"I saw them this morning before I left."

"Well?"

"They say the time is not ripe. We'll have to wait and see."

She took a deep breath, let it out slowly.

"What did you . . . ," she started, blinking.

"I said they'd made a deal with me, surely they would honor it? I told them they'd promised if I got rid of Nelson they'd let Bernard go."

"Yes?"

"They insisted it wasn't quite like that. They'd told me they wanted to let Bernard go. Use their generosity as a weapon against the U.S. They couldn't do it while Nelson yelped at their heels."

"Well, now he's out of their way."

"Yes. And they're very glad about that. They send you their compliments, by the way. But they say the time is not ripe. The pressure is off for the moment, the West is distracted by the Middle East, the arms race, terror in Europe. They want to choose the right minute, gain the maximum advantage. They say they don't know when that will be, they can't predict. We'll have to wait and see."

There was a long silence. Images of Bernard danced in her mind, Bernard proud behind the wheel of his car, Bernard's head high above all the others on the steps of Great Hall, his voice passionate, certain, Bernard murmuring phrases of Greek aloud, Bernard in sunshine, light slanting across his narrow, lively face, memories merged with imagining.

"Are you surprised, Ruth?" said Gerald tentatively.

"No. Not really." It was only a whisper.

She looked up again. Over Gerald's shoulder she saw Nelson, leaning against a gnarled tree on the lawn beyond the verandah, watching her with Gerald, thinking himself unobserved. If it weren't for the stripes of the long palm leaves shadowing his face he might have been Bernard.

The tea was cold by now. Ruth poured it anyway.